EXTREME ISLAM

Acknowledgments

The editor wishes to thank Linda Hayashi, Laura Smith-Guerrero, Sean Tejaratchi, Ghazi Barakat, Mattias Gardell, Michael Moynihan, Mel Gordon, Lance Tilford, Bill White and Marti Singer for their help.

ISBN: 0-922915-78-4

FERAL HOUSE
P.O. BOX 13067
LOS ANGELES, CA 90013

WWW.FERALHOUSE.COM
INFO@FERALHOUSE.COM

DESIGN BY LINDA HAYASHI

10 9 8 7 6 5 4 3 2 1

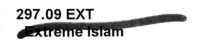

DISCARD

EXTREME ISLAM
Anti-American Propaganda
of Muslim Fundamentalism

EDITED BY ADAM PARFREY

FERAL HOUSE

CONTENTS

INTRODUCTION By Adam Parfrey

Muslim academics and clerics express alarm when the words "extreme" and "fundamentalist" are used to describe the more orthodox of their co-religionists.

Dr. Omar Abdul Rahman, the blind cleric jailed for his participation in the 1993 World Trade Center attack, wrote a paper about the media code words describing militant or orthodox Islamic belief. Says Rahman, the root word of fundamentalism is *fundamental*, meaning a structure, a foundation. If you are a fundamentalist, you cannot also be an extremist. Therefore the media code word is a distortion.

What the media wishes to do, says Rahman, is destroy Islam through its assaults and distortions. Other Muslims have posted essays on websites saying that the word "extremist" has served to brew the sort of hate taken up by the grotesque morons who used 9/11/01 as an excuse to brutalize anyone they imagined to fit the description of "Arab."

So there really isn't an "extreme Islam," claims Dr. Rahman, since Islam is by definition centered upon a strict reading of The Qur'an. As Asaf Hussain explains in "Islamic Awakening in the Twentieth Century" in the April 1988 issue of *Third World Quarterly*:

> The mainstream of fundamentalist thought (*al-salafiyya* or *al-usauliyya*) espouses a reading of Islam that is far from extremist. As expounded by Jamal el-Din, al-Afghani and Muhammad Abdu in the later part of the nineteenth century and early part of the twentieth century, fundamentalism prides itself on being the epitome of "moderation." The *umma* is a moderate or Middle Nation (*ummatun wasta*) among all nations. The "straight path" of Islam is the path that forms the geometric center between extremes.

The purpose of *Extreme Islam* is not to harm, but to understand. Understanding requires asking hard questions, and the reading of all relevant material. If the "epitome of moderation" has believers guiding jets into skyscrapers; if certain practitioners of the "straight path" force a woman, under penalty of death, to never go out in public unless she wears a stifling suit of wool armor that does not allow one hair or square inch of flesh to be seen; if the most desirable afterlife is achieved through sacrificing oneself through the mass murder of political enemies, then perhaps we should ask ourselves whether or not The Holy Qur'an is itself the voice of moderation, or an extremist document.

The Qur'an doesn't allow straggling. To question whether its verses and its commands are truly a supernatural statement by a higher power and, to ask whether Prophet Muhammad's marriage to a nine-year-old girl is worthy of emulation and respect, is to commit the unpardonable sin of elevating "self" above "God" — and in some moderate lands that is an apostasy worthy of execution.

"Moderate" Muslims, always regarded with deep respect by the western media, pick and choose from the Qur'an as if it were a buffet of ideas that allows verses to be adhered to or discarded, depending upon what's considered properly democratic. The "moderate" Reform Jew belongs to a branch so hated in Israel that he is not even considered Jewish. The "moderate" Christian, like a Unitarian, or a Quaker, is so despised by fundamentalists that he is thought of as being Satanic. Monotheism ≠ moderation.

The psychological security provided by fundamentalist absolutism must be quite a relief to troubled souls. I wonder, though, if belief is intensified by a queasy distrust of what lurks beneath.

Because the editor of this collection does not believe that flying aircraft into the World Trade Center towers can be defined as moderate, I've elected to use the words "extreme" and "fundamentalism" to suggest the type of Islamic belief that embraces the present-day jihad against America and its allies.

Perhaps use of the word "propaganda" in the title ought to be explained. Iran, the prophetic forefather of Islamic revolution, considers it important to have a "Minister of Islamic Propagation," or, as they put it in the west, propaganda. Most of the contents propagates a particular view. And not always Islam. A couple articles in this book also put across Zionist and Christian Zionist views of the Palestine crisis for contrast and perspective.

I must confess that I love Islamic propaganda. After putting my hands on a bound volume of Iran's English-language Echo of Islam magazines, so full of remarkable posters, including those making Jimmy Carter look like the veritable Antichrist, I spent a considerable amount of time trying to locate similar material. It's damn hard to find. Hardly anyone I knew possesses it. Americans would do well to study the arguments of those who despise us rather than parading around in a patriotic haze. Fearing that opposition propaganda is riddled with secret code unnecessarily gives it a lot more power.

The late '90s saw an explosion of militant Muslim websites. A few days after the War on Terrorism was engaged, many of these websites were abruptly shut down, unavailable to researchers or the curious.

www.taleban.org or www.azzam.com were not even accessible as cached material on Google.com. I feel lucky to have downloaded material from these and other sites before their unceremonious removal from the internet.

Knowledge, as they say, is power. I wish that our intelligence agencies, with their $40 billion a year budgets, had enough sense to realize that after the 1993 bombing of the World Trade Center, the destruction of American embassies and Naval ships, and Usamah Bin-Laden released his 1998 fatwa urging the murder of all Americans, that he and his comrades were biding time before 9/11/01 could happen.

After viewing, like everyone in the United States, its surreal results on television, I began to wonder if the planners of the attack had thought of the following Qur'anic verses:

> "That Day some faces will be radiant, laughing, rejoic-
> ing. That Day some faces will be dust-covered, over-
> cast with gloom. Those are the dissolute disbelievers."
> (Surah Abasa: 38-42)

and

> "Wherever you are, death will find you out. Even if
> you are in towers built up strong and high."
> (al-Nisaa 4:78)

Adam Parfrey
November, 2001

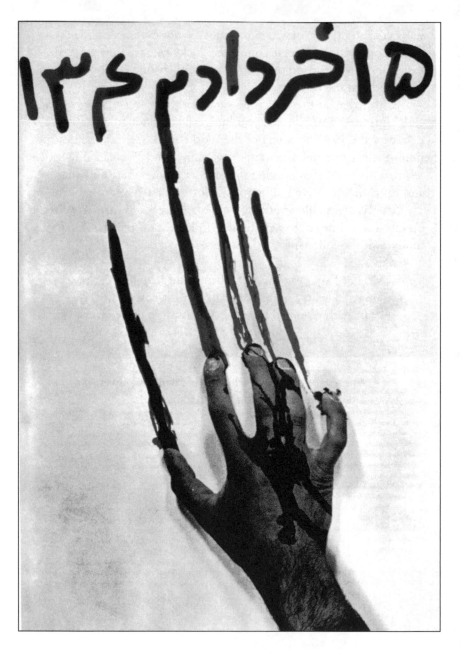

The theme of the bloody hand writing on the wall was taken up by the Islamic Republican Party of the city of Mashhad which in 1979 commissioned a poster commemorating the 15th of Khordad (5 June 1963) showing the date written in blood of a dying martyr. Here the Revolution pays tribute to its forerunner, the uprising of 1963.

THE SECOND COMING
by William Butler Yeats

TURNING and turning in the widening gyre
The falcon cannot hear the falconer;
Things fall apart; the centre cannot hold;
Mere anarchy is loosed upon the world,
The blood-dimmed tide is loosed, and everywhere
The ceremony of innocence is drowned;
The best lack all conviction, while the worst
Are full of passionate intensity.

Surely some revelation is at hand;
Surely the Second Coming is at hand.
The Second Coming! Hardly are those words out
When a vast image out of Spiritus Mundi
Troubles my sight: somewhere in sands of the desert
A shape with lion body and the head of a man,
A gaze blank and pitiless as the sun,
Is moving its slow thighs, while all about it
Reel shadows of the indignant desert birds.
The darkness drops again; but now I know
That twenty centuries of stony sleep
Were vexed to nightmare by a rocking cradle,
And what rough beast, its hour come round at last,
Slouches towards Bethlehem to be born?

ARE APOSTATES EXECUTED?

Q: Where is the line drawn of when an apostate should be executed or should not be?

A: Some time back Dr. Liyakat Takim gave an excellent dissertation on apostasy on the Alim Network. I can not do better than quote from his response: "Apostasy (irtidad) is the act of turning away from Islam having accepted it. This involves the rejection of *tawheed* and *nabuwwah* and the essentials of Islam (e.g. that the Qur'an is a book of God).

There are two types of *murtad* — *fitri* and *milli*.

A *fitri murtad* is one who was born of Muslim parents (or at least one parent) and then rejects Islam. If he rejects Islam, then, according to the fatwa of our *maraji* (including Ayatollahs al-Khu'i and Khomeini) he is to be killed.

A *milli murtad* is one who converts and then rejects Islam — he is to be given three days to repent and accept Islam again. If he does not accept by the fourth day he is to be killed.

A *murtad* has to be *baligh*, be sane, be free in his rejection of Islam. A woman *murtad* (whether of the *fitri* or *milli* type) is not to be killed. She is to be imprisoned."

For those who are murtad, since the hudud can not be practiced in the west, it is merely better, in my humble view, to show them the true and unadulterated teachings of Islam through our actions. *Insha-allah*, one day they will see the light again.

The punishments prescribed above are to be applied when a person voluntarily renounces Islam. A person who is a kafir is not an apostate but a disbeliever.

Contemporary Legal Rulings in Shi'i law in Accordance with the Rulings (fatwa) of Ayatullah al-Uzma al-Sayyid Ali al-Husayni al-Seestani

The Qur'an and the corpus of *hadith* literature constitute a comprehensive legal resource that is invoked to regulate the various aspects of a Muslim believer's life. New situations and contingencies have prompted the experts in the field to delve into the sources and to devise methodological devices in *usul al-fiqh* to enable them to deduce fresh juridical rulings (*fatwa*) in order to deal with novel problems and issues. Consequently, the door of independent research (*ijtihad*) — deducing legal rulings in the area of human-divine (*ibadat*) and human-human (*mu'amalat*) relationships — has remained open in the Ja'fari/Shi'ah Ithna Ashari/Imami school of thought. This is not a peculiar feature of the Ja'fari school, and it is presently being argued in Islamic scholarship that, contrary to the commonly held opinion, the gate of *ijtihad* was not considered closed by Sunni jurists of the 4th/10th century.

This work contains [excerpts from] my translation of a selection of new legal rulings that are based on the opinion of the eminent jurist Ayatullah al-Uzma al-Sayyid Ali al-Husayni al-Seestani, who resides in Najaf, Iraq, and is the point of reference, or *marja*, for a good part of the Shi'ah Ithna 'Ashari community of believers, who revert to him for guidance. Three of his works, *Al-Fatawa al-Muyassarah* (*FM*), *al-Mustahdathat min al-Masa'il al-Shar'iyyah* (*MMS*) and *Minhaj al-Salihin, vol. 1* (*MS*) were used in compiling the list of questions and answers and organizing them under appropriate subjects. The source is clearly marked in regular brackets after the response to each question to facilitate easy reference to the original Arabic text. . . .

Wa Bi-l-laahi-t-tawfiq, Hamid Mavani (Translator)
Q: Some people throw newspapers, magazines and some respected books in the garbage, although they contain some verses of the Qur'an or names of Allah (s.w.t.).
A: This is not permissible and it is obligatory to take them out of such places and to purify them if they have come into contact with some ritual impurity. (FM, p. 419)

Q: What is the ruling on blood that coagulates under the fingernail, this being the result of a blow or some other cause? This blood then moves gradually to the outside and it is not possible to remove it. Is this blood ritually impure or ritually pure? And how is it treated if it is considered ritually impure?

A: If it does not change (into something other than blood), it is to be considered ritually impure, and it is obligatory to remove it if there is no difficulty in doing so. But if it presents a problem, then that which seems apparent is to substitute *tayammum* for *wudu* and *ghusl*. God knows best. (MMS, p. 21, Q33)

Q: Is a man permitted to have relations with his wife after her nifas period lasting 10 days has ended, while being aware that blood continues, with the characteristic of *istihadah*, to flow from her for more than 18 days?

A: It is permissible, although it is preferable to take precautions from the 10th until the 18th day. (MMS, p. 20, Q29)

Q: Is it permissible to have a sexual relationship without a *shar'i* contract with women who are unbelievers from People of the Book, or without a religion, knowing that the government and state of their country are in a state of war with the Muslims, either directly or indirectly?

A: That is not permissible. (MMS, pp. 26–27, Q48)

Q: You mentioned in a previous dialogue that masturbation is forbidden. Are the male and female alike in this ruling?

A: Yes. As it is forbidden for the man to titillate his genitalia until he ejaculates, so too it is not permissible for the woman to titillate her genitalia to orgasm. (FM, p. 431)

Q: Certain illnesses require that the doctor may request the patient's semen for examination, and discharging it by the *shar'i* way is difficult because it must be discharged in the presence of the doctor.

A: If the patient is in dire need to do so, then he is allowed. (FM, pp. 431–32)

Q: If a person desires to test his ability to have children and the doctor asks him to discharge the semen to examine it.

A: As long as he is not obliged to do that, it is not permissible for him to masturbate. (FM, p. 432)

Q: A man cannot impregnate (sterile) and asks the doctor to determine the reason for his sterility through an examination of his sperm. The emission (of such semen) is obtained by the use of an instrument attached to his genitals and, by its movements, causes a discharge. Is this to be considered as masturbation and thus forbidden, or is it allowed for the purpose of the examination? And does it matter whether the patient is in difficulty or is acting out of necessity?

A: Yes, it is considered as masturbation. It is not allowed unless the examination requires it. It is equally so for reliance upon that except under the previous two situations (difficulty and necessity), assuming, as does your question that some definitive result can be determined from it. God knows best. (MMS, p. 14, Q11)

Q: Thinking intentionally about women other than one's wife with an image in mind of having sexual intercourse, if the penis becomes erect without discharge of semen.

A: It is not prohibited if it does not lead to a forbidden act. (FM, p. 431)

Q: These days women go out on public streets while some parts of their body that should be covered are exposed. Is it permissible to look at them without lust and sexual pleasure?

A: Yes, this is permissible if they do not desist from exposing themselves if asked to do so. (FM, p. 430)

Q: Is a Muslim permitted to go to mixed swimming pools [men and women] without a suspicious motive, especially when they (women) remove the dress of modesty from themselves and would not desist if asked to do so?

A: Although looking without a suspicious motive and lust at those who are scantily dressed and would not desist if asked to do so is permissible, presence in these places of moral depravity is absolutely not permissible based on precaution. (MMS, p. 25, Q45)

Q: Is it permissible to make a statue in the shape of a human being or an animal?

A: No, it is not permissible. (FM, p. 410)

Q: Some students of the faculty of fine arts study sculpturing and similar things relating to corporeal objects of creation that possess souls. If they refuse to participate in making them, then they will be prevented from passing and graduating from the faculty. Is it permissible for them to do that?

A: Being denied success if they abandon it (i.e. refuse to participate in this activity) is not an appropriate justification for committing this act (which is forbidden by *shari'ah*). (FM, p. 434)

Q: Giving a film, to a non-*mahram* man for developing and printing, that contains pictures of women who observe *hijab* but are unveiled (in the photos).

A: This is permissible if the one who will develop and print the pictures does not know the women pictured in the film, and such pictures are not suggestive or will not cause any attraction. (FM, p. 420)

Q: Is she allowed to have a picture of herself taken without the *hijab* to place on a passport, for example?

A: If she is forced to place the uncovered picture on her passport or other official documents, then it is permissible. But, the one who takes her picture must be her husband or her mahram. However, should the need arise, it is permissible for her to have the picture taken by a *non-mahram* photographer. (FM, p. 420)

Q: How about a woman who comes out in public and the upper part of her feet are exposed to the sight of non-*mahram*?

A: This is not permissible for her. (FM, p. 430)

Q: Some husbands who are not religiously committed demand that their wives neglect prayers, remove the *hijab*, serve alcoholic beverages to guests, participate in gambling games, shake hands with guests, etc., forcing them (wives) to do it if they refuse. Is it permissible for the wife to leave his house in order to preserve her *shar'i* obligatory duties?

A: Yes, it is permissible for the wife to leave his house at that time to the extent required by the circumstances, and in spite of that, she is entitled to full maintenance. (FM, p. 427)

Q: A woman faithfully observes the *hijab* but her husband prevents her from this and gives her a choice between abandoning the *hijab* and divorce.

A: It is not permissible for her to abandon her *hijab* even if the matter ends in divorce. (FM, pp. 427–28)

Q: But divorce would entail for some of them (women) great difficulty, distress and hardship.

A: She should endure the difficulty and hardship, and recollect His saying, the Exalted: ". . . and whoever is careful of (his duty to) Allah, He will make for him an outlet, and give him sustenance from whence he thinks not . . ." (Qur'an, 65:2-3). (FM, p. 428)

Q: Some men shave their beard and leave some hair on the chin alone. Is this sufficient by the *shari'ah*?

A: It is not sufficient. (FM, p. 434)

Q: It is normal these days for a woman to put on mascara and make-up, wear rings, necklaces and bracelets for beauty and then go out in front of people in the markets and streets?

A: This is not permissible for her except for mascara and rings provided that she is safe from falling into forbidden activities and does not intend by it to excite non-*mahram* men. (FM, p. 430)

Q: Is it permissible for a woman to go out of her house for some errands perfumed, with the fragrance of her perfume reaching *non-mahram* men?

A: She ought not do that. It is not permissible if it tempts a non-mahram man or normally causes him excitement. (FM, p. 439)

Q: Does all fluid which issues forth from a woman during the state of passion or sexual arousal require performance of *ghusl* for her? Or are there distinguishing characteristics for it as some *ulama* have indicated? Does her *ghusl* exempt her from performing *wudu*?

A: It is obligatory for her to perform *ghusl* when the fluid is discharged in a state of passion without regard to other characteristics — like languor — and it exempts her from *wudu*. God knows best. (MMS, p. 20, Q27)

Q: Is it permissible to donate the eye or kidney of a living human being for another?

A: It is not permissible to donate the eye. As for donating a kidney, for one who has another healthy one, it is permissible. (FM, p. 415)

Q: Dissection of a corpse after death, if it is done for a reasonable purpose such as criminal investigation, teaching of medicine or similar purposes.

A: It is not permissible to dissect a Muslim corpse for these kinds of reasons. The dissecting of the body of an unbeliever whose blood is not protected during his lifetime is permissible, and likewise when the protection of his blood is doubtful, if there is no *shar'i* sign of it being so (protected). (FM, p. 416)

Q: Is it permissible to listen to religious songs?
Follow up: You mean religious phrases that are composed with musical tunes that are common amongst the people of amusement and entertainment?
Response: Yes.
A: It is prohibited to listen to them. The same ruling applies to all phrases that are not for pleasure and amusement — such as supplication or *dhikr* — but composed with these musical tunes. (FM, p. 437)

Q: Classical music is believed to soothe excited nerves, and is also prescribed at times for treatment of some psychological ailments. Is it permissible for me to listen to it?
A: Yes, it is permissible to listen to music which is not suited for the gatherings of amusement and entertainment. (FM, p. 438)

Q: Is it permissible to play chess and backgammon without placing a bet?
A: It is not permissible to play them. (FM, p. 436)

MARTYR'S BLOOD
By Morteza Motah-Hary

What does a martyr do? His function is not confined to resisting the enemy, and in the process, either giving him a blow or receiving a blow from him. Had that been the case, we could say, that when his blood is shed, it goes waste. But at no time is a martyr's blood wasted. It does not flow on the ground. Every drop of it is turned into hundreds and thousands of drops, nay into tons of blood, and is transfused into the body of his society. That is why the Holy Prophet has said: "Allah does not like any drop, more than the drop of blood shed, in His way." Martyrdom means transfusion of blood into a society, especially a society suffering from anemia. It is the martyr who infuses fresh blood into the veins of the society.

MARTYR'S COURAGE AND ZEAL
The distinctive characteristic of a martyr, is that he charges the atmosphere with courage and zeal. He revives the spirit of valor and fortitude, courage and zeal, especially divine zeal, among the people who have lost it. That is why Islam is always in need of martyrs. The revival of courage and zeal is essential for the revival of a nation.

MARTYR'S IMMORTALITY
A scholar serves the society through his knowledge. It is on account of his knowledge that his personality is amalgamated with the society, just as a drop of water is amalgamated with the sea. As the result of this amalgamation a part of personality, namely his thoughts and ideas, become immortal. An inventor is amalgamated with the society through his inventions. He serves the society, by making himself immortal, by virtue of his skill and inventions. A poet makes himself immortal through his poetic art, and a moral teacher through his wise sayings.

Similarly, a martyr immortalizes himself in his own way. He gives invaluable fresh blood to the society. In other words, a scholar immortalizes his thoughts, an artist his art, an inventor his inventions, and a moral teacher his teachings. But a martyr, through his blood, immortalizes his entire being. His blood for ever flows in the veins of the society. Every other group of people can make only a part of its faculties immortal, but a martyr immortalizes all his faculties. That is why, the Holy Prophet said: "Above every virtue, there is another virtue, but there is no virtue higher than being killed in the way of Allah."

MARTYR'S INTERCESSION

There is a *hadith* which says, that there are three classes of people who will be allowed to intercede with Allah on the Day of judgement. They are the prophets, *ulema* and martyrs. In this *hadith*, the *Imams* have not been mentioned expressly, but as the report comes down from our Imams, it is obvious that the term, "*Ulema*," stands for the true divines, who par excellence include the *Imams* themselves.

The intercession of the prophets is quite apparent. It is the intercession of the martyrs, which we have to comprehend. The martyrs secure this privilege of intercession because they lead the people onto the right path. Their intercession will be portrayal of the events which took place in this world.

The Commander of the Faithful, Imam Ali (P) says: "Allah will bring forward the martyrs, on the Day of Judgement, with such pomp and splendor, that even the prophets if mounted, will dismount to show their respect for them." With such grandeur, will a martyr appear on the Day of Judgment.

THE BOILERPLATE ISLAMIC WILL

I, _____, being of sound mind and memory, do hereby revoke any and all of my former wills and amendments, and declare this my last Will and Testament.

THE *SHAHADAH* — TESTIMONY OF FAITH
Ash-hadu alla ilaha illallah, wa ash-hadu anna Muhammadan rasulullah. I testify that there is no true deity except Allah, and that Muhammad is Allah's messenger. I bear witness that Allah is the Creator of the Heavens and Earth, and the God of Adam, Nuh (Noah), Ibrahim, Musa (Moses), and 'Isa (Jesus). I bear witness that Allah's promises are true and we will certainly meet with Him, Paradise is true, the Day of Judgement is coming without any doubt, and Allah (exalted be He) will surely resurrect those in the graves.

COUNSEL TO MY BELOVED ONES
The following is my counsel to my beloved spouse, children, relatives, friends, Muslim brothers and sisters, and all those who survive me:

+ Strive to be true Muslims. Worship our Creator as He alone is to be worshipped. Direct your absolute fear, hope, love, and submission to Him alone. I exhort you with what Ibrahim and Ya'qub exhorted their children:
+ "O my children, Allah has chosen for you this true religion, so do not die except in the faith of Islam."
+ Revere Allah and be conscious of Him. Be prepared for departure from this life. Take provision of good deeds. Keep the company of the scholars and righteous Muslims. Let your appearance and behavior reflect Islam in the best way. Strive to spread and establish the religion of Islam.
+ Obey Allah and His Messenger (peace be upon him). Hold fast to the Messenger's Sunnah (teachings), and the guidance of the *salaf* (righteous early Muslims). I exhort you with the Messenger Muhammad's last exhortation to his followers: "The prayer . . . the prayer . . ." So, maintain the prayers at their prescribed times.
+ Always supplicate for me and ask Allah to forgive me and have mercy on me.

◆ Avoid all acts of disobedience. Beware of innovations or altering any of the teachings of Islam. I disown before Allah any act of disobedience or innovation that anyone might commit after me.

WHAT TO DO WHEN DEATH COMES

When death approaches me, have Muslims of knowledge and piety attend me, and let them remind me of maintaining good thoughts about my Lord, hoping for His mercy and forgiveness, and constantly uttering the *Shahadah*.

Remove from my presence anything that dispels the angels of mercy, such as pictures or statues of humans and animals, dogs, bells, improperly attired women, music, smoking, etc.

After my soul departs, I ordain the following to my family or those who are present:

◆ Close my eyes.
◆ Make good supplications for me (without raising their voice), invoking mercy and forgiveness for me.
◆ Take measures to quickly prepare me for the burial.
◆ Avoid announcing my death on loudspeakers or in newspapers.
◆ Stop prompting me to say the *Shahadah* after my soul had departed from my body.
◆ Hasten to pay off my debts.

No person dies before his appointed time. So, I ordain to my family the following:

◆ Do not preoccupy yourselves with my death, but instead make the proper preparations for your own.
◆ Maintain patience, self-composure, and submission to Allah's decree.
◆ Do not raise your voice, wail, strike your cheeks, or call out with the calls of ignorance that reflect dissatisfaction with Allah's decree.
◆ Women may not mourn over me for more than three days, except for a widow who is allowed to mourn over her husband for four months and ten days — until her *'iddah* (period of waiting until she can consider remarriage) is completed.

FUNERAL

I ordain that all of my funeral and burial procedures be performed by Muslims in full compliance with the Islamic religion and the Sunnah of the Messenger. Absolutely no non-Islamic religious services or observances may be conducted upon my death, or on my body. In particular:

- Autopsy or embalmment may not be performed on my body — unless required by law.
- My burial may not be delayed for reasons Islamically unjustifiable, such as awaiting a specific day, or the arrival of a particular person.
- My body should be washed three or five times (or more if needed) with soap and water, adding camphor or perfume on the last time.
- My body should be wrapped with three plain white perfumed sheets of cloth that are free of ornaments and other articles.
- I should be buried where I die; my body may not be transported over any unreasonable distance except as needed to reach the nearest Muslim cemetery.
- My funeral procession should be expedited.
- Women and incense burners may not accompany my funeral procession.
- During my funeral, voices may not be raised with reciting Qur'an, uttering the *Shahadah*, or any supplications. Silence should be maintained, and those present should contemplate over the event and supplicate for me in their hearts.
- The funeral prayer upon me should be conducted outside the graveyard, and not among the graves.
- The largest possible number of Muslims should be invited to pray upon me, they should be arranged in a minimum of three rows, and they should be instructed to supplicate for me sincerely and extensively.

BURIAL AND THE GRAVE

I ordain that:

- My grave should be dug in accordance with the specifications of the Sunnah.
- If possible, my grave should be made as a *lahd*. (Near the bottom of the grave, in its wall facing Qiblah, a horizontal niche made large enough for the body to be placed in it.

- My body should be buried without a casket or any other encasement that separates the wrapped body from the surrounding soil. In the event that the local laws require casket encasement, I ordain that such encasement be of the simplest, most modest, and least expensive type.
- My body should be laid in the lahd on the right side, with the face to the *Qiblah*, and my back supported with bricks.
- The men who lay down my body should say: *Bismillahi, wa'ala millati Rasulillah* (with Allah's name, and upon the religion of Allah's Messenger).
- No pillow may be placed under my head, no perfumes or decorations may be sprinkled in my grave, and no worldly possession may be buried with me.
- Each one attending my burial should pour three handfuls of dust into the head end of my grave.
- After finishing my burial, the Muslims should be urged to stay for about fifteen minutes around my grave, supplicating for me quietly, and asking Allah to grant me mercy, forgiveness, and firmness of words when questioned by the angels in the grave.

I ordain that:
- No structure may be built over my grave.
- The soil over my grave should be raised no more that a hand span.
- No fence may be built around my grave.
- No writing, or symbols may be placed on my grave, except for a simple rock or inscription of my name to mark it so that other family members may later be buried in it.

VIOLATIONS TO ISLAM

I ordain that innovations, violations to Islam, and practices of the non-Muslims should all be prevented at my funeral. In particular:

- No one may wear black as a sign of mourning.
- No pictures, decorations, flowers, wreaths, flags, or symbols may be included at any stage of my burial, nor be placed at the site of my grave.
- Recitation of Qur'an (even *Surat ul-Fatihah* or *Yasin*) may not be done over my body during the funeral procedures.

CONDOLENCES

I ordain that:

- The people should be instructed to express their condolences in proper Islamic terms and manner.
- My family may not prepare food for the people who visit to comfort them, nor are they to hire or appoint men to recite Qur'an for the occasion.
- Gatherings may not be arranged for the specific purpose of receiving condolences, especially those made on Fridays, on the third day, after one week, forty days, annually, etc.

I disown before Allah, the Most High, every action or saying that conflicts with the Sunnah of the noble Messenger.

Finally, I ask all my relatives, friends and all others, whether they choose to believe as I believed or not, to honor my right to these beliefs. I ask them to honor this document, and not to obstruct it or change it in any way. Rather, let them see that I am buried as I have indicated above, and let my estate be divided as I indicate below.

SETTLEMENT OF DEBTS AND EXPENSES

I direct that all trust properties in my possession be returned to their rightful owners. I further direct that my Executor first applies the assets of my estate to the payment of all my legal debts, including such expenses incurred by my last illness and burial, as well as the expenses of the administration of my estate. I direct said Executor to pay any outstanding obligations that are binding on me before Allah, including unpaid *zakah* (obligatory Islamic charity), vows, *kaffarat* (expiating Islamic obligations), and unperformed *Hajj* (pilgrimage to Makkah).

I direct that all inheritance, estate and succession taxes (including interest and penalties thereon), payable by reason of my death, shall be paid out of, and be charged generally against, the principal of my residuary estate without reimbursement from any person; except that this provision shall not be construed as a waiver of any right which my Executor has, by law or otherwise, to claim reimbursement for any such taxes which become payable on account of property, if any, over which I have a power of appointment.

DISTRIBUTION OF THE RESIDUARY ESTATE

I direct and bequeath all of my residuary estate only to my Muslim heirs whose relationship to me, whether ascending or descending, has occurred, at each and every stage, through blood relationship or lawful marriage. The distribution of my residuary estate shall be made strictly in accordance with the Islamic Law of inheritance, as is summarized in the table attached herewith.

I direct that no part of my residuary estate shall be inherited by a non-Muslim relative, except legatees specifically named.

Should I die as a result of murder, I direct that the adjudged murderer, principal or accessory in the murder, shall be disqualified from receiving any part or share of my estate.

I direct that no part of my estate shall be given to relatives whose relationship to me, whether ascending or descending, has only occurred through non-Islamic marriage, illicit contact, or adoption, except: (a) legatees specifically named, or (b) individuals who are related to me through their biological mother. I further direct that a relationship based on a well-established Islamic marriage shall be accepted whether or not the marriage had been confirmed with the legal authorities.

I direct that any fetus, conceived before my death, whose relationship to me qualifies it to be a legal heir according to Islam, shall be considered an heir, provided that it is born alive, and within a reasonable term after my death. In such a case, the distribution of my residuary estate shall be delayed until after the birth of the fetus. If some of the other heirs are in urgent financial need, a disbursement may be extended to them not to exceed their minimum possible share after taking the fetus's share into consideration.

I direct that any residuary estate, after the execution of other Articles in this will, to the following tax-exempt Islamic organization:

This is my will, which I have laid out.

"Whoever changes the bequest after hearing it, the sin will be upon those who make the change. Truly, Allah is Hearing and Knowing." (Al-Baqarah 2:181)

I ask Allah to guide me and all the Muslims and grant us righteousness, a good end, and death upon the testimony of Islam.

DEATH'S COMELY REWARD
The Suicide Bomber's Erotic Afterlife

Hadith Tirmzi, Volume Two, gives details of the houris:

A *houri* is a most beautiful young woman with a transparent body. The marrow of her bones is visible like the interior lines of pearls and rubies. She looks like red wine in a white glass.

She is of white color, and free from the routine physical disabilities of an ordinary woman such as menstruation, menopause, urinal and offal discharge, child bearing and the related pollution.

A *houri* is a girl of tender age, having large breasts which are round, and not inclined to dangle. *Houris* dwell in palaces of splendid surroundings.

Now add to this description of *houris* what *Mishkat* says, Volume Three:

If a *houri* looks down from her abode in heaven onto the earth, the whole distance shall be filled with light and fragrance. . . .

A *houri's* face is more radiant than a mirror, and one can see one's image in her cheek. The marrow of her shins is visible to the eyes.

Every man who enters paradise shall be given 72 houris; no matter at what age he had died, when he is admitted into paradise, he will become a 30-year-old, and shall not age any further.

Tirmzi, Volume Two, states:

A man in paradise shall be given virility equal to that of 100 men.

PURIFICATION AND PRAYER
From IslamOnline.net

Before attempting any sort of prayer, our bodies should be totally purified. In order for us to be in this state, he or she must perform something called *Wudu* (Ablution). Again, the best way to learn *Wudu* is to
watch others face to face. Here are the steps for *Wudu*:

The first step in performing *Wudu*, is to have the intentions of purifying your heart.

Rinse your palms up the wrist three times; right palm first then your
left.

Rinse your mouth three times. (Preferably with three gargles.) Wash
nose by sniffing in it three times.

Wash the face three times making sure that water reaches all the areas
of your face. Then wash each hand up to the elbow three times, right
hand first then your left hand. Wipe your hand (hair) with wet hands,
and then rub the ears with wet hands.

Finally, wash your feet up to the ankle three times starting with the
right foot.

You are able to maintain the state of *Wudu* unless you attend the call
of nature, pass wind, sleep, or become unconscious. Now, if a person
was in a major state of impurity resulting from actions like, i.e. intercourse or semen discharge, then he must perform *Ghusl* (Bathing)
Women should also carry out this cleansing to purify themselves after
intercourse, wet dreams, or recovering from menstrual period and
child birth.

The procedure for *Ghusl* (bathing) is as follows:

Make the intention for *Ghusl* (ceremonial bath).
Wash the private parts,
Perform ablution (*Wudu*) as you do before prayer,
Pour water over the head,
Wash the whole body, head and hair thoroughly so as not to leave a
dry spot.

Wash feet before getting out of bathing area.

Thank and praise Allah and supplicate him. It is required that a Muslim perform *Ghusl* once a week, that is on Friday before the congregational prayers but a daily bath is hygienically preferred. Women are excused from prayers on days of menstruation and childbirth period.

PRAYER

After reciting the *Shahadeh*, the creed to Islam which is translated into: "I bear witness to that there is no deity worthy of worship, except Allah and I bear witness that Muhammad is the Prophet of Allah," praying five times a day becomes obligatory for all Muslims. A great way to master the performance of *Salaat* (prayer) is to learn from other Muslims face to face. Each prayer of the day must be performed according to its time slot in the day. Here is the following order:

Fajr (Morning Prayer) begins about one hour and twenty minutes before sunrise and ends about ten minutes before sunrise.

Duhr (Noon Prayer) begins when the sun passes the meridian and ends about two and a half hours afterwards.

Asr (Afternoon Prayer) begins from the time the noon prayer time ends and ends about 10 minutes before sunset.

Maghrib (Sunset) begins soon after sunset ends and ends before darkness approaches.

Isha (Night Prayer) begins from the time the sunset prayer ends and extends till just before the morning prayer.

For exact timings of each prayer, obtain a prayer timetable from your nearest masjid or any Muslim website.

HOW TO PERFORM PRAYER

Prayer is the difference from the believer and the non-believer and should be done in complete humility and submissiveness to Allah. Prayer requires a person to have complete concentration when performing prayer. Also, performing prayer should not converse, look around or attend to any worldly matters during the prayer. Certain prayers of the day are performed differently from one another. First, let's see how the morning prayer is performed. The first thing one should do is face the *Kaba* (The Holy House of Allah).

Raise hands to behind your ears and say *Allahu Akbar*.
Then lower your hands and place the right hand over the left one above the navel. Then recite the *Fatiha* (Opening chapter of the Qur'an): *Bismillah ir Rahman ir Raheem. Alhamdullah Rabbil Alameen. Ar Rahman ir Raheem. Maliki yawmid deen. Iyyaka nabudu wa iyyaka nasta'een. Ihdinas siratal mustakeem — siraatal ladeena an amtaalayhim gayril maghdoobi alayhum, Waladdaallin Ameen.*

Following the *Fatiha*, one should recite any *Sura* from the Qur'an.

For example is chapter 112 (*Sura Ikhlas*). *Qul hu wallahu ahad, Allahus Samad, lam yalid wa lam yulid, walaam yakin lahoo qufuwan ahad.* After the completion of the *Sura*, say *Allahu Akbar* and then bow down, bending your hands and knees. This position is called *Ruku*, and in this position recite three times: *Subhana Rabbiyaal Azeem.*

After that, the standing position is resumed with three words, "*Sami Allahu liman Hamidah, Rabbana Wa lakal Hamd.*" Then say *Allahu Akbar* and prostrate yourself down with your forehead touching the ground. This position is called Sujud. In this position, recite three times, *Subhana Rabiyaal Ala.* Saying *Allahu Akbar*, resume the erect sitting position while saying Allahu Akbar, then again prostrate by saying *Allahu Akbar* and repeating three times, *Subhana Rabiyaal Ala* while in prostration. Then stand upright saying *Allahu Akbar*. This completes one unit or one *Rakah*.

After the first *Rakah*, perform the second one exactly the same way you did the first one. In the second one, after you say perform your second prostration recitals, you remain in the erect sitting position and repeating the following of what is called *Tashahhud; Attahiyatt lilahi wa'salawat wa tayyibat. Asaalamu Alaika Ayyuhan nabi wa rahmutullah wa barakat. Asaalaam alayna wa ala ibadillahis saliheen.* Pointing your index finger straight, say *Ashadu Ana la ihlahi illallah, wa ashadu anna Muhammadan was abduhoo wa rasoolooh.*

Following this, you then recite the following of what is called *Durud: Allahuma salli ala Sayyiddna Muhammad wa ali Sayyiddna*

Muhammad, kama sallayta ala sayyiddna Ibraheem wa ala ali Sayyiddna Ibraheem Wa barik ala Sayyiddna Muhammad, wa ala ali Sayyiddna Muhammad, kama barakta ala Sayyiddna Ibraheem wa ala ali Sayiddna Ibraheem, fil alameen innaka hamidun majeed After this, you turn your head to the right and say *Asalaam Alaykum wa Rahmatullah wa baraktu* and then turn your head to the left and repeat the same.

This completes the morning prayer of two *Rakah* (units).

NUMBER OF *RAKAH* (UNITS) IN THE FIVE OBLIGATORY PRAYERS
PRAYER AND NUMBER OF UNITS
Fajr: Early Morning 2
Duhr: Early Afternoon 4
Asr: Late Afternoon 4
Maghrib: After Sunset 3
Isha: Night 4
The first two *Rakah* of these prayers are performed in the same manner as the morning prayer. But after reciting the *Tashahhud* you should stand and continue to pray the third Rakah (unit) reciting only *Sura Fatiha* and not joining it with other passages of the Qur'an. Then in the fourth *Rakah*, after the second sajdah (prostration) sit down as you do in the second *Rakah* and recite *Tashahhud, Durud*, supplication and ending the prayer as above.

The *Maghrib* prayer (Sunset) consists of three *Rakah*. First two *Rakah* are the same as above. Stand up for the third *Rakah* reciting *Sura Fatiha*, then complete this *Rakah* as you did the fourth *Rakah* above.

It is highly recommended that all people perform the five daily prayers in congregation in a Mosque and we should make our world activities revolve around the five daily prayers.

On Fridays, the Muslims perform Prayers in congregation, the *Juma* Prayer. A *Khutba* or sermon precedes this prayer. It consists of two *Rakah* during which the *Imam* recites Sura Fatiha and then follows up with another verse. This prayer replaces the noon prayer and it is obligatory for all Muslims to attend the Friday prayers. All mosques hold the Juma prayers each Friday.

PHYSICAL PURITY

Physical Purity means cleanliness of the body, clothing and the environment. According to the rules of Islam, Muslims should keep their bodies and clothing clean from any impurity. Impurity is excretion from anything human or animalistic.

It is a must for humans to wipe off the last drops of urine from their bodies with tissue paper and to not allow specks of dried feces to cling to any parts of their bodies, even on clothing. After wiping with tissue paper, Muslims should find water and wash away thoroughly all the impurities on them. Also applying to this rule are semen discharges and ejaculations.

Muslims should wash away any and all discharges received from animals during play, etc. This includes the saliva from dogs on the human body, clothing, or on dishes used by humans for food. Also considered impure is unnecessary hair on the body.

Hair of the underarms and pubic area is considered unnecessary and undesirable and should be removed regularly. Circumcision for Muslims is strongly recommended because of its health advantages such as cleanliness and reducing the risk of cancers in that area of the body. It is not required for Muslim women to do the same though.

HITLER'S PROMISES TO THE GRAND MUFTI OF JERUSALEM

RECORD OF THE
CONVERSATION
BETWEEN THE FÜHRER
AND THE GRAND
MUFTI OF JERUSALEM
ON NOVEMBER 28,
1941, IN THE PRESENCE
OF REICH FOREIGN
MINISTER AND
MINISTER GROBBA IN
BERLIN, AS PRINTED IN
*THE ISRAEL-ARAB
READER,* EDITED BY
WALTER LACQUER.

The Mufti with Hitler in Germany.
A German leaflet dropped over Egypt at
the time of battle of al-Alamein in 1942, in
order to win Arab sympathy for the Nazis.

The Grand Mufti began by thanking the Führer for the great honor he
had bestowed by receiving him. He wished to seize the opportunity to
convey to the Führer of the Greater German Reich, admired by the
entire Arab world, his thanks for the sympathy which he had always
shown the Arab and especially the Palestinian cause, and to which he
had given clear expression in his public speeches. The Arab countries
were firmly convinced that Germany would win the war and that the
Arab cause would then prosper. The Arabs were Germany's natural
friends because they had the same enemies as had Germany, namely
the English, the Jews, and the Communists. They were therefore prepared to cooperate with Germany with all their hearts and stood ready
to participate in the war, not only negatively by the commission of acts
of sabotage and the instigation of revolutions, but also positively by
the formation of an Arab Legion. The Arabs could be more useful to
Germany as allies than might be apparent at first glance, both for geo-
graphic reasons and because of the suffering inflicted upon them by
the English and the Jews. Furthermore, they had had close relations
with all Moslem nations, of which they could make use in behalf of
the common cause. The Arab Legion would be quite easy to raise. An
appeal by the Mufti to the Arab countries and the prisoners of Arab,
Algerian, Tunisia and Moroccan nationality in Germany would
produce a great number of volunteers eager to fight. Of Germany's

victory Arab world was firmly convinced, not only because the Reich possessed a large army, brave soldiers, and military leaders of genius, but also because the Almighty could never award the victory to an unjust cause.

In this struggle, the Arabs were striving for the independence and unity of Palestine, Syria, and Iraq. They had the fullest confidence in the Führer and looked to his hand for the balm on their wounds which had been inflicted upon them by the enemies of Germany. The Mufti then mentioned the letter he had received from Germany, which stated that Germany was holding no Arab territories and understood and recognized the aspirations to independence and freedom of the Arabs, just as she supported the elimination of the Jewish national home.

A public declaration in this sense would be very useful for its propagandistic effect on the Arab peoples at this moment. It would rouse the Arabs from their momentary lethargy and give them new courage. It would also ease the Mufti's work of secretly organizing the Arabs against the moment when they could strike. At the same time, he could give the assurance that the Arabs would in strict discipline patiently wait for the right moment and only strike upon an order from Berlin.

With regard to the events in Iraq, the Mufti observed that the Arabs in that country certainly had by no means been incited by Germany to attack England, but solely had acted in reaction to a direct English assault upon their honor.

The Turks, he believed, would welcome the establishment of an Arab government in the neighboring territories because they would prefer weaker Arab to strong European governments in the neighboring countries, and, being themselves a nation of seven million, they had moreover nothing to fear from the 1,700,000 Arabs inhabiting Syria, Transjordan, Iraq, and Palestine.

France likewise would have no objections to the unification plan because she had conceded independence to Syria as early as 1936 and had given her approval to the unification of Iraq and Syria under King Faisal as early as 1933.

In these circumstances he was renewing his request that the Führer make a public declaration so that the Arabs would not lose hope, which is so powerful a force in the life of nations. With such hope in their hearts the Arabs, as he had said, were willing to wait. They were not pressing for immediate realization of their aspirations; they could easily wait half a year or a whole year. But if they were not inspired with such a hope by a declaration of this sort, it could be expected that the English would be the gainers from it.

The Führer replied that Germany's fundamental attitude on these questions, as the Mufti himself had already stated, was clear. Germany stood for uncompromising war against the Jews. That naturally included active opposition to the Jewish national home in Palestine, which was nothing other than a center, in the form of a state, for the exercise of destructive influence by Jewish interests. Germany was also aware that the assertion that the Jews were carrying out the function of economic pioneers in Palestine was a lie. The work there was done only by the Arabs, not by the Jews. Germany was resolved, step by step, to ask one European nation after the other to solve its Jewish problem, and at the proper time direct a similar appeal to non-European nations as well.

The Mufti visiting volunteers from Bosnia whom he had recruited and organized for service in a Nazi S.S. division.

Germany was at the present time engaged in a life and death struggle with two citadels of Jewish power: Great Britain and Soviet Russia. Theoretically there was a difference between England's capitalism and Soviet Russia's communism; actually, however, the Jews in both countries were pursuing a common goal. This was the decisive struggle; on the political plane, it presented itself in the main as a conflict between Germany and England, but ideologically it was a battle between National Socialism and the Jews. It went without saying that Germany would furnish positive and practical aid to the Arabs involved in the same struggle, because platonic promises were useless in a war for survival or destruction in which the Jews were able to mobilize all of England's power for their ends.

The aid to the Arabs would have to be material aid. Of how little help sympathies alone were in such a battle had been demonstrated plainly by the operation in Iraq, where circumstances had not permitted the rendering of really effective, practical aid. In spite of all the sympathies, German aid had not been sufficient and Iraq was overcome by the power of Britain, that is, the guardian of the Jews.

The Mufti could not but be aware, however, that the outcome of the struggle going on at present would also decide the fate of the Arab world. The Führer therefore had to think and speak coolly and deliberately, as a rational man and primarily as a soldier, as the leader of the German and allied armies. Everything of a nature to help in this titanic battle for the common cause, and thus also for the Arabs, would have to be done. Anything, however, that might contribute to weakening the military situation must be put aside, no matter how unpopular this move might be.

Germany was now engaged in very severe battles to force the gateway to the northern Caucasus region. The difficulties were mainly with regard to maintaining the supply, which was most difficult as a result of the destruction of railroads and highways as well as of the oncoming winter. If at such a moment, the Führer were to raise the problem of Syria in a declaration, those elements, in France which were under de Gaulle's influence would receive new strength. They would interpret the Führer's declaration as an intention to break up France's colonial empire and appeal to their fellow countrymen that they should rather make common cause with the English to try to save what still could be saved. A German declaration regarding Syria would in France be understood to refer to the French colonies in general, and that would at the present time create new troubles in western Europe, which means that a portion of the German armed forces would be immobilized in the west and no longer be available for the campaign in the east.

The Führer then made the following statement to the Mufti, enjoining him to lock it in the uttermost depths of his heart:

1. The Führer would carry on the battle to the total destruction of the Judeo-Communist empire in Europe.

2. At some moment which was impossible to set exactly today but which in any event was not distant, the German armies would in the course of this struggle reach the southern exit from Caucasia.

3. As soon as this had happened, the Führer would on his own give the Arab world the assurance that its hour of liberation had arrived. Germany's objective would then be solely the destruction of the Jewish element residing in the Arab sphere under the protection of British power. In that hour the Mufti would be the most authoritative spokesman for the Arab world. It would then be his task to set off the Arab operations which he had secretly prepared. When that time had come, Germany could also be indifferent to French reaction to such a declaration.

Once Germany had forced open the road to Iran and Iraq through Rostov, it would be also the beginning of the end of the British world empire. The Führer hoped that the coming year would make it possible for Germany to thrust open the Caucasian gate to the Middle East. For the good of their common cause, it would be better if the Arab proclamation were put off for a few more months than if Germany were to create difficulties for herself without being able thereby to help the Arabs.

The Führer fully appreciated the eagerness of the Arabs for a public declaration of the sort requested by the Grand Mufti. But he would beg him to consider that the Führer himself was the Chief of State of the German Reich for five long years during which he was unable to make to his own homeland the announcement of its liberation. He had to wait with that until the announcement could be made on the basis of a situation brought about by the force of arms that the Anschluss had been carried out.

The moment that Germany's tank divisions and air squadrons had made their appearance south of the Caucasus, the public appeal requested by the Grand Mufti could go out to the Arab world.

The Grand Mufti replied that it was his view that everything would come to pass just as the Führer had indicated. He was fully reassured and satisfied by the words which he had heard from the Chief of the German State. He asked, however, whether it would not be possible, secretly at least, to enter into an agreement with Germany of the kind he had just outlined for the Führer.

The Führer replied that he had just now given the Grand Mufti precisely that confidential declaration.

The Grand Mufti thanked him for it and stated in conclusion that he was taking his leave from the Führer in full confidence and with reiterated thanks for the interest shown in the Arab cause.

GLUBB PASHA ON THE MIDDLE EAST CRISIS

GLUBB PASHA, BORN SIR JOHN BAGOT GLUBB (1897–1986), A BRITISH SOLDIER CALLED ON IN 1939 TO COMMAND THE ARAB LEGION OF TRANS-JORDAN DUE TO HAVING SERVED THE FIRST WORLD WAR IN IRAQ, WHERE HE LIVED WITH BEDOUINS AND LEARNED THEIR LANGUAGE.

TODAY IT'S NEARLY FORGOTTEN THAT ENGLAND, THROUGH GLUBB PASHA AND HIS ARAB LEGION, FOUGHT AGAINST ZIONISM AND ITS CONTINUING LAND GRAB THROUGHOUT THE '30S AND '40S. ARAB IN-FIGHTING, COMBINED WITH BRITISH MISCOMMUNICATIONS, ASSURED THE FAILURE OF ITS BATTLES AND THE 1948 CAPITULATION TO THE STATE OF ISRAEL.

MORE THAN A DECADE AFTER BEING DISMISSED FROM DUTY BY KING HUSSEIN OF JORDAN, GLUBB PASHA PUBLISHED HIS THOUGHTS ON THE "MIDDLE EAST CRISIS" IN BOOKLET FORM AFTER THE WAR OF 1967. IN THE BOOKLET HE CLAIMS, "I DO NOT THINK THAT I HAVE ANY REMAIN-ING PASSIONS, HATREDS, JEALOUSIES OR AMBITIONS. I DO NOT WISH TO GO TO MY MAKER WITH HATE IN MY HEART. I HAD NEVER DREAMED THAT I WOULD RETURN TO THESE BITTER STRUGGLES." THEN HE WRITES OF HIS LOVE OF JORDANIANS AND AMERICANS, AND SAYS THAT HE DOES NOT DISLIKE ANYONE ELSE, INCLUDING SYRIANS, LEBANESE, EGYPTIANS OR ISRAELIS. "MANY JEWS DO NOT LIKE THE AGGRESSIVE MILITARY ATMOSPHERE OF ISRAEL AND ADHERE TO THE OLD GENEROUS, CUL-TURED, LIBERAL JEWRY. I HAVE MANY JEWISH FRIENDS ALSO." THE "AGGRESSIVE, MILITARY ATMOSPHERE OF ISRAEL" IS THE SAME ONE THAT SHOWED HIM UP AND PLAYED HIM FOR A FOOL. ONE OF THE LAST THINGS GLUBB PASHA EVER WROTE WAS A FOREWORD TO THE BRITISH EDITION OF SKYJACKER LEILA KHALED'S MEMOIRS; ONE WOULD THINK THAT THIS BETRAYS HIS SYMPATHIES.

King Hussein of Jordan, Glubb's boss.

I do not propose to discuss the early stages of Zionism in Palestine, but British people may like to be reminded of the two pledges contained in the Balfour Declaration of 1917. Firstly, "His Majesty's Government view with favor the establishment in Palestine of a National Home for the Jewish people and will use their best endeavors to facilitate this object." Such was the promise made to the Jews.

The second part of the declaration contained a promise to the Arabs of Palestine. ". . . it being clearly understood that nothing shall be done which may prejudice the civil and religious rights of existing non-Jewish communities in Palestine."

Foreign Office,
November 2nd, 1917.

Dear Lord Rothschild,

I have much pleasure in conveying to you, on behalf of His Majesty's Government, the following declaration of sympathy with Jewish Zionist aspirations which has been submitted to, and approved by, the Cabinet.

"His Majesty's Government view with favour the establishment in Palestine of a national home for the Jewish people, and will use their best endeavours to facilitate the achievement of this object, it being clearly understood that nothing shall be done which may prejudice the civil and religious rights of existing non-Jewish communities in Palestine, or the rights and political status enjoyed by Jews in any other country"

I should be grateful if you would bring this declaration to the knowledge of the Zionist Federation.

The Jews who were in Palestine in 1917 were living peaceably with the Arabs. They represented seven percent of the population, the Arabs providing 93 percent.

Before 1914, when a Palestine Arab wanted particularly to emphasize the truth of a statement he was making, he would add, "word of an Englishman, what I say is true." Prior to the First World War, an Englishman's word was believed to be his bond. The phrase quoted is now no longer used by Palestinians.

During the First World War, the Balfour Declaration was not the only pledge given. Britain, France and the United States promised that all the peoples previously governed by the Turks should have the right to choose their own form of government. This pledge was also one of President Woodrow Wilson's Fourteen Points, which aroused such intense enthusiasm all over the world for the noble ideals of the people of the United States.

The peoples to whom these promises were made ultimately obtained their fulfillment. The people of Palestine alone were an exception. They were never allowed to choose their own government.

After the Second World War, the Arabs of Palestine, realizing their own weakness and unable to present their own case, not being a sovereign state, called upon other Arab states for help.

I frankly do not know the legal precedents — if any exist — for one independent state representing an entirely different country. Suffice it to say that the Arab states who represented the Arabs of Palestine before the United Nations were not parties to the dispute and in some cases at least, knew little or nothing about it.

In any case, at the vital session at which the partition of Palestine was eventually accepted, the Arab states decided to boycott the proceedings. As a result, the Arab-Palestine case was never put to the Assembly.

Fighting broke out immediately after the end of the British Mandate in May, 1948, and Israel gained a sweeping military victory, and was allowed to enjoy the fruits of her armed success. Thus the rights and wrongs of the case were never stated by the Palestinians. Armed force was the means used for settlement.

The justification usually urged for this procedure was that the Egyptians were the aggressors, because they invaded the area allotted to Israel by the United Nations. The argument is of somewhat doubtful validity.

Firstly, the admission of hundreds of thousands of Jewish immigrants into Palestine under the protection of the British army during the mandatory period, against the bitter opposition of 93 percent of the people of the country, is rightly or wrongly regarded by the Palestinians as military aggression.

Secondly, it may be questioned whether the United Nations had the legal power to order that half the territory of a country be taken from the inhabitants and given to a completely foreign race of immigrants.

Thirdly, the Egyptians are an entirely different race from the Palestinians. If, let us suppose, the Egyptians commit a breach of international law, there is no apparent reason why the Palestinians should be driven from their homes.

It is not my object to say that these arguments, or any others, are valid or not. The point which I wish to make is that the Palestinians genuinely believed that they had a grievance, which, they felt, had never received an impartial hearing.

WHAT IS AN ARAB?

The justification for the Israeli seizure, in 1948, of considerably more territory than was allotted to them by the United Nations was, therefore, that the Egyptians were the aggressors and so "the Arabs" got what they deserved. (The Jordanians did not enter territory alloted by U.N.O. to Israel but defended the area allotted to the Arabs.)

It must be realized that "the Arabs," as the word is used today, are not a single race but a cultural group of entirely different races. This is not a political opinion but a scientific fact, which anthropologists can prove by such means as skull shapes, physical measurements, hair, eyes, blood tests and so on.

The Arab world may be compared to the Latin-American world, which forms a linguistic and cultural group often acting in unison, but consisting of many sovereign and independent states. Nobody would agree to an American annexation of Nicaragua on the grounds of the hostility of Cuba. Why not? They are all Latin-Americans, aren't they?

The relationship of Egypt to Palestine may be compared to that of Germany or Holland to Britain, if the North Sea were full of sand instead of water. Racially, the Germans, Dutch and British may probably be about as closely related as the Egyptians to the Palestinians.

But they all speak Arabic, don't they? Yes, though with considerable variations. But the Latin-Americans speak Spanish, but are different nations. West Indians and the colored people in the United States speak English as their mother tongue, but can scarcely be said to be English.

Many of these linguistic affinities are due to military conquests centuries ago and do not signify any racial relationship. Let us, therefore, appreciate that Egypt is an independent state, separated from Palestine by two hundred miles of sand and having virtually no racial affinity with the Palestinians. It is, therefore, on the face of it, not just to drive the Palestinians from their homes, using the behavior of the Egyptians as a pretext.

It is true that the Palestinians, weak and helpless as they felt themselves to be in face of the powers opposed to them, claimed to be of the same race as the other Arabic-speaking peoples. Their claims, however, do not alter the physical facts. Moreover, in actual practice, the intervention of the other Arab states did them more harm than good.

THE PALESTINE REFUGEES

In 1948, about a million Palestinians were driven from their homes by force. It has been alleged that some or all of them left their homes voluntarily on the instructions of their leaders. No one has ever said what leader gave this order, on what occasion, or by what means. Personally, I do not believe that this order was ever given and I am not an intentional liar.

However, I am prepared, for the sake of argument, to assume that these statements were correct. Let us agree that the people of Palestine left their homes on orders from their leaders, who told them that they would subsequently be able to return. ("Their leaders," incidentally, were self-appointed politicians, not elected or representative.) In fleeing from their homes, they abandoned their shops, their houses, their businesses, their farms and their livelihood.

In 1940, great numbers of French people left their homes before the advancing German armies and fled in the clothes they stood up in. Nobody has ever suggested that they thereby forfeited their right to return to their homes when the war was over. The million-odd Palestinians who fled in 1948 have never been allowed to return. Most of them are still living in sordid camps, where they have been for 19 years.

It is quite essential vividly to grasp the unique conditions of the struggle in Palestine. We have witnessed many wars in this century, in which one country seeks to impose its power on others. But in no war,

I think, for many centuries past, has the objective been to remove a nation from its country and to introduce another and entirely different race to occupy its lands, houses and cities and live there. This peculiarity lends to the Palestine struggle a desperate quality which bears no resemblance to any other war in modern history.

WHY DON'T THE OTHER ARAB COUNTRIES TAKE THEM?

When the pitiable state of the Palestine refugees is mentioned, this question is often asked. Perhaps the Palestinians or "the Arabs" as a whole have laid themselves open to this rebuke, by claiming to be all of one homogeneous race. We have already seen that "the Arabs", as the expression is used today, are a cultural and linguistic group of many different racial origins. What would be said if the United States seized Cuba and evicted all the Cubans from their homes, introducing an equal number of American immigrants to replace them? They could be re-absorbed in Venezuela, couldn't they? After all, they are all Latin-Americans.

Or let us take an example nearer home. Suppose Hitler had won the Second World War, had conquered Britain and decided to move all the Jews from Germany to England. For this purpose, he took over the counties of Kent, Surrey and Sussex and ordered the area to be cleared of its inhabitants to accommodate the immigrants. The persons evicted

were told that they could find new homes for themselves in other parts of England. It was pointed out to him, however, that there was already unemployment in other parts of England.

Well, why cannot Canada and Australia take them? They are British too, aren't they?

Can we honestly say in this twentieth century that human beings should be driven against their will from one country to another like human cattle?

But this is how Hitler treated the Jews, many of whom have now at last found a home in Israel.

This is true. But the Arabs have never persecuted Jews. There does not, therefore, seem to be any justification why the terrible sufferings of Jews in Europe should be atoned for by the infliction of similar tortures on the people of Palestine.

The question of the other Arab countries taking refugees has many facets, too various to enumerate here. It may, however, be pointed out that half the refugees were in Jordan, which not only accepted them but gave them full Jordanian citizenship.

Secondly the refugees did not want to leave their country. In that part of Palestine which has been in Jordan since 1948, the refugees felt

themselves still in their own country and within a few miles of their old homes. The well educated refugees did indeed find employment in other countries, some of them in Saudi Arabia. Many of the others could not have been made to leave what they considered to be their native country.

Sometimes it has even been said that the miseries of the refugees are not Israel's fault but that of the other Arab countries which did not accommodate them.

If the landlord were to evict the tenants from a house and leave them shivering in the gutter, a court of law would scarcely accept the plea that the fault lay with the neighbors, who should have taken them in, not with the landlord who turned them out. The case of the Palestine Arabs, however, was far stronger for they were the owners of the houses from which they had been evicted.

Moreover, Jordan accepted half the total number of refugees without hesitation and gave them Jordan citizenship, but the economy of Jordan was not capable of absorbing them and no financial aid was given to her to enable her to do so except by Britain and the United States, the alleged villains of the piece. The United Nations supplied only subsistence rations and medical care.

The refugees admitted and welcomed by Jordan amounted to one-third of the population of the country. This influx of refugees was equivalent to the arrival of seventeen million destitute people in Britain or eighty million in the United States. Their presence has constituted a major social and economic threat to the continued existence of Jordan ever since. In these circumstances, it can scarcely be claimed that the continued existence of refugees is the fault of "the Arabs" and not of Israel.

A Minority In Israel

In the course of the present crisis, the Israeli army has occupied all Palestine down to the Jordan. In so doing, they have overtaken most of the refugees who left their homes in 1948 and who have been living for nineteen years in the Gaza Strip or in the Jordan part of Palestine. There are also a million other Palestinians, who are still living in their own homes in the Arab part of Palestine, which has now been occupied by the Israeli army.

It would, therefore, appear that there must now be a million and a half or a million and three quarters Palestine Arabs, in territory controlled by the Israeli army. The number of Israelis in Israel is two and a half million.

What is to become of a million and a half or more Palestine Arabs, whose ancestors have been living in their homes in the country for centuries, perhaps for millennia? Can they be just pushed out into neighboring countries to live for another 20 years in refugee camps on United Nations' bare subsistence rations?

The alternative suggested is that they remain as a minority in Israel, perhaps even with local semi-autonomy in certain areas. The Israelis, it is alleged, are a democratic community, the Arabs would receive the right to vote and would become happy Israeli citizens. Is this a possible solution?

A glance at the world of today is sufficient to prove that some of the world's most intractable problems are caused by mixed races living in one country. The colored population in the United States, the Turks and the Greeks in Cyprus, the British in Rhodesia and the Indians and Pakistanis in Kashmir are a few examples. In none of these cases were the two races at bitter enmity, yet their inclusion in one state leads to endless problems, often giving rise to international complications.

The Palestine problem is immensely worse. The Israelis and the Arabs are divided by intense hatred. The neighbors of Palestine have all been involved in the struggle. It is perfectly obvious that so large a minority (one and a half millions out of a total of four millions) would be looked upon by the Israelis as a dangerous security risk. They would certainly be closely watched, disarmed, controlled and suppressed — a hated and despised subject race.

But are not all our modern idealisms directed precisely at preventing the subjection of one race to another? How could the British government object so strongly to white rule in Rhodesia and yet connive at Israeli rule over more than a million and a half Arabs in Palestine? When two races are inflamed with such bitter hatred against one another, is it possible to place a million and a half of one such race under the rule of another?

THE RIGHT OF CONQUEST
Until modern times, all nations recognized the right of conquest. A victorious nation had the right to annex the territory of another and to reduce the inhabitants to the status of a subject race. But this very problem is what most of our idealisms are about.

Jews, it is said, are good citizens, capable businessmen, civilized, cultured, charming, artistic, wonderful musicians. Much of this is true, at least of west European Jews. But surely the objection to the rule of one race by another is not that the rulers are unpleasant people, but merely that they are a different race.

For centuries the English ruled Ireland, but eventually they abandoned the attempt and gave independence to the Irish. Yet some English people are quite nice, civilized citizens! But the point was that, nice or nasty, the Irish did not want to be ruled by them and so it was recognized that British rule ought not to be imposed on them.

But the Israelis are enterprising and efficient. They would develop the Arab areas and the Arabs themselves would have a higher standard of living. The same arguments were used in 1936 when Italy invaded Abyssinia. The country was poor and backward, the Italians would develop it, establish industries, and make good roads. The Abyssinians themselves would be the chief beneficiaries. But the world at large rejected these arguments with vehemence.

JEWS ALSO HAVE A RIGHT TO LIVE
Of course they have. The same right as Christians, Muslims and Hindus.

The wildness of Egyptian and Syrian demagogy, their neglect of facts and their empty threats have done the Palestinians more harm than good. Silly boasts about pushing Israel into the sea have been the best Israeli propaganda.

Once again, however, we must remember that "the Arabs" are a linguistic and cultural group of many different races. It is unjust to reduce the Palestinians to subjection or to drive them from their homes because the Egyptians are carried away by their own verbosity.

In any case, Israel has amply proved that she is in no danger of being pushed into the sea. She is more likely to push the Arabs into the sea or the desert. Anyone with any knowledge of the area has known this for the last nineteen years.

THE CRUSADER PRECEDENT

I am no lawyer and I have merely surveyed something of the problem from the Balfour Declaration until now, in order to explain, to some extent, how the Arabs of Palestine think. If they have a persecution complex, there are reasons for their mental state. Whether their treatment was or was not unjust, these things have happened and we cannot put the clock back.

However, the fact that Israel is today supreme, does not mean that she always will be. The Crusaders in the twelfth century held three or four times as much territory as the Israelis hold. For 45 years they defeated all comers. Israel has only been in existence for 19 years.

The Crusaders, however, depended for their existence on the support of the West, as Israel depends now on the U.S.A. After 80 years, the West tired of contributing and the Crusaders suffered a disastrous defeat. But the West again returned to their help and the states were re-established for a further century. After 190 years, they were exterminated. Throughout the whole 190 years, the Middle East was torn by continual wars.

DICTATION OR NEGOTIATION

Peace can be made by dictation or negotiation. Israel may now want peace but she wishes to dictate it. This is human nature — victory is heady wine. We made the same mistake in 1918 and had to fight again in twenty years.

Voices are already to be heard, "We Great Powers cannot settle this. It is best for the Middle East nations to settle their own affairs." When Egypt announced her control of the Straits of Tiran, the United States and Britain did not adopt this attitude of philosophic detachment.

To discuss terms of peace would be too long and only a few points can be mentioned.

1. Everyone in the area needs security, which would free them from the crippling burden of armaments. Security, it seems to me, can only be secured by a guarantee of all frontiers, given by the Great Powers. If the United States, Britain, France and Russia were to join, the solution would be complete but we must remember that Russian policy seems to be to embroil the Western Powers with the Arab world.

2. If the Great Powers could impose a solution, I submit that Egypt, Syria and other states should not act for the Palestinians. Their intervention has done the latter much more harm than good.

3. A bi-national state of Israelis and Arabs could not succeed. Therefore Israel must give back that part of Palestine which formerly was united to Jordan, for the Arabs to live in. Money should be provided from outside, so to develop a reconstituted Jordan that all the refugees could be settled there. They cannot be driven away like human cattle to Syria, Iraq or other countries.

4. In 1948, the United Nations made a resolution that Jerusalem should be international, but it was never implemented. I believe that the Old City and Bethlehem with a small area of countryside should be internationalized, but not the Israeli city. Old Jerusalem is sacred to Christians and Muslims as well as to Jews. Its retention by Israel would greatly aggravate the resentment already felt against her throughout the Muslim world.

The dangerous thing about the Palestine grievance is that they have a case which they have never been able to state. The voice of the Palestinians has been drowned by propaganda, or their defense conducted by other Arab states with their own axes to grind, or they have been driven out by military action.

I have not written propaganda. To the best of my ability, I have written only the absolute and unvarnished truth. "Word of an Englishman, what I say is true."

JEWS IN MUSLIM LANDS
By Adam Parfrey

As the nineteenth century began, the vast majority of Middle Eastern
and North African Jewry, like the vast majority of the general populace,
was poor. In addition to their poverty, however, the Jews had to bear
the burden of social isolation, inferiority, and general opprobrium.
Over the preceding four centuries, then had become increasingly confined into overcrowded ghetto-like quarters, which were called by a
variety of names throughout the Muslim world (for example, Mellah,
Harat al-Yahud, and Mahallat al-Yahud). European travelers of the
eighteenth and nineteenth centuries were unanimous in their reports of
the overall debasement of the Jews living in Islamic lands. The Italian
Jewish poet and traveler Samuel Romanelli, who spent four years
among his co-religionists in Morocco in the late eighteenth century,
described them as "oppressed, miserable creatures, having neither the
mouth to answer an Arab, nor the cheek to raise their head." And the
Englishman Edward William Lane, who lived in Cairo during the
1820s and 1830s and was a keen and sympathetic observer of native
life, depicted the Jews of Egypt as being "held in the utmost contempt
and abhorrence by Muslims in general."

No native group benefitted more from Europe's intrusion into the
Middle East than did the non-Muslim minorities. They were quick to
see that increased European influence and penetration meant a weakening of the traditional Islamic norms of society that had defined
their social and political status for more than a millennium. . . . The
non-Muslim minorities were inclined to view the process of modern-
ization as a means for their own betterment. Jews and Christians
accepted the trappings of Westernization earlier and with greater ease
than did most Muslims.

> — *The Jews of Arab Lands in Modern Times*
> by Norman A. Stillman, Jewish Publication Society, 1991.

The emerging Zionist movement, resulting in mass and sudden emigration of Jews to Palestine, alarmed Arab natives. "The Sephardi Jews
(Jews who were originally from Spain, North Africa and Arab countries) spoke Arabic and had a cultural connection to their Arab neighbors," writes Shira Schoenburg for the Jewish Virtual Library. "In the
mid-1800s, Ashkenazi (native European) Jews started moving to

Hebron and, in 1925, the Slobodka Yeshiva, officially the Yeshiva of Hevron, Knesset Yisrael-Slobodka, was opened. Yeshiva students lived separately from the Sephardi community, and from the Arab population. Due to this isolation, the Arabs viewed them with suspicion and hatred, and identified them as Zionist immigrants."

Jewish immigrants urged British, Italian, Spanish and French authorities of their North African and Middle East colonies not to relinquish power to Arab governments. But the British rule of Palestine failed to restrain anti-Jewish rioting in 1929 and 1936 inspired by the prophetic warnings of Haj Amin al-Husseini, the Mufti of Jerusalem, that Jewish immigration would bring on a Jewish state in Arab homeland. Al-Husseini was actually appointed Mufti by the British Jew Herbert Samuel, the high commissioner of Palestine who inspired the Balfour declaration — the British promise for a Jewish national home.

Many prominent Sephardic Jews of North Africa and the Middle East did not agree with the Zionist cause (led and promoted by European Ashkenazim Jews), declaring solidarity with the Palestinian Arab cause, to which they often made monetary contributions, as seen in a letter sent by a prominent Tunisian Jew to Zionist leaders. Arabs, angered by the usurpation of their lands, did not care to make fine distinctions about Jewish backgrounds, and their violence knew no boundaries.

The rioting of 1929 in Jerusalem was directed against Jews praying at the Western (Wailing) Wall, which was seen as the Jewish attempt to take over sacred Muslim sites. Rioters massacred 129 Jews and severely injured over 300 more, most of them members of the religious communities in Hebron and Safed. British troops in turn killed more than 100 Arabs to suppress the riots. Published accounts of the massacre, such as Maurice Samuel's 1929 book *What Happened in Palestine?*, demonstrated that British troops were warned in advance of the coming mayhem, and did little to suppress this early violent reaction to Zionism:

> Dr. Elkana of Hebron:
> For many days before the horror began, the poison of incitement was felt everywhere. The Arabs spoke openly, shamelessly, and fearlessly of the massacre of the Jews to be arranged in the near future. They did not hesitate to reveal their whole detailed plan . . . Facts and evidence are in the hands of the survivors. The landlord of the Hotel, Nachman Segal, said to the lessee of the hotel on Thursday: "Pay me the rent today, because tomorrow no one among you will be saved."

An unidentified Jewish resident of Hebron:
At about half past two on Friday (August 23) we saw a young Arab arrive by motorcycle from Jerusalem. He alarmed the Arab inhabitants of Hebron, saying that the blood of thousands of Moslems in Jerusalem was being shed like water. He called to the Arabs to avenge this blood. The unrest among the Arabs of Hebron was very strong, particularly after the motor cars began to arrive from Jerusalem with news of disturbances.

Davar newspaper of August 20, 1929:
Incitement of feeling against the Jews goes on, particularly round Jerusalem and Hebron. Rumors are being spread by unknown persons that on Saturday last the Jews cursed the Moslem religion and that it is the duty of Moslems to take revenge.

Excerpted from a telegram from the Arab Executive to the British High Commissioner for Palestine (after the pogrom):
The world will see (as a result of an impartial inquiry) that Jews, whose aggressions have surpassed political aims to religious ones, whose provocations have lately become insupportable, as admitted by [British Mandatory] Government, etc., were responsible for the present troubles, together with the policy supporting them.

From *The Memorial Book of the Jewish Community of Hebron:*
On Friday morning, the day of the outbreak in Jerusalem, the Jews of Hebron were already alarmed. The day before, Aref el-Aref, Arab Governor of Be'ersheva, had been in the City and had preached in the Mosque (Ha' Machpelah). His words were repeated to the Jews; in the midst of open incitement to riot recurred those familiar and sinister words: "The Government is with us!'"

The visit of Aref el-Aref to Hebron on Thursday bore very early fruit. On Friday morning the Jews of Hebron received, from an Arab source, the news that the Arabs were arming. Rabbi Ya'acov Slonim, head of the Sephardic Jewish community, and Rabbi Frank, head of the Ashkenazic community, turned to the Arab Governor of Hebron, Abdullah Kardos. The Governor calmed us and said: "There is no fear of anything happening. The British Government knows what it has to do. In the place where two soldiers are needed, it sends six." And he added: "I tell you in confidence that they have many soldiers in the streets, in civilian clothes; these soldiers circulate among the crowds, and in the hour of need they will fulfill their duty."

On Friday afternoon, an Arab mob broke into the Yeshiva, and killed the only student who had remained there — Samuel Rozenholtz, known among the Jews of Hebron as a matmid, a name given to those who distinguish themselves by their devotion to study. On Saturday morning, before the slaughter began, the Rabbis again appealed to the Governor for help. Again they received the same astounding assurances. Bewildered, they turned to Mr. Cafferata, the British officer in charge of the Police. From him, too, they received assurances of safety. I find such difficulty in believing this story, that I have looked at every record of eyewitnesses, without finding a contradiction.

For two hours on the morning of Saturday, August 24, there raged in Hebron a scene which is not easy to parallel even in the medieval annals of the Jewish people. For two hours neither the Governor of Hebron nor the British officer interfered. From English papers I cull a story of the heroism of Mr. Cafferata in attempting to stop the massacre. Newspaper reports speak of Mr. Cafferata being decorated for "heroism." However, I could not find an account of such heroics or even any attempt to stop the attack. The author does state that a certain Commander Partridge of Gaza treated the wounded and dying. The Memorial book and survivors does mention the heroism of some of their Arab friends and landlords: "The family Moshe Masha, the family Borowsky, the family of Rabbi Slonim, the family Schneersohn were thus rescued." They recall even the unsuccessful efforts of one Arab, Nassar El-Din, to protect Jews in his own home. However, with regard to Mr. Cafferata, both the Memorial Book and the testimony of the survivors record, with damning unanimity, that Mr. Cafferata did nothing for two hours. The Memorial book records:

From our knowledge, we say with certainty that it would have sufficed to issue a warning, or to fire some shots into the air, and the crowd would have scattered. It was only after there had been sufficient butchery, plunder and rape, and the pogromists were about to attack an English officer, that some shots were fired, and the mob dispersed at once.

One eyewitness stated:

The massacre lasted an hour and a half. There were then heard six shots and the murderers scattered. Those that would not scatter were fired on by the English commander. Then 25 Arabs fell.

The Memorial of the Jews of Hebron, as submitted to the High Commissioner of Palestine closes with these tragic words:

In the name of 65 slaughtered, 58 wounded, and many orphans and widows; in the name of the remnants of the plundered and tortured we accuse:

The [British Mandatory] Government, which did not fulfill its duty and provide protection for its peaceful and defenseless charges.

The Governor, Abdullah Kardos, and the Commander, Cafferata, who deprived us of the means of appealing for help and defense, betrayed us with empty promises and gave the murderers and robbers their opportunity.

The police, which did not fulfill its duty, and behaved with contemptible baseness.

The emissaries of the Mufti and the Moslem Council, in particular the Sheikh Talib Narka and his colleagues, those mentioned above, as well as those who have not been mentioned, who proclaimed the massacre and permitted murder and rape.

Also the inhabitants of Hebron (with the exception of some families) who did not rise up to help their brothers and neighbors in accordance with the commandments of the Koran . . .

Like most Western media accounts of Islamic terror, including ones following the 9/11/01 attacks, Maurice Samuel rebukes Muslims for disobeying their own holy book. But did they? The Koran says, "Slay them wherever you find them" (4:89) and, "Fight the idolators utterly" (9:36). Jihad, as defined by *Reliance of the Traveller*, the standard Islamic legal reference, reminds all believers that Jihad is a "communal obligation," particularly in the case of non-Muslims entering into Muslim territory. "Fight those who do not believe in Allah and the Last Day and who forbid not what Allah and his messenger have forbidden — who do not practice the religion of truth, being of those who have been given the Book — until they pay the poll tax out of hand and are humbled" (Koran 9:29).

Jews lived in Muslim lands for centuries; sometimes valued and treated well, but most often as "oppressed, miserable creatures." According to Islamic law, "The indemnity paid for a Jew or Christian is one-third the indemnity paid for a Muslim," but certainly this wasn't as valueless as the Zoroastrian, who was worth one-fifteenth the indemnity paid for a Muslim, but closing in on the value of a female Muslim, worth "one-half the indemnity paid for a man."

Israel law does not goes so far as to stipulate the value of a Palestinian life, but at the funeral of Baruch Goldstein, who murdered 29 Palestinians in prayer at Tomb of the Patriarchs, Orthodox rabbi Yaacov Perrin said, "One million Arabs are not worth a Jewish fingernail." Goldstein's February 1994 massacre was not dissimilar from the suicidal terror of the Islamic "martyrs," and Jews erected a shrine in his name and produced books in his memory, including one titled "Blessed is Baruch." Goldstein devotedly followed Meir Kahane, the Brooklyner who founded the militaristic Jewish Defense League, and led the Kach party, now outlawed in Israel, and who wrote books telling Jews why all Arabs should be evicted from Israel and occupied territories. Son Binyamin and his wife Talia, residents of a West Bank settlement and inheritors of father Meir's anti-Arab program, were gunned down in November 2000 by a group called "Intifada Martyrs."

Goldstein's murderous rampage provoked a vast escalation of Arab suicide bombings within Israel in the mid-to-late 1990s. On websites, and in books, Palestinians remember the Goldstein massacre, as well as Deir Yassin, with the kind of language meant to inspire payback, like Meir Kahane's nauseous detailing of the 1929 Hebron massacre, used here as the rationale to expel all Arabs from the state of Israel, dead or alive:

The mob is drunk on murder and brutality. Its cruelty is fed by atrocity. The scholar Reb Bezalel Smarik, from Zhitel in Lithuania, is seventy-three. The Arabs drag him outside and kill him obscenely on the doorstep of his home. Inside they murder three North American yeshiva students: Binyamin Halevi Horowitz, twenty, of New York; Tzvi Halevi Freuman, twenty-one, from Canada; and twenty-two-year-old Memphis-born David Scheinberg.

They now burst into the adjoining home of Shlomo Unger. The twenty-six-year-old Unger is a huge man, a mechanic, from Zgug, Poland. He looked like a Gentile and the mob pauses. One shouts at him: "Are you a Christian?" He can say yes and save his life. He looks with contempt at the mob of Arabs and says, "I am a Jew!" They leap on him with fury, his courage maddening them. They attack his wife; she loses her mind and dies a few days later. They leave two orphans, one two years old and the other two months . . .

More, more! The baker Noah Imerman, from Slutzk and Slobodka, is killed as the Arabs thrust his head into the oven. Nahman Segal, thirty, of Skola, Poland, watches in horror as his Arab landlord opens the doors for the mob. He is holding his three-year-old child, Menachem. An Arab ax cuts through his hand, wounding the child fatally. Segal dies a few hours later. His wife has three fingers cut off, and a yeshiva student in the house loses his left hand. In the same house the great *masmid* ("eternal learner of Torah") of the yeshiva, Simcha Yitzhak Broida, twenty-eight, of Vilkomir, Lithuania, is

Arab volunteers with the skull of a Jew and with bodies of dead Jews, near Jerusalem.

dangled head down from the window and tortured to death. With him dies sixteen-year-old Brooklyn-born Chaim Krasner and a couple that have come to Hebron for a Sabbath visit, Asher Moshe and Chaya Gutman of Tel Aviv.

The Hebron yeshiva is looted and totally destroyed. All its records are ripped to shreds and the furniture destroyed in an orgy of madness. The home of the Rosh Yeshiva, Rabbi Epstein, is a major target of the murderers. They attack in a large force, throwing huge stones through the windows. The families inside are gripped by terror. The men desperately try to hold the doors against the mob, and the women cry out in panic. Across the street stands the home of the governor of Hebron. The cries of anguish move him to come out onto the balcony and order the police, who have been standing by the whole time, to chase the mob away. The mob is not impressed. Three times they return, and three times the governor calmly orders them to be dispersed. It is easily done, but not before sixty-eight-year-old Elimelech Zev Lichtenstein is murdered. The day before, when the first victim of the Arabs was killed in the yeshiva, Lichtenstein was in a side room. Today he has just been called up to the Torah, where he gave the traditional blessing of thanks, *Hagomel*, for having been saved. Now, fifteen minutes later, he is dead.

The day of horrors nears its end. Outside the small hotel, according to *The Book of Hebron* (edited by Oded Avisar, 1970), Eishel Avraham, Sheikh Talib, the Muslim religious leader of the town, walks up to the building in which dozens of Jews sit huddled in terror. He looks inside to see how many people he can count, then leaves. Some moments pass, and suddenly the sound of a large mob is heard. The Jews look out the windows to see hundreds of Arabs following the Sheikh. They stand around him, now, as he speaks to them: "You, Muslims! Inside are ten Americans whose parents are millionaires. Slaughter the Jews! Drink their blood! Today is the day of Islam! This is the day that the Prophet has commanded you! Allah and the prophets have commanded you to avenge the blood of your dead brethren in Jerusalem! Allah is great! Come with me and kill the Jews! Inside are beautiful Jewish women; take them!"

The mob attacks the home of the Cheichal family near the hotel. The yeshiva students, inside, fight wildly to hold the doors. At the very moment that they begin to splinter, the students see what they take to be a miracle: a British officer with five Arab policemen suddenly appears on horseback! The two Cheichal sons, Yisrael-Aryeh, twenty, and Eliyah Dov, seventeen, rush out past the surprised mob to the policemen. They plead with them to save the Jews inside. The policemen stare. The mob now angrily rushes at the two Jews who are standing and imploring the British officer to save their lives. They attack Yisrael-Aryeh. Bloodied, he turns like a madman on his attackers, smashing them with his fists, until he falls dead at the feet of his "rescuers."

The younger brother seizes the reins of the Britisher's horse and pleads for his life. As he does so the mob stabs him again and again, one Arab laughing and shouting, "Does it hurt, Jew?"

The two brothers die, but their deaths enable the other Jews, whose presence the Arab murderers have momentarily forgotten, to flee to safety.

And in the Jewish quarter, the Jewish ghetto, every house is looted, every synagogue destroyed. Reb Alter Platshy, the twenty-nine-year-old Sephardic sexton, is brutally murdered. He is a poverty-stricken plasterer, sole supporter of his six children and elderly widowed mother. Another pauper, elderly Yitzhak AbuHana, sixty-nine, dies a terrible death, and two other destitute Jews, Avraham Yani, fifty-nine, and his wife, Vida, both born in Constantinople, also fall victim to the killers.

The famous Sephardic synagogue, Avraham Avinu, built in the year 1501, is totally destroyed. The Arabs take the Torah Scrolls and with shouts of animal joy rip them to pieces and burn the shreds. This is the synagogue that will later be turned into a sheep pen. It is the synagogue that, after Israeli liberation of Hebron, will remain a sheep pen for years, with the Arab shepherd paying IL 60 a year for the "privilege" to the Israeli military government! It is the synagogue that the Israeli government will refuse for more than ten years to repair, out of fear of changing the "status quo," giving in only after Russian Jewish hero Professor Ben Zion Tavgar single-handedly drives out the sheep.

Only ghosts haunt the buildings today: the ghosts of Jews whose intestines were ripped out. The ghosts of Jews whose skulls were so viciously chopped that their brains poured out. The ghost of the elderly Jew who was castrated before being killed, of the young Jewish student whose body was found with a piece of flesh ripped from his throat, of the barber whose head was stuffed into a toilet, where he died. Of the woman who was hanged by her legs and whose hair was ripped from her head. Of the baker whose head was thrust into a lit oven. Of Rabbi Grodzinski, whose left eye was ripped out and whose skull was broken, even as the blood spattered the ceiling. Of the young woman teacher who was raped by thirteen Arabs before her parents' eyes. Of the young girl who was stripped naked and saved from rape only when she pleaded to be killed. The "merciful" Arabs agreed: they ripped open her belly before the eyes of her tiny sister, who hid under a bed . . .

Hebron: where six more Jews die by Arab bullets in May 1980; nothing has changed. Hebron: where the impossibility of Arab-Jewish coexistence is written in blood.

Muslim fervor against Zionism was stoked by the Wailing Wall riots and the Hebron massacre. According to Norman Stillman, "The more traditional religious groups within Egyptian society, such as the Young Men's Muslim Association, the Society of Islamic Guidance, the students at the Azhar, merchants in the bazaar, and members of the professional class, were deeply affected by what was happening in Palestine . . . [responding] with impassioned manifestos, newspaper articles and fund-raising campaigns on behalf of the Palestinian Arabs. Their appeals were filled with accounts of Zionist aggression and wild accusations concerning Jewish attempts to destroy the Aqsa Mosque in order to replace it with a new Temple*. . . The most violent reactions came, not surprisingly, in Syria and Iraq . . . the press in both countries constantly issued hyperbolic reports filled with lurid details of the happenings in Palestine. . . . Trucks with Jewish-owned merchandise were attacked and destroyed by mobs. Rumors were spread by posters and in the press that Jews were giving poisoned candy to Muslim children, some of whom had died as a result."

---

* **Editor's note:** As seen in the chapter "Ground Zero for Holy War," accusations of Zionist attempts to destroy the Aqsa Mosque and replace it with a new Temple weren't as wild as Norman Stillman believed.

In the late 1930s, Nazi and Fascist anti-Jewish propaganda made its way to Arab countries. Fascist propaganda broadcasts in Arabic "were the monopoly of the Italian radio station at Bari." Sami al-Jundi, an early Baathist leader, wrote in his memoirs:

"We were racialists. We were fascinated by Nazism, reading its books and the sources of its thought, especially Nietzsche's *Thus Spake Zarathustra,* Fichte's *Addresses to the German Nation,* and Houston Stewart Chamberlain's *Foundations of the Nineteenth Century.*"

Arabic translations of *Mein Kampf,* with anti-Arab passages expunged, were available in the Middle East and North Africa during these years. Arabic youth groups (the Green Shirts of Misr al-Fatat, the Phalanxes of the Muslim Brotherhood, the Iron Shirts of the Syrian National Bloc, the Phalanges Libanaises of the Maronites and the Muthanna Club and the Futuwwa of Iraq) affected paramilitary attire like the Italian and Germans. And so did their rhetoric:

"[The Jews] are the secret of this moral desolation throughout the Arab and Islamic worlds. They are the secret of this cultural squalor and filthy arts. They are the secret of religious and moral decay . . . search for the Jew behind every depravity." (Ahmad Husayn, leader of Misr al-Fatat, quoted in *The Influence of German National Socialism on Radical Movements in Egypt* by Shimon Shamir.)

World War II was traumatic for the Jewish communities in the Middle East and North African. In Iraq, on June 1, anti-Jewish rioting resulted in the murder of 200 Jews. 911 buildings housing 12,000 Jews were pillaged, and 586 businesses were looted. Thousands of Jews died in Libya after being sent to desert internment and labor camps. Prison camps containing many Jews operated in Algeria, Tunisia and Morocco.

In the postwar years the Jewish communities were nearly swept clean from Arab land. "A concatena-

Soldiers with mantle of a torah scroll.

tion of forces and events set in motion . . . would totally undermine the position of the Jewish communities in the Arab world and result in their almost total dissolution," writes Norman Stillman. "Within a decade, the overall Jewish population in Arab countries was reduced by half through emigration. In several countries the decline was far greater. By the end of 1953, Iraq, Yemen and Libya had lost over 90 percent of their Jews, and Syria approximately 75 percent."

The number of Jews removed from Arab territory, by emigration, disease, or murder is variously depicted as being 500,000 to one million. Zionist propagandists eagerly point out that Jews forced out of Arab land comprise a nearly equal number of Palestinians who fled their land during the first Arab-Israeli war, and thus should be seen as a righteous exchange. The propagandists neglect to mention that Jews comfortably and successfully possess their own country, and are likely not to be anxious to return to lands that treated them as second-class citizens. Palestinians are denied the ability to return and forced into the disease-infested Warsaw ghettos of the Middle East.

British attempts to pacify Arabs by suppressing Zionism to keep order in Palestine failed miserably. For reasons stunningly similar to Western culture's inability to stop Islamic revolution, postwar Zionism, particularly following the nasty business of a European Holocaust, used messianic determination — a polite way of saying "terror" — to get its way.

Menachem Begin and Yitzhak Shamir, future Prime Ministers Israel, made names for themselves by not being unwilling to practice terror against England — the apogee of Western civilization and Parliamentary law. Begin and his Irgun organization are notably responsible for bombing the British Mandate's headquarters, The King David Hotel, killing nearly 100 formidable citizens of the free world. Shamir and his Lehi "Stern gang" are noted for murdering Baron Moyne, Britain's minister of State in Cairo, and Count Folke Bernadotte, the United Nation's mediator in Palestine, whose partition plan displeased Zionists and their plans that would brook no disappointment.

Caving in to practitioners of terror, the British thought best to allow the United Nations to offer the Zionists their own state. On November 29, 1947, a partition offer divided Palestine into two states — one Jewish, the other Palestinian. The peculiar partitioning layout favorably provided Jews, who at the time comprised one-third of the population, approximately 56% of Palestine. The hot zones of Jerusalem and Bethlehem were designated an international zone to be shared by both states.

The partition plan begged another question for the Zionists: what to do with all the Arabs occupying what they saw as their land? The answer: Terror. Get them to run. Writes Menachem Begin in *The Revolt*:

"Arabs throughout the country, induced to believe wild tales of 'Irgun butchery' were seized with limitless panic and started to flee for their lives. This mass flight soon developed into a maddened, uncontrolled stampede. Of the almost 800,000 who lived on the present territory of the State of Israel, only some 165,000 are still there. The political and economic significance of this development can hardly be overestimated."

Begin's Irgun crew is held responsible for the April 9, 1948 massacre of over 100 Arab civilians, including more than 50 women and children at Deir Yassin, a village located outside of the area that the United Nations recommended be included in a future Jewish State. The Deir Yassin massacre is held by Arabs as symbolic of inhuman Zionist terror, and because of its iconic status, some Israeli nationalists say the crime, though admitted and apologized for by Zionist leaders of the time, never happened — a kind of flipside to Holocaust Denial.

The way Uncle Sam was depicted as participating in the Jewish-Arab War.

The United States is a dog who hides after the Jewish dog is lanced.

Arab newspaper's view of Arab supremacy and caricatures of Jewish weakness in 1948.

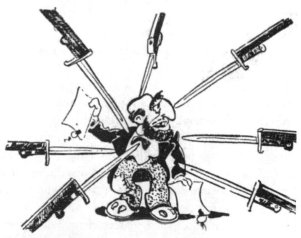

OCCIDENTOSIS: A PLAGUE FROM THE WEST

By Jalal Al-I Ahmad

SUPPRESSED BY THE SHAH OR IRAN WHEN FIRST PUBLISHED IN 1963, OCCIDENTOSIS — MEANING "A PLAGUE FROM THE WEST" — IS A SARCASTIC BLAST ON IRAN'S UPPER-CRUST SOCIETY, PARTICULARLY THOSE INFLUENCED BY THE PAHLAVI FAMILY. ITS AUTHOR WAS A MARXIST WHO DIED IN 1969, AND CONSEQUENTLY HAD VERY LITTLE TO DO WITH ISLAMIC REVOLUTION, THOUGHT MANY OF ITS TOP INTELLECTUAL CORE, INCLUDING ALI SHARIATI, WERE INSPIRED BY ITS RIP ON WESTERN MATERIALISM, AND THE WAY IT WAS RUINOUSLY TAKEN UP IN IMITATION BY IRAN'S SECULAR SOCIETY. OCCIDENTOSIS WAS PUBLISHED IN ENGLISH BY MIZAN PRESS, HAMID ALGAR'S BERKELEY COMPANY THAT HAS TAKEN UP THE CAUSE OF ISSUING BOOKS BY MAJOR FIGURES INVOLVED WITH ISLAMIC REVOLUTION.

From the chapter, "Asses in Lions' Skins, or Lions on the Flag":

The occidentotic has no character. He is a thing without authenticity. His person, his home, and his words convey nothing in particular, and everything in general. It is not that he is cosmopolitan, that the world is his home. He is at home nowhere rather than everywhere. He is an amalgam of singleness without character and character without singularity. Because he has no security, he dissembles. In the very act of being so polite and sociable, he mistrusts whom he is speaking to. And because suspicion dominates our age, he must never open his heart to anyone. The only palpable characteristic he has is fear. In the West individuals' characters are sacrificed to their field of specialization, but the occidentotic has neither. He has only fear: fear of tomorrow, fear of dismissal, fear of anonymity, fear of discovery that the warehouse he has weighing down his head and tries to foist off as a brain is empty.

The occidentotic is effete. He is effeminate. He attends to his grooming a great deal. He spends much time sprucing himself up. Sometimes he even plucks his eyelashes. He attaches a great deal of importance to his shoes and his wardrobe, and to the furnishings of his home. It always seems he has been unwrapped from gold foil or come from some European maison. He buys the latest prodigy in automotive engineering every year. His house, which once had a porch and a cellar, a pool, awnings, and a vestibule, now looks like something different every day. One day it resembles a seaside villa with picture windows all around, and full of fluorescent lamps. Another day it resembles a cabaret, full of gaudy junk and bar stools. The next day all the walls are painted one color and triangles of all colors cover every surface. In one corner there is a hi-fi, in another a television, in another a piano for the young lady, in others stereo loudspeakers. The kitchen and other nooks and crannies are packed with gas stoves, electric washers, and other odds and ends. Thus the occidentotic is the most faithful consumer of the West's industrial goods. If he should rise one morning and find that the hairdresser, the tailor, the shoeshiner, and the repairman have all closed up shop, he would turn to the qibla in desperation (that is, he would do so if he knew where the qibla was).

All his preoccupations and Western products are more essential to him than any school, mosque, hospital, or factory. It is for his sake that we have an architecture with no roots in our culture, and counterfeit cities! It is for his sake that our city streets and intersections have turned out looking like barbers' shops with all their brazen fluorescent and neon lighting. It is for his sake that a cookbook called *The Way to the Heart* (*Rah-i Dil*) has been published, full of detailed recipes for all the doughy and meaty dishes that one absolutely cannot eat in this sort of hot, dry climate, dishes that are no more than a justification for using gas stoves made in Europe. It is for his sake that they are destroying the bazaars' roofs. It is for his sake that the state Takya is demolished. It is for his sake that the senate building has such a monstrous design. It is for like reasons that soldiers wear so much gaud and gook, that enough goods to stock a haberdashery hang from their chests, shoulders, and aiguillettes.

The occidentotic hangs on the words and handouts of the West. He has nothing to do with what goes on in our little world, in this corner of the East. If perchance he is interested in politics, he is cognizant of the faintest right or left tendencies in the British Labor Party and is more familiar with the current U.S. senators than with the ministers in his own government. And he knows more about the staff of *Time* or the *News Chronicle* than about some nephew way off in Khurasan. And he supposes them more veracious than a prophet because all these have more influence on the affairs of his country than any domestic politician, commentator, or representative. If he is interested in letters, his only concern is knowing who won this year's Nobel Prize or who was awarded the Goncourt or Pulitzer prizes. And if he is interested in research, he folds his hands and closes his eyes to all the problems within the country that could be studied. He seeks to learn only what some orientalist has said and written about the questions within his field. If he is one of the ordinary people who read the weeklies and the pictorials, we have seen what a sorry lot they are.

If there used to be a time when one could silence opponents and end all arguments by citing one verse of the Qur'an or one tradition transmitted in Arabic, now one does so by relating one sentence by some European, whatever the subject under discussion. This matter has reached such scandalous proportions that the predictions of Western fortune-tellers and astrologers throw the whole world headlong into tumult and dread. Now revelation is sought not in scriptures but in European books or from the lips of reporters for Reuters, United Press, and so forth — these great corporate makers of news (counterfeit or otherwise).

Granted that one may seek to familiarize oneself with the scientific method, the methods of machine manufacture, and the basic assumptions of Western philosophy only through European or Western books, but an occidentotic has no concern with the basic assumptions of Western philosophy. Even when he wants to learn about the East, he resorts to Western sources. It is for this reason that orientalism (almost certainly a parasite growing on the root of imperialism) dominates thought and opinion in the occidentotic nations. On the subject of Islamic philosophy, the customs of Yogis in India, the prevalence of superstitions in Indonesia, the national character of the Arabs, or any other Eastern subject, the occidentotic regards only Western writings as proper sources and criteria. This is how he comes to know even himself in terms of the language of the orientalist. With his own hands he has reduced himself to the status of an object to be scrutinized under the microscope of the orientalist. Then he relies on the orientalist's observations, not on what he himself feels, sees, and experiences.

This is the ugliest symptom of occidentosis: to regard yourself as nothing, not to think at all, to give up all reliance on your own self, your own eyes and ears, to give over the authority of your own senses to any pen held by any wretch who has said or written a word as an orientalist. I haven't the foggiest notion when orientalism became a "science." If we say that some Westerner is a linguist, dialectologist, or musicologist specializing in Eastern questions, this is defensible. Or if we say he is an anthropologist or sociologist, this again is arguable to an extent. But what does it mean to be an orientalist without further definition? Does it mean to know all the secrets of the Eastern world? Are we living in the age of Aristotle? This is why I speak of a parasite growing on the root of imperialism. This orientalism attached to UNESCO has its own organizations in turn, its biennial or quadrennial congress, its member bodies, its comings and goings. The misfortune is that our contemporaries of prominence — especially those engaged in both politics and letters (this happens to be one of the characteristics of politics and politicians in the occidentotic countries, that politicians generally are drawn from among the literati, and the venerable ones, and accordingly that the converse is also true, that every leading politician must write books) — are often those who have been taken for a ride by the Western orientalists. These orientalists having no vocation in their own Western country, knowing nothing of any science, technology, trade, or talent, learned an Eastern language, secretly or openly entered the service of their country's foreign ministry, and were exported to this part of the world along with the European-made machine, or as an advance party for it, along with the technical specialists, to hum some poem to himself while the goods were being sold. Then the faithful purchaser could say, "Did you see? Did you hear that? How well so-and-so speaks Persian!" This is how we come to have orientalists, with books, researches, excavations, poetics, musicologies. In such a going market for the machine and the transformation it offers, the Western orientalist writes a study of Mulla Sadra, pontificates on belief and want of belief in the Imam of the Age, or does research on the wondrous deeds of Shaykh Pashm ad-din Kashkuli. Then not only do all occidentotics everywhere invoke this opinion, but many a time I have heard in the mosques, from the pulpits (supposedly the last bastion against the West and occidentosis), Carlyle, Gustave Le Bon, Gobineau, Edward Browne, or others cited as the final authority on the veracity of some person, course of action, or religious school.

We might say that the Westerner, with his university and research facilities and well-stocked libraries, has a better grasp of the scientific method, a freer hand, and a broader outlook than his Eastern counterpart even when it comes to the study of Eastern languages, religions, and customs. Thus his opinion is necessarily weightier than those of the Easterners themselves, who lack this scientific method and these research facilities. Perhaps also, because the museums, libraries, and universities of that side of the world have been packed with the plundered relics, antiquities, and libraries of this side, a Western researcher necessarily has more material at his disposal than his Eastern counterparts. For this reason, one must turn to the West to consult most Eastern sources. It may be because the Easterner has yet to attain to these worlds or is still caught up in problems of obtaining daily bread and clothing that he has yet to find time to discourse on the spiritual and the worldly. There are a thousand more maybes. I accept them all as inevitable. But what do you say of those cases in which both the Easterner and the Westerner have offered views — and with one method but two separate outlooks? Do you not concede that, in the eyes of the occidentotic, the view of the orientalist or the Western researcher is in every case preferable to that of the Eastern specialist? I have experienced this time after time.

Finally, the occidentotic in this country knows absolutely nothing about the oil question. He doesn't sound off about it, because his own well-being is not involved. Even if in some cases he does gain his living through this means, he never gives himself a headache over oil. He has utterly given up when it comes to oil. If the opportunity arises, he will work as a servant and broker for the oil interests. He writes magazines for them and makes films for them. But they just look the other way. The occidentotic is not an imaginative man or idealist. He deals with reality, and reality in this country means the easy and automatic income provided by oil.

DO NOT CALL JIHAD A DEFENSE
from *Milestones*, the book that killed its author By Sayyid Qutb

QUTB'S ENORMOUS IMPACT WITH REVOLUTIONARY ISLAM IS PERHAPS BEST ARTICULATED BY A WRITER WITH A MILITANT'S SYMPATHY.

REMEMBERING SAYYID QUTB, AN ISLAMIC INTELLECTUAL AND LEADER OF RARE INSIGHT AND INTEGRITY
BY ZAFAR BANGASH
IT IS PERHAPS INDICATIVE OF THE PRESENT STATE OF THE *UMMAH* THAT, OUTSIDE HIS NATIVE EGYPT AND A SMALL CIRCLE OF ISLAMIC ACTIVISTS, FEW MUSLIMS ARE AWARE THAT AUGUST 29 [1999] MARKED THE 33RD ANNIVERSARY OF THE MARTYRDOM OF SAYYID QUTB. HE WAS NO ORDINARY MUSLIM. A MAN OF IMPECCABLE ISLAMIC CREDENTIALS, HE MADE AN IMMENSE CONTRIBUTION TO MUSLIM POLITICAL THOUGHT AT A TIME WHEN THE MUSLIM WORLD WAS STILL MESMERIZED BY SUCH WESTERN NOTIONS AS NATIONALISM, THE NATION-STATE AND FATHERS OF NATIONS. NATIONALIST RHETORIC LACED WITH SOCIALIST SLOGANS WAS THE VOGUE.

IT WAS IN THIS ATMOSPHERE THAT SAYYID QUTB RAISED HIS VOICE — INDEED HIS PEN — AGAINST THESE FALSE IDEOLOGIES AND IN ONE CLEAN SWEEP DENOUNCED THEM AS THE MODERN-DAY *JAHILIYYAH* (THE PRIMITIVE SAVAGERY OF PRE-ISLAMIC DAYS). IN THIS SAYYID QUTB DEPARTED FROM MAULANA MAUDOODI'S ARTICULATION OF "PARTIAL *JAHILIYYAH*" IN WHICH THE LATE PAKISTANI SCHOLAR WAS PREPARED TO CONCEDE TO THE SYSTEMS PREVALENT IN MUSLIM SOCIETIES SOME ROOM FOR MODIFICATION AND HENCE A DEGREE OF RESPECTABILITY. SAYYID QUTB WOULD HAVE NONE OF IT; HE INSISTED THAT, BEING A COMPLETE SYSTEM OF LIFE, ISLAM NEEDS NO ADDITIONS FROM MAN-MADE SYSTEMS.

IT WAS THIS FORTHRIGHT FORMULATION WHICH SENT HIM TO THE GALLOWS ON AUGUST 29, 1966 TOGETHER WITH TWO OTHER IKHWAN AL-MUSLIMOON [MUSLIM BROTHERHOOD] LEADERS, MUHAMMAD YUSUF AWASH AND ABD AL-FATTAH ISMAIL. THE SPECIFIC CHARGE AGAINST SAYYID QUTB WAS BASED ON HIS NOW-CELEBRATED BOOK, *MA'ALIM FI'L-TAREEQ* (*SIGNPOSTS ON THE ROAD*, ALSO TRANSLATED AS *MILESTONES*). THE BOOK DENOUNCED THE EXISTING ORDER IN MUSLIM SOCIETIES AS *JAHILIYYAH*, PROVIDES GUIDELINES FOR MUSLIM ACTIVISTS, AND DESCRIBES THE STEPS THEY MUST TAKE TO ESTABLISH A SOCIETY BASED ON DIVINE GUIDANCE.

THE IKHWAN AL-MUSLIMOON IS NO LONGER THE MOVEMENT THAT SAYYID QUTB HAD JOINED WHEN HE RETURNED FROM THE US IN 1950. IT HAS SINCE BEEN REDUCED TO A SHELL, BEING LITTLE MORE THAN A POLITICAL PARTY WITH AN ISLAMIC FLAG. EVEN THIS MILD VERSION OF ISLAMIC EXPRESSION IS NOT TOLERATED BY THE PHARAOHS OF EGYPT, WHO ARE BEHOLDEN TO THEIR MASTERS IN WASHINGTON AND TEL AVIV. YET IT IS THE MUSLIM ACTIVISTS WHO ARE ACCUSED OF "INTOLERANCE."

SAYYID QUTB WAS A PROLIFIC WRITER. HIS BEST WORKS, HOWEVER, WERE PRODUCED AFTER HIS SUDDEN RETURN FROM THE US. WHAT DISAPPOINTED HIM MOST THERE WAS THE INFATUATION OF AMERICAN SOCIETY WITH MATERIALISM AND THE WIDESPREAD SEXUAL ANARCHY. HE COULD HAVE GONE ON TO STUDY FOR HIS DOCTORAL THESIS, BUT DECIDED INSTEAD TO RETURN TO EGYPT AND DEVOTE HIS LIFE TO THE ISLAMIC MOVEMENT.

IF THERE WAS ONE PARTICULAR MOMENT IN HIS LIFE WHICH PROVED CRUCIAL IN THIS DECISION, IT WAS HIS PAIN AT THE MANNER IN WHICH HASAN AL-BANNA'S MARTYRDOM WAS REPORTED IN THE AMERICAN PRESS. *CRESCENT INTERNATIONAL* READERS WILL NOT BE SURPRISED AT THE MANNER IN WHICH THE *NEW YORK TIMES* REPORTED THE MARTYRDOM OF IMAM HASAN AL-BANNA. IT WROTE: "IN CAIRO THE LEADER OF THE OUTLAWED TERRORIST MOSLEM BROTHERHOOD HASAN EL-BANNA, WAS KILLED BY AN ASSASSIN" (FEBRUARY 13, 1949). IT WENT ON TO SAY: "SHEIKH HASAN EL-BANNA, 39-YEAR-OLD HEAD OF THE OUTLAWED MOSLEM BROTHERHOOD EXTREMIST EGYPTIAN NATIONALIST MOVEMENT THAT WAS BANNED AFTER AUTHORITIES HAD DECLARED IT RESPONSIBLE FOR A SERIES OF BOMBING OUTRAGES AND KILLINGS LAST YEAR, WAS SHOT FIVE TIMES BY A GROUP OF YOUNG MEN IN A CAR AND DIED TONIGHT IN HOSPITAL."

THE "TERRORIST" APPELLATION FOR ISLAMIC ACTIVITY IS NOT A PHENOMENON OF THE '80S OR '90S. IT HAS BEEN IN CIRCULATION FOR MORE THAN 50 YEARS. ONE CAN IMMEDIATELY SEE THE EMOTIONALLY-LOADED EXPRESSIONS — "TERRORIST," "EXTREMIST," "OUTLAWED," ETC — USED FOR THE IKHWAN AL-MUSLIMOON BY THE MOUTHPIECE OF THE ZIONIST ESTABLISHMENT IN AMERICA. QUTB'S DISAPPOINTMENT AT SEEING THE SUPPOSEDLY RESPECTABLE ORGANS OF PUBLIC OPINION INDULGING IN A VICIOUS ATTACK ON THE CHARACTER OF A LEADING ISLAMIC LEADER CAN BE IMAGINED.

WHEN SAYYID QUTB RETURNED TO EGYPT, HE STARTED WORKING WITH THE IKHWAN AL-MUSLIMOON, WHICH HE HAD NOT PREVIOUSLY BEEN A MEMBER OF, AS WELL AS CONTINUING TO THINK AND WRITE. AT THE TIME, THE IKHWAN WERE WORKING WITH THE "FREE OFFICERS" PLOTTING TO OVERTHROW THE MONARCHY OF KING FAROUK. AMONG

THE FREE OFFICERS WERE SUCH FIGURES AS COLONEL GAMAL ABD AL-NASSER AND COLONEL ANWAR SADAT. ACCORDING TO THE SADAT'S OWN ACCOUNT, SAYYID QUTB WAS THE MAIN IDEOLOGUE OF THE FREE OFFICERS' "REVOLUTION." HAD THE COUP FAILED, IT IS CLEAR THAT SAYYID QUTB WOULD HAVE PAID WITH HIS LIFE. SADAT, AGAIN ACCORDING TO HIS OWN ACCOUNT, HAD GONE TO THE CINEMA ON THE DAY OF THE COUP IN ORDER TO HAVE AN ALIBI IN THE EVENT THAT 'THINGS WENT WRONG.' HE WENT ON TO BECOME THE PRESIDENT OF EGYPT AFTER NASSER'S DEATH FROM A HEART ATTACK IN SEPTEMBER 1970.

THE FREE OFFICERS, HOWEVER, SOON FELL OUT WITH THE IKHWAN. THAT CAN BE NO SURPRISE TO THOSE WITH EVEN A SUPERFICIAL FAMILIARITY WITH SUCH INSTITUTIONS AS THE MILITARY IN THE MUSLIM WORLD. THE COUP-PLOTTERS WERE YOUNG AND INEXPERIENCED; THEY NEEDED A FATHER-FIGURE AND AN INTELLECTUAL GUIDE; SAYYID QUTB FIT THE BILL WELL. BUT ONCE THE COUP HAD SUCCEEDED, THE FREE OFFICERS HAD OTHER PLANS.

WITHIN TWO YEARS OF THE COUP, NASSER HAD TAKEN FULL CONTROL OF THE STATE. HE THEN CAME DOWN HARD ON THE IKHWAN. TWO EVENTS IN PARTICULAR CONTRIBUTED TO THE BREAK: THE IKHWAN'S INSISTENCE ON AN ISLAMIC CONSTITUTION AND A FREE PRESS; AND THEIR DENUNCIATION OF THE JULY 1954 ANGLO-EGYPTIAN AGREEMENT PERTAINING TO THE SUEZ CANAL. THIS TOTALLY EXPOSED NASSER'S FALSE REVOLUTIONARY CREDENTIALS. THE TREATY ALLOWED BRITISH TROOPS TO ENTER EGYPT IF BRITISH INTERESTS WERE THREATENED IN THE MIDDLE EAST. IN FACT, IT ACTUALLY PERMITTED THE PRESENCE OF BRITISH TROOPS ON THE SUEZ CANAL.

FROM THE BEGINNING OF 1954 UNTIL HIS EXECUTION, SAYYID QUTB SPENT MOST OF HIS TIME IN PRISON. IN EARLY 1954, WHEN THE EGYPTIAN SECRET SERVICE CAME TO ARREST HIM, SAYYID QUTB WAS RUNNING A HIGH FEVER. THEY INSISTED ON PUTTING THE HANDCUFFS ON HIM AND FORCING HIM TO WALK TO PRISON. ON THE WAY, HE FAINTED SEVERAL TIMES FROM WEAKNESS. ONCE INSIDE THE PRISON COMPOUND, A SPECIALLY-TRAINED DOG WAS UNLEASHED UPON HIM WHICH DRAGGED HIM AROUND FOR MORE THAN TWO HOURS. HE WAS THEN INTERROGATED FOR SEVEN HOURS WITHOUT A BREAK.

AT HIS TREASON TRIAL IN 1966, HE WAS ACCUSED OF PLOTTING TO BRING ABOUT A MARXIST COUP IN THE COUNTRY. THIS LUDICROUS CHARGE WAS MADE BY A REGIME THAT WAS ALREADY A CLOSE ALLY OF THE ERSTWHILE SOVIET UNION. THE RULERS OF EGYPT KNEW THAT THEY WERE TRYING A MAN ON WHOLLY FALSE CHARGES. THE REAL REASON FOR THE PROSECUTION WAS SAYYID QUTB'S DENUNCIATION OF THE SYSTEM AND REGIME AS *JAHILIYYAH*. NASSER KNEW THAT IF SUCH IDEAS WERE ALLOWED TO CIRCULATE, THEY WOULD THREATEN HIS RULE AND ULTI-

MATELY LEAD TO HIS OVERTHROW. SAYYID QUTB HAD TO BE ELIMINATED.

SHORTLY BEFORE HIS SCHEDULED EXECUTION, AN EMISSARY OF NASSER CAME TO SAYYID QUTB ASKING HIM TO SIGN A PETITION SEEKING MERCY FROM THE PRESIDENT. SAYYID QUTB'S REPLY WAS FORTHRIGHT: "IF I HAVE DONE SOMETHING WRONG IN THE EYES OF ALLAH, I DO NOT DESERVE MERCY; BUT IF I HAVE NOT DONE ANYTHING WRONG, I SHOULD BE SET FREE WITHOUT HAVING TO PLEAD FOR MERCY FROM ANY MORTAL." THE EMISSARY WENT AWAY DISAPPOINTED; NASSER WAS DENIED THE PLEASURE OF TURNING DOWN SAYYID QUTB'S "APPEAL" FOR MERCY.

SAYYID QUTB WROTE A NUMBER OF BOOKS, INCLUDING THE WELL-KNOWN *TAFSEER, FI ZILAL AL-QUR'AN (IN THE SHADE OF THE QUR'AN)*, IN WHICH HE EXPLAINS QUR'ANIC *AYAAT* WITH REFERENCES TO OTHER *AYAAT* OF THE NOBLE BOOK. THIS HE COMPILED DURING HIS LONG CONFINEMENTS IN PRISON ON SPURIOUS CHARGES. SIMILARLY, HIS CONTRIBUTION TO MUSLIM POLITICAL THOUGHT WAS IMMENSE. HE CATEGORICALLY REJECTED ANY BORROWINGS FROM THE WEST AND INSISTED THAT ISLAM IS SELF-SUFFICIENT.

THAT SUCH A WORTHY SON OF ISLAM SHOULD BE SO MISTREATED AND HUMILIATED IN A MUSLIM COUNTRY SHOWS THE DEPTHS OF DEPRAVITY TO WHICH THE REGIMES IN THE MUSLIM WORLD HAVE SUNK. PERHAPS THIS WAS PARTLY THE REASON THAT NASSER'S ARMY FACED SUCH AN IGNOMINIOUS DEFEAT AT THE HANDS OF THE ZIONIST FORCES A YEAR LATER, IN THE SIX DAY WAR OF JUNE 1967.

SAYYID QUTB LIVES IN THE HEARTS OF MILLIONS OF MUSLIMS WORLDWIDE. HIS BOOKS HAVE BEEN TRANSLATED INTO VIRTUALLY EVERY LANGUAGE THAT MUSLIMS READ, AND REMAIN HUGELY INFLUENTIAL. THE MAIN TRANSLATIONS INTO FARSI HAVE BEEN DONE BY THE RAHBAR OF THE ISLAMIC REPUBLIC, AYATULLAH SEYYED ALI KHAMENEI, HIMSELF. THIS IS A GREAT TRIBUTE TO THE MARTYRED SCHOLAR OF ISLAM.

MARTYRED SCHOLAR OF ISLAM
From *Milestones* by Sayyid Quib

Those who look for causes of a defensive nature in the history of the expansion of Islam are caught by the aggressive attacks of the orientalists at a time when Muslims possess neither glory nor do they possess Islam. However, by God's grace, there are those who are standing firm on the issue that Islam is a universal declaration of the freedom of man on the earth from every authority except God's authority, and that the religion ought to be purified for God; and they keep writing concerning, the Islamic Jihad.

But the Islamic movement does not need any arguments taken

from the literature, as it stands on the clear verses of the Qur'an:

"They ought to fight in the way of God who have sold the life of this world for the life of the Hereafter; and whoever fights in the way of God and is killed or becomes victorious, to him shall We give a great reward. Why should not you fight in the way of God for those men, women and children who have been oppressed because they are weak and who call: 'Our Lord! Take us out of this place whose people are oppressors, and raise for us an ally, and send for us a helper'. Those who believe, fight in the cause of God, while those who do not believe, fight in the cause of tyranny. Then fight against the friends of Satan. Indeed, the strategy of Satan is weak." (3:74–76)

"Say to the unbelievers that if they refrain, then whatever they have done before will be forgiven them; but if they turn back, then they know what happened to earlier nations. And fight against them until there is no oppression and the religion is wholly for God. But if they refrain, then God is watching over their actions. But if they do not, then know that God is your Ally and He is your Helper." (8:38–40)

"Fight against those among the People of the Book who do not believe in God and the Last Day, who do not forbid what God and His messenger have forbidden, and who do not consider the true religion as their way of life, until they are subdued and pay Jizyah. The Jews say: 'Ezra is the Son of God', and the Christians say: 'The Messiah is the Son of God'. These are mere sayings from their mouths, following those who preceded them and disbelieved. God will assail them; how they are perverted! They have taken their rabbis and priests as lords other than God, and the Messiah, son of Mary; and they were commanded to worship none but One God. There is no deity but He, glory be to Him above what they associate with Him! They desire to extinguish God's light with their mouths, and God intends to perfect His light, although the unbelievers may be averse." (9:29–32)

The reasons for Jihad which have been described in the above verses are these: to establish God's authority on the earth; to arrange human affairs according to the true guidance provided by God; to abolish all the Satanic forces and Satanic systems of life; to end the lordship of one man over others, since all men are creatures of God and no one has the authority to make them his servants or to make arbitrary laws for them. These reasons are sufficient for proclaiming

Jihad. However, one should always keep in mind that there is no compulsion in religion; that is, once the people are free from the lordship of men, the law governing civil affairs will be purely that of God, while no one will be forced to change his beliefs and accept Islam.

The Jihad of Islam is to secure complete freedom for every man throughout the world by releasing him from servitude to other human beings so that he may serve his God, Who is One and Who has no associates. This is in itself a sufficient reason for Jihad. These were the only reasons in the hearts of Muslim warriors. If they had been asked the question, "Why are you fighting?" none would have answered, "My country is in danger; I am fighting for its defense," or, "The Persians and the Romans have come upon us" or, "We want to extend our dominion and want more spoils."

They would have answered the same as Raba'i bin 'Amer, Huzaifa bin Muhsin and Mughir abin Sh"ba answered the Persian General Rustum when he asked them one by one during three successive days preceding the battle of Qadisiyyah: "For what purpose have you come?" Their answer was the same: "God has sent us to bring anyone who wishes from servitude to men into the service of God alone, from the narrowness of this world into the vastness of this world and the Hereafter, and from the tyranny of religions into the justice of Islam. God raised a Messenger for this purpose to teach His creatures His way. If anyone accepts this way of life, we turn back and give his country back to him, and we fight with those who rebel until we are martyred or become victorious."

These are the reasons inherent in the very nature of this religion. Similarly, its proclamation of universal freedom, its practical way of combating actual human conditions with appropriate methods, its developing new resources at various stages, is also inherent in its message from the very beginning — and not because of any threat of aggression against Islamic lands or against the Muslims residing in them. The reason for Jihad exists in the nature of its message and in the actual conditions it finds in human societies, and not merely in the necessity for defense, which may be temporary and of limited extent. A Muslim fights with his wealth and his person "in the way of God" for the sake of these values in which neither personal gain nor greed is a motive for him.

Before a Muslim steps into the battlefield, lie has already fought a great battle within himself against Satan — against his own desires and a ambitions, his personal interests and inclinations, the interests of his family and of his nation; against anything which is not from Islam:

against every obstacle which comes into the way of worshipping God and the implementation of the Divine authority on earth, returning this authority to God and taking it away from the rebellious usurpers.

Those who say that Islamic Jihad was merely for the defense of the "homeland of Islam" diminish the greatness of the Islamic way of life and consider it less important than their 'homeland'. This is not the Islamic point of view, and their view is a creation of the modern age and is completely alien to Islamic consciousness. What is acceptable to Islamic consciousness is its belief, the way of life which this belief prescribes, and the society which lives according to this way of life. The soil of the homeland has, in itself, no value or weight. From the Islamic point of view, the only value which the soil can achieve is because on that soil God's authority is established and God's guidance is followed; and thus it becomes a fortress for the belief, a place for its way of life to be entitled the 'homeland of Islam,' a center for the movement for the total freedom of man.

Of course, in that case the defense of the "homeland of Islam" is the defense of the Islamic beliefs, the Islamic way of life, and the Islamic community. However, its defense is not the ultimate objective of the Islamic movement of Jihad but is a means of establishing the Divine authority within it so that it becomes the headquarters for the movement of Islam, which is then to be carried throughout the earth to the whole of mankind, as the object of this religion is all humanity and its sphere of action is the whole earth.

As we have described earlier, there are many practical obstacles in establishing God's rule on earth, such as the power of the state, the social system and traditions and, in general, the whole human environment. Islam uses force only to remove these obstacles so that there may not remain any wall between Islam and individual human beings, and so that it may address their hearts and minds after releasing them from these material obstacles, and then leave them free to choose to accept or reject it.

We ought not to be deceived or embarrassed by the attacks of the orientalists on the origin of Jihad, nor lose self-confidence under the pressure of present conditions and the weight of the great powers of the world to such an extent that we try to find reasons for Islamic Jihad outside the nature of this religion, and try to show that it was a defensive measure under temporary conditions. The need for Jihad remains, and will continue to remain, whether these conditions exist or not!

REVOLUTIONS ARE NEVER BROUGHT ABOUT BY COWARDS AND THE IMBECILIC

By Maulana Maudoodi

MAULANA MAUDOODI (1903–1979) NOT ONLY HAD A GREAT NAME, BUT IS REVERED AS BEING ONE OF THE ORIGINAL INTELLECTUALS TO PROMOTE THE QUEST OF THE TRULY ISLAMIC STATE. IN 1920 HE JOINED THE KHILAFAT MOVEMENT, WHICH SUGGESTED THAT ALL MUSLIMS ESCAPE BRITISH RULE IN INDIA BY MOVING TO AFGHANISTAN TO ESTABLISH THEIR QUR'AN-BASED STATE. BACK IN PAKISTAN IN THE LATE '40S AND '50S, HE WAS OFTEN ARRESTED AND JAILED, AND BARELY AVOIDED MARTYR STATUS IN THE MID-'50S, WHICH MAY HAVE BEEN A MORE MEMORABLE CONCLUSION TO HIS CAREER, RATHER THAN PASSING AWAY IN AN AMERICAN HOSPITAL AS KHOMEINI CAME TO POWER. THE CURIOUS RACISM OF MAUDOODI'S DIATRIBE FROM *WEST VS. ISLAM* BELOW REVEALS THE ARISTOCRATIC PREJUDICES PREVALENT IN '30S INDIA.

Islam does not need such Muslims who do not like to adhere to Islam in their views, their morals, their social life, their means of living and their education. They are not at all interested in remaining Muslim, and are by no means any asset for Islam; rather they are a burden and liability for Islam and Muslims. They do not believe in Allah and follow their own whims and desires. They will never hesitate to bow before idols and deities if they find the idolaters dominating the society. If nudism becomes the fashion of the world, they too will get rid of their dress. If people start taking filth, they will blindly follow them and try to prove that filth alone is clean and pure and cleanliness and purity is nothing but filth and refuse. Their hearts and minds are subjugated and nothing suits them except slavery.

As West dominates today, they want to become European every inch from top to bottom. They will turn negroes, beyond doubt, if negroes dominate the world. They will blacken their faces, fatten their lips, curl their hair like negroes and start worshipping every thing that comes from Ethiopia the land of negroes. Islam does not need such slaves at all. Islam will be far more powerful if all such hypocrites with slavish mentality are removed from the list of Muslims in the census register, leaving only a few thousand Muslims behind, whom the Qur'an defines as:

"God loves them and they love God, (they are) humble towards the believers, stern towards unbelievers striving in the way of Allah fearing not the blame of any reproacher." (5:54)

Such a purge of even millions and millions of so-called Muslims will give much more strength to Islam, just as the purge of pus from the body relieves the patient. The hypocrites are portrayed saying:

"We fear lest a turn of fortune befall us." (5:52)

This is no new apprehension. The hypocrites have, since times immemorial, expressed this apprehension quite loud. This apprehension exposes the old disease hidden in the hearts of hypocrites. These hypocrites have always tried to seek refuge in the anti-Islam camp. They considered the Divine limits always as chains and fetters, and compliance of divine and Prophetic command as a burden. They have always been afraid of the loss of life and property in submission and expected all worldly gains in insubordination. The Divine law was neither changed for them before nor now, and shall never be changed in future. This Shariah or the Divine law is not meant for the cowards and the imbecile. It is neither for the slaves of material and mundane urges nor for those who have no courage to stand against odds and who change themselves with the changing circumstances.

The Shariah is meant for those who are brave and courageous like the lions, determined to face all oppositions and turn the tide in their own favor. They regard the will and pleasure of Allah over and above every other thing, and struggle to make the world submit to the will of Allah. A Muslim is not meant to adopt the ever-changing patterns of the world, he is supposed to change the world according to the will of Allah and his own faith and conviction. Anybody who lets himself float on the mainstream and is ready to change himself with the changing times is a liar and is not honest in his claim of Islam. A true Muslim, in fact, would fight tooth and nail against everything that is wrong and contrary to the will of Allah without caring at all for the consequences. He will never lose heart nor accept defeat even if he is deprived of all physical resources and, cooperation in his struggle against evil and wrong, and even if he is extradited helplessly from his own society. He will never regret his so-called failure and bad luck or envy the achievements of the non-believers or the hypocrites.

The holy Qur'an is before you. The sacred lives of the holy Prophets as well as the lives of the outstanding believers in Islam from the very beginning up-to-date are open to you. Do these examples exhort you to change with the changing circumstances? Had this been the ultimate aim of life, the world would have never needed any Prophet and any book from Allah. The changing times and trends could have been enough to make the people change themselves accordingly like the chameleon changing his color as and when needed. Allah Almighty never revealed any Divine book for such a humiliating purpose, nor was any prophet sent down for such petty cause. No revelation has been made from Allah but to warn the mankind about all the ways and paths misleading and destructive, and lead them to the only right path to eliminate all the wrong paths, push aside the people from such paths and form a group of the faithful who not only tread the right path themselves but call others also to it. The holy Prophets and their followers have always struggled for it, have suffered hardships and tribulations. They have sacrificed their lives and suffered heavy losses, but none of them ever thought of changing themselves with the changing times to save themselves from hardships or to gain worldly comforts. If any body, individually or as a group, apprehends losses, difficulties and dangers in adopting the path pointed out to them through Divine guidance, and, because of such apprehensions and fears, prefers the path apparently leading to prosperity, success and exaltation, he is free to choose that option. But let not such a coward and greedy fellow try to deceive himself or the world at large that he is still a follower of Allah and the holy Prophet (SAW) even after discarding it. Disobedience in itself is a serious crime. What is the good of further adding falsehood, fraud and duplicity to it?

It is quite wrong and illogical to presume that the tide of life cannot change its direction. Observation and experience both testify against it. The world has undergone a number of revolutions and changes and every revolution has changed the trends. Islam itself is the most outstanding and eloquent example. What were the ways and trends of life when the holy Prophet Muhammad (be peace upon him) came into the world? Was not the entire world dominated by infidelity and pantheism? Did not despotism and oppression rule supreme? Was not the mankind torn and split into various classes? Were not the ethical values overshadowed by lewdness, sensuality, feudalism, capitalism and injustice. A single individual stood up and challenged the whole world, refuted their irrational beliefs and claims commonly accepted and adopted all the world over, put forward a faith and creed of his own before the world and, within no time, changed the world's trends, way of thinking and mode of activities by appealing commonsense and reason and asserting conviction and continuity.

But be it revolution or evolution, it has always occurred as a result of force, and force always moulds others, but is not moulded itself. It does not bow before others, but makes others to bow before it. Revolutions are never brought about by cowards and the imbecilic. History never acknowledges those who have no principles, no aim and no ideal of life; who never dare to stake their life for a high and noble cause; who cannot face dangers and hardships, who live for nothing but worldly comforts and amenities; who are ever ready to change with the changing times; who can be cast in every mould and who yield to all sorts of pressure. It is only the brave and the daring who make history. They are the people who have always turned the tide of life with their heroic struggle and sacrifice, changed the concepts and ideals of the world and revolutionized their course of action. They have changed the world instead of being changed themselves with the changing world.

Never say that the course of events cannot be changed and there is no way out except following the trends of time. Do not take the cover of the lame excuse of helplessness. Admit your weakness straight away. And when you admit your weakness, you will also have to concede that principles, codes and religion have no meaning and sense for the weak. He will have to bow before every one who is powerful. He cannot take stand on any principle and cannot claim any code. And no religion is worth the name if it goes on changing its principles for such weaklings.

It is also an illusion that restrictions imposed by Islam are a drag on your progress and prosperity. Is there any restriction imposed by Islam and honored by you. Have you not crossed all limits, and openly defied them. Is any of the things damaging you allowed by Islam? If you are facing destruction, it is because of your own extravagance. You are paying millions of rupees as interest to the money-lenders and losing your precious properties. Did Islam permit you this extravagance? You are suffering because of your own bad habits. Cinemas and operas are crowded with Muslims even in the state of poverty. Every Muslim lives beyond his means and wastes lots of money on dress and fashions. Millions of rupees are wasted on absurdities never permitted by Islam. The most serious fault on your part is evasion of *Zakat* and lack of the spirit of mutual help. Did not Islam make it obligatory for you?

Thus it is established beyond doubt that it is not observance but violation of Islamic restrictions that has ruined you financially. As for the prohibition of interest who cares to observe it. More than 95% take loans on interest without any genuine hardship. Is this the implementation of Islamic tenets. Most of the moneyed Muslims are drawing interest in one form or the other. May it not be regular money-lending, but Muslims draw interest from banks, insurance policies, government bonds and the provident fund. Where is that prohibition of interest honored and observed? Why then blame Islam for your financial collapse?

It is argued that the prestige and national strength depends on wealth which in its turn depends on permissibility of interest. Perhaps they are still unaware of the real source of their prestige and power. Mere wealth cannot bestow honor and power upon a nation. If every individual of a community becomes a millionaire or multi-millionaire but they lack character, they carry no weight in the world. But if you possess Islamic character, if you are veracious and trustworthy, if you are above fear and favor and firm in your principles, if you are fair in your dealings, regard right as right and duty as duty, discriminate between the lawful and the unlawful in every matter, and possess enough moral strength to rise above fear of loss and temptation for gain, refuse to deviate from the straight path and prove your faith and conviction priceless, you will establish your credibility in the world. Your word shall carry weight much more than the entire wealth of a millionaire, you will command much more respect than those residing in palaces although you may be living in huts and putting up patched dresses. Your nation shall become too strong to be ever humbled.

The companions of the Holy Prophet were very poor. They lived in huts and tents, unacquainted with the luxuries and niceties of culture. They had no proper dress, no good food, no modern weapons, no impressive means of conveyance. But their goodwill and their terror all over the world could never be matched even by the grandeur of Umayyads and Abbassids nor in any later period till now. They had no wealth but possessed such a character that established their respect and their greatness all over the world. After them, the Muslims no doubt achieved much wealth and power, pomp and show of culture, but nothing could cover the deficiency of character.

You cannot find even a solitary example of any nation in history attaining power and prestige through easy going, lotus eating and gain seeking, if you are not ready to learn any lesson from Islamic history. No nation could attain respect and prestige in the world without observing some principles and discipline, without taking pains and suffering want and hardships for a sacred cause, and without the spirit to sacrifice its ambitions and its own interests. This discipline, this commitment to principles and sacrifice of luxuries, comforts and benefits could be noticed in one form or the other in the progressing nations.

Islam puts it in one way while other progressing nations put it in some other forms. Visit any of the people, you will have to follow their rules and regulations and bear the rigors of their discipline. Anywhere you go, you will be required to follow a set of principles and to offer sacrifice for some objectives and principles. If you are fond of easy going and relaxation and lack the stamina to endure any rigor and bitterness, then you can be free from the bondage of Islam and go anywhere, but you will get no position of respect anywhere, neither shall you find any source of strength.

The holy Qur'an describes this formula in a few words and the known human history establishes it as a universal truth.

"After every hardship there is ease and prosperity."

One who cannot bear hardship cannot achieve prosperity.

THE MUSLIM BROTHERHOOD
By Medea Institute and ummah.com

The first Islamic political-religious movement to be born in an Arab country under European rule, the movement of the Muslim Brothers (Al-Ikhwan Al-Muslimun) was created in 1929 by Hassan al-Banna of Egypt.

Its first goal was to fight against the secular Egyptian constitution of 1923 to obtain the creation of an Islamic society on the pattern of the one set up in the Arabian peninsula by the Wahhabites Ikhwans. The Muslim Brothers wanted to be a quasi-monastic brotherhood preaching the return to the strict and fundamental values of Islam together with the fight against King Farouk's government.

After the defeat of Egypt and other Arab states facing Israel in 1948, they begin an open revolt against the regime and participated in the revolution that led to Gamal Abd al-Nasser's rule.

Nasser, a nationalist willing to modernize Egypt along socialist lines, quickly came into conflict with the Muslim Brothers who, after an attempted murder, were forced to go underground or to leave Egypt (mainly for Saudi Arabia). Sayyed Qutb, the Muslim Brotherhood's most widely read propagandist of the Islamic state rather than the Nationalist state, was sentenced to death by hanging in 1966 by the Nasserites on charges of treason. A couple years after losing the 1967 war, and losing great amounts of Egyptian land to Israel, Nasser died of a heart attack. When Sadat came to power afterwards, he began distancing Egypt from the USSR and became friendly with Saudi Arabia, giving the Brotherhood semi-official status. The more severe branch calling itself "The Excommunicated of Hegira" (*Takfir Al-Hijra*) later assassinated Sadat after signing the peace treaty with Israel which in turn isolated Egypt from the Arab world. Later the Muslim Brothers were used by President Mubarak as unofficial contacts between Egypt and Saudi Arabia. Today they are tolerated, without being formally authorized, and divided into several branches: some being ready to play according to democratic rules, others choosing violence.

The Muslim Brothers spread very early in many Arab countries. Although their Jordanian branch killed King Abdallah in Jerusalem in 1952, they are now authorized to take part in the political life of the country. They presented candidates for election to the House of Representatives for the first time in 1989 and won 20 seats.

The Syrian branch organized an armed uprising in Hama in 1982, which was brutally crushed by the army, killing thousands of members and sympathizers. In February 1995, on the 25th anniversary of Hafez Assad's rule, members of the banned Muslim Brotherhood were released from Syrian jail. The following is from the official Muslim Brotherhood website.

Allah is our objective.
The messenger is our leader.
Quran is our law.
Jihad is our way.
Dying in the way of Allah is our highest hope.

HISTORY

Soon after the biggest calamity happened in 1924 with the collapse of the "Khilafa," and the declaration of war against all shapes of Islam in most of the Muslim countries, the Islamic "revival" entered into the movement phase in the middle east by establishing "Al-Ikhwan Al-Moslemoon" (Muslim Brotherhood) in Egypt, 1928 [1]. Soon after that date, it began to have several branches outside Egypt [2]. Al-Ikhwan, since that date, began to spread the principal Islamic idea that Islam is "Creed and state, book and sword, and a way of life" [3]. These principles were uncommon at that time even among many muslim "scholars" who believed that Islam is restricted within the walls of the mosque [2]. The Ikhwan, after a few years, were banned and tortured in most of the Muslim countries [2]. However, the "mother movement" kept growing and working. Its first leader and guide (murshid) — Hassan Al-Banna — preferred "gathering men over gathering information in books" [1], and so he emphasized building the

Ikhwanic organization and establishing its internal rules so that it would keep going, unaffected by his absence. And that's what happened after his shahada in 1949 in Cairo.

ORGANIZATION

Al-Ikhwan has branches in over 70 countries all over the world. The movement is flexible enough to allow working under the "Ikhwan" name, under other names, or working according to every country's circumstances. However, all Ikhwan groups, in all countries are characterized by the following with respect to their method [3]:

1. Following the *Salaf:* Rejecting any action or principle which contradicts the Qur'an or *Sunna,* and inviting people to nothing but them both.
2. Establishing the *Sunna*: Working — as much as possible — to spread the *Sunna* in every aspect of life.
3. Increasing the *Iman*: By concentrating on the purity of hearts, loving Muslims in the sake of Allah, and remembrance (plus being away of any Sufi mistakes).
4. Political Activism: By putting political programs for "Islamising" government in different countries (after realistic studies), and establishing these programs through the convenient ways which do not conflict with Islam.
5. Stressing Physical Health: By forming sports clubs and committing members to regular exercises.
6. Enriching Scientific Study: By enhancing the knowledge of members and others about Islam. Members with Shari'a major have special study programs.
7. Establishing a Sound Economic Infrastructure: By supporting and/or sponsoring any Islamic project and facing its fiqh problems. By the way, the ONLY accepted source of money to the Ikhwan is its members' OWN money [3].
8. Fostering Social ties: By maintaining brotherhood links among the members of the Islamic society.

MAIN OBJECTIVES

A huge tree of "sub-goals" branches from these main objectives which are derived from the Qur'an and the tradition of the prophet [3, 4]:

1. Building the Muslim individual: brother or sister with a strong body, high manners, cultured thought, ability to earn, strong faith, correct worship, conscious of time, of benefit to others, organized, and self-struggling character [3].
2. Building the Muslim family: choosing a good wife (husband), educating children Islamically, and inviting other families.
3. Building the Muslim society (through building individuals and families) and addressing the problems of the society realistically.
4. Building the Muslim state.
5. Building the *Khilafa* (basically a shape of unity between the Islamic states).
6. Mastering the world with Islam.
Objectives 1 to 4 are parallel and interlinked, and continuous even after reaching 4, 5 or 6.

MAIN METHODS OF EDUCATION (*TARBIAH*):
The main (not the only) way of "building" is the Islamic education tarbiah.

Establishing the Islamic government:
Al-Ikhwan believe that ruling a government should be the step which follows preparing (most of) the society for accepting the Islamic laws. Otherwise, ruling a totally corrupt society through a militant government-overthrow is a great risk [5]. Preparing the society is achieved thru plans for: spreading the Islamic culture, the possible media means, mosques, and da'wa work in public organizations such as syndicates, parliaments, student unions . . . [6]. Parallel to that, distinct muslims should be trained to administer political, economical, social, and student organizations efficiently (and Islamically), as another preparation step. Moreover, the Ikhwan don't demand the rule for themselves; they welcome any leader who wants to establish a TRUE Islamic government to have all the Ikhwanic support and help.

ACHIEVEMENTS OF IKHWAN
1. Liberating Muslim lands
Throughout their history, the Ikhwan have had many accomplishments. However, their philosophy is that they prefer action and work over words and propaganda. The Ikhwan have played and continue to play a major role in the struggle to liberate Muslims lands. The

Ikhwan's bravery in the 1948 Palestine war has been recorded by all sides. The total number of volunteers from the Ikhwan in 1948 numbered 10,000 from Egypt, Syria and other countries. In addition to participating in the battle to liberate Palestine, they served to raise the consciousness of Muslims all over the Islamic World and restore to them the spirit of struggle and dignity. The Ikhwan have played a role in liberating Muslim lands from colonialist powers in almost every Muslim country. The Ikhwan were active amongst Muslims in Central Asian Muslim republics since the '70s, and their involvement can be seen recently in such republics as Tajikistan. More recently they had a major role in the struggle for Afghanistan and Kashmir.

2. Intellectual development
The school of Ikhwan counts amongst its graduates many of the thinkers, scholars and activists of this century. To list but a few:
+ Hassan Al-Banna
+ Sayyed Qutb
+ Abdel Qader 'Audah, Mustapha al-Siba'yi, Hassan al-Hudaybi, Umar al-Tilmisani, Yusuf al-Qaradhawi, Sa'eed Hawwa, Abdullah 'Azzam, Muhammad Hamed Abul-Nasr, Rached al-Ghannoushi, Mahfouz al-Nahnah, Muhammad Ahmad Al-Rashid, Fathi Yakan, Shaikh Abdul-Fattah Abu Ghuddah, Shaikh Ahmad Yaseen, Mustapha Mashhour, Muneer al-Ghadban, Shaikh Abdul-Majeed al-Zindanee, Shaikh Syed Sabiq, Shaikh Muhammad al-Ghazali . . . and many others.

The contributions of these thinkers, scholars and activists to Muslim thought existence in the twentieth century is well-known. Stemming from the notion that Islam is comprehensive for all areas of life, the thinkers and activists who have gone through the training of the ikhwan have branched out to address as many areas of Muslim life as possible. Theories have been developed in areas of fiqh, finance & economics, political systems . . . etc.

3. Development of Institutions
Beginning in the late '50s and early '60s and up till now, the Ikhwan contributed to establishing firm basis for Islamic communities in Europe and North America. This was done mainly through fostering the establishment of local community organizations, Islamic schools, national associations, and special interest organizations (Medical, Scientific, Cultural . . . etc.)

The Ikhwan were the main motivators behind setting up experiments in Islamic financing on a nationally and internationally viable scale. The theory and practical requirements needed to set up an Islamic banking system came from amongst the ranks of the Ikhwan. From the earliest years, establishing an Islamic Economic system was a priority for the Ikhwan. Hassan al-Banna, Sayyed Qutb, Yusuf al-Qaradhawi and numerous other scholars laid down some of the groundwork for practical theories of Islamic finance. Further specialized writers such as provided the practical basis for Islamic Financial Institutions, a number of which were developed in Muslim countries.

[1] Diary of *Da'wa* and *Dai'iah*, Hassan Al-Banna.
[2] *Al-Ikhwan Al-Muslimoon: Events That Made History*, Mahmoud Abdel-Haleem.
[3] The Messages of Al-Imam-u-shaheed, Hassan Al-Banna.
[4] *An introduction to the Da'wa of Al-Ikhwan Al-Muslimoon*, Saiid Hawwa.
[5] *Means of Education of Al-Ikhwan Al-Muslimoon*, Ali Abdel-Haleem.
[6] *The Path*, Muhammed Ahmed Ar-Rashed.

Memoir of Hassan Al-Banna Shaheed
Founder of the Muslim Brotherhood

Like Sayyid Qutb, Hassan al-Banna (1906–1949), founder of the Muslim Brotherhood in 1929, was killed by the Egyptian government, which saw him as a threat due to the militancy of his organization. The Muslim Brotherhood is one of the first groups to adopt a Pan-Islamic attitude, one going beyond Nationalism to Qur'an for its precepts. As you can see from the memoir below, al-Banna's innate puritanism was revered as much as his militancy.

The Achievements of Hasan al-Banna
By N. M. Shaikh

Hassan al-Banna was born in 1906 in a deserted village. He came of a poor village family. He was martyred in 1949 on the biggest road of Cairo. The British, the Jews and the Government had prepared the conspiracy of his murder. He lived only 43 years. Al-Ikhwanul Muslimoon was formed in 1928. Thus we see that this soldier of God started a movement in 1928 and in two decades only he brought about a revolution in the culturally, politically and religiously decayed society of Egypt and put the society on the Islamic anvil. New slogans like Allah's pleasure is our aim, Qur'an is our Constitution, jihad is our method and sacrifice of our lives in the way of Allah is our motto, etc., had become the favorite pastime of those who were allergic with Islam before the movement.

When Imam Hassan Al Banna Shaheed was studying in school at his small village, he had formed a society of the children of his age and named it "Jamiat-e-Akhalq-e-Adabia." He was elected its president. The aim of the society was to create good habits in the little students. However, he was not satisfied with the limited activities of this small society and had formed another society outside the school and called it "Jamiat-e-Insdad-e-Muharramat."

Once, when Imam Hasan Al Banna was a student, he happened to pass by a river in Mahmoodiya. At the bank there was a yacht. A nude wooden statue was stuck on it. It was a place from where a lot of women used to pass. When he saw this offensive image he could not bear it. He at once went to the police station and protested against the exhibition of the statue. The Police Officer was very much impressed with the feelings of the little preacher. He went to the sailor and ordered him to remove the statue from the mast. The Police Officer visited his school the next day and praised the little student before the Principal.

THE MEMOIR OF HASSAN AL-BANNA
Reflections of Ismailiya
Ismailiya created very strange feelings in my heart. The British Cantonment on its West was casting its influence over the city, and created the feeling of sadness in every respectable and dignified Muslim. It makes him realize its historical background and the horrifying activities which is carried on in Ismailiya in order to deprive the Muslims of their golden chance of acquiring higher education and other material gains. It also reminded him how it had become an obstacle in the progress of Egypt and how it hindered the unity and fraternity of the Muslims for over 60 years.

This beautiful and grand building of the officers of the Suez Canal Company still stands there. The Egyptians work in this office. They treat them just like slaves. But the foreigners are accorded full respects and given the status of officers and rulers. The Office has the sole monopoly of the affairs of the people. The supply of water, health, sanitation and other affairs which are usually managed by the Councillors, have been taken over by this Company. Even the management of the roads is under this company. No one can enter or leave this city without obtaining a permit from this company.

The beautiful bungalows and buildings form the colony of the foreigners. The foreign employees of this Company live in these bungalows. Just opposite this colony there are the narrow and dark hutments of the Arab labourers. All sign boards on the highways are written in European languages. Even the name of Share Masjid was written "Rue De Le Mosque." Thus the European names are being popularized on permanent basis through these sign boards.

All these factors were constantly at work on my heart. These effects became more severe when I sat in the thick gardens or jungle or at the bank of Al Tamisah Lake and pondered over these matters. Undoubtedly, the environment of Ismailiya created very deep impression on my mind and these impressions helped me a great deal in the determination of my mission and my career as a preacher.

AL IKHWAN AL MUSLEMOON

As far as I remember it was the month of Ziqadah, 1347 and March 1928 when six friends — Hafiz Abdul Hamid, Ahmad Al Hasri, Fowad Ibrahim, Abdur Rehman Hasabullah, Ismail Izz and Zaki Al Maghribi — came to see me. These gentlemen were greatly influenced by the lectures and sermons which I delivered in Ismailiya. They began to discuss about the mode of preaching Islam. Their faces looked bright with their determination; their eyes were shining and their voices were very forceful. They said:

"We have heard your speech, pondered over it with heart and soul and felt extraordinarily impressed. But we do not know what to do practically. We are disgusted with the present way of life. This is the life of captivity and disgrace. You say that the Arabs and Muslims have no respectable place in this country. They are just the most obedient servants of the foreigners. And we have hot blood running in our veins. We possess the vitality of faith (*Iman*) and sense of honor. We have brought these Dirhams after curtailing the expenses of our families. You know better than we do how best to serve Islam, the Muslim Ummah and the country. We have come to you to present to you whatever we possess so that we can feel relieved of our duties towards Allah. It is for you to guide us. The group which determines to serve the cause of Islam and Muslims does it simply to cam the pleasure of Allah and nothing else. Such a group deserves success, however small it may be and its resources."

Their sincere utterances impressed me very much. I could not escape the responsibility which was thrown on my shoulders. But it was the same responsibility for which I was struggling through and I told them in emotional voice, "May Allah accept your prayer and bless you all for your good intentions. May Allah give us strength to do good deeds, to earn His pleasure and serve the cause of the Muslim Ummah. Our duty is to try and work hard and leave the result to Allah. Let's wear

before Allah that we shall be the soldiers of Islam and in the fulfillment of this mission lies the prosperity of our nation."

Consequently, the oath of allegiance was taken by all of us. We determined on solemn oath that we shall live as brethren; work for the
glory of Islam and launch Jihad for it.

One of the friends got up and said, "What shall we call ourselves?
Shall we go by the name of any society or club or religious sect or
association? Let us do so for the sake of formal identity."

I replied, "We shall not be any of them. It is better to be away from
the show business and traditionalism. The basis of our unity and
organization should be our ideology and faith. Our moral thinking
and particular way of its implementation. We are united to serve the
cause of Islam and, therefore, we are brethren and shall be known as Al
Ikhwanul Muslemoon." Thus with the co-operation of these six gentlemen, the first organization in the name of AL IKHWANUL MUSLE-
MOON came into existence. Its emergence was sudden and simple
and its aims and objects were those defined above.

East and West—Shall They Meet?

By Anwar Sadat

"I killed the Pharaoh," shouted the assassin of Anwar Sadat. Although this extract from Sadat's 1957 book, *Story of Arab Unity*, praises Egypt's "pharaonic" civilization (Sadat perhaps neglects what this implies to the average worker), it also follows the lead of Islamists Sayyed Qutb and Hassan Al-Banna, decrying Western Civilization as a violent pirate culture. When Sadat kissed Western Civilization on both cheeks he got his violent payback from Qutb and Al-Banna's ideological brethren.

The West sees in the East only swarming millions of starving, naked, and ignorant people, toward whom it has the duty to assume the role of tutor according to the principles of humanity, the Christian religion, and European civilization!

There again, the West runs counter to truth, to history, and to human values. Has it, in effect, the prerogative of carrying the Christian message? Has it the right to interpret it in a manner contradictory to its fundamental principles, to enlist it in the colonial adventure founded on hate and discord between the sons of humanity? No, that is one thing we do not accept, we in the East, for we know Christianity and its principles: The Christians are people like ourselves; our land is the cradle of this religion; it is from our soil that the new message went forth to conquer pagan Europe!

The diversity of our beliefs and our laws does not prevent us in the East from recognizing Christianity, from respecting it and separating it from all the West would add to it. The Buddhists, the Hindus, the Muslims, the Confucians, the Christians of the East, and the Copts know Christianity better than the West knows it or claims to know it.

In pronouncing the puerilities about Christianity, the West forgets that the millions of orientals, whom it sees naked and starving, knew civilization, religion, and wisdom while Europe was still wandering in the blackness of ignorance and living under the influence of witchcraft and myth. The East, the cradle of Christianity, knows that it is founded on the two principles of faith and charity. Do these figure in what the West calls Christianity?

The East, the cradle of Christianity, knows that the basis of its message is not to separate men, but to urge them to love one another for all time. If, then, a man of black or yellow race should approach a Christian to ask him to cure him, the Christian will treat him exactly as if he were white. Does the West really understand Christianity as we understand it in the East?

Qaddafi, Sadat and Sudan's Nimery

No, for the West wallows in the materialism that penetrates all its principles and shames the letter and the spirit of Christianity. It is the West that has created the myth of the white man and his superiority over the "colored"; it is the West that undertakes the killing of the innocent, assuming the right to determine the destiny of their countries; it is the West that calls piracy courage, for whom the stripping and subjugation of man are established rights.

That is the fundamental point of conflict between East and West. For us orientals, religions are a spiritual refuge where our souls find peace from the cares of this world. The West, on the other hand, enlists religion in its plans for domination.

For us orientals, Christianity has a universal message of mercy which in principle does not differ from other religions and beliefs that we practice, for they all teach love, brotherhood, and peace. The Westerners, on the other hand, consider themselves as the privileged guardians of Christianity, and those who are not Christians as illiterates, sorcerers, and barbarians.

It is thus that the West has gone astray, that Christianity and its principles are mixed with the acts of this sinful world, forgetting that the East is the cradle of Christianity and the source of all religions . . .

But Western civilization and its heritage, for which Europe and America fear so much, live only on the debris of the East and would not flourish if they had not sucked its blood. That is the astonishing truth.

Western civilization is not today a civilization [*hadara*] as the term is understood by science and theory, but only a way of life [madaniyya], and there is a big difference between a civilization and a way of life. A civilization, in fact, is characterized, above all by its ideals and spiritual principles, and material institutions come only in second place; we see therefore, that it is not concerned with appearances but is above all founded on the spirit.

85

A way of life, on the other hand, is not concerned with ideals or spiritual principles, and in the life of the individual or of the group, it presents only a purely material and readily artificial face, as if life itself were as mechanical as machines or pushbuttons. There is no value in a way of life that ignores the very essence of human life.

Civilization, therefore, is defined and will always be defined by the highest human values, while a way of life interprets human values in terms of material progress. By virtue of this argument and what we see all around us, we can appreciate the distance that extends between a civilization and a way of life, and can identify the so-called civilization of the West as the Western way of life. And there, as I see it, is another conflict between West and East: The West claims the right to impose its present way of life; it claims that the basis of the new message is to make the Eastern peoples receive only some examples of this Western "civilization" in well-defined and restricted form — for example, when the West introduces a democratic system to an Eastern people it is not in the same form as in the West. Westerners content themselves with imposing on the people [of the East] a system designed to ensure Western authority and domination, finally baptizing it democracy and calling it the outcome of modern Western civilization.

When the West introduces modern science to an Eastern country under the yoke of colonialism, this knowledge is not transmitted by natural stages, for the Western concept of civilization is that the East should not have more than the outer shell of Western science, the preservation and usages of knowledge being reserved for the white man.

Hence many peoples, victims of colonialism, have thus far been suffering and have been incapable of growth, since they have neither medicine nor geometry — these skills being reserved, in the Western theory of civilization, for the white man, the chosen man. That is how the West ensures its domination. One last illustration of this state of affairs: England invites military missions to come to England from various Western and Eastern states. It happened that in 1950 some Egyptian officers formed part of one of these missions. On their return, they told how the main meetings were barred to them and to other delegations from Eastern countries, because those meetings dealt with military secrets reserved for the English and the Europeans . . . These examples illustrate what is understood in the West by civilization, or, rather, way of life.

The Eastern idea of civilization differs radically. The East is proud of the fact that the greatest civilizations known to man were nurtured on its soil: the Chinese civilization, which discovered wisdom and light; the pharaonic civilization, which astonished and continues to astonish the world by its brilliant past in science and the arts; the Indian civilization, which, since antiquity, has plumbed the secrets of the spirit and of matter and presented to humanity a philosophy and science whose glorious heritage will remain until the end of time.

The East, therefore, interprets civilization as founded on spiritual rather than material values. We believe that the Chinese, Egyptian, or Indian civilizations invented ethics and humanities and arts, honored the family, organized the relationships of individuals with one another, and the relationships of individuals to society or to the government — the Chinese civilization remaining unsurpassed in its theory of power and the applications of power, on the one hand, and of subjects and their essential politeness, on the other.

But the sole result of these civilizations has not been the establishment of human values. Science, art, mathematics, and architecture remain as testimonials to the permanence of the superiority of these civilizations over thousands of years. The East conceives civilization as an edifice where coexistence reigns for the good of all, and that is why it is proud of its civilization, which it deems superior to the Western way of life.

Everything was therefore abundantly clear to the East when it threw off the vestiges of colonialism and Western domination. It now desires to make up for lost time. It feels an ardent desire for the civilization which is part of its lifeblood and which will devour it like a fire; and the civilization engrained in it burns with a flame which cannot be extinguished.

The West finds itself — with its "civilization" built by the sword, by fire, by piracy, and by violence — faced with people who possess a pure and genuine civilization, faced with people who would live honorably and rescue their spiritual strength from the grip of Western "civilization."

The struggle will continue until the true civilization triumphs over the false — in other words, until supreme values replace base methods of force.

> "WHEN YOU MEET THOSE
> WHO HAVE DISBELIEVED,
> LET THERE BE SLAUGHTER."
> —Excerpt from *The Neglected Duty*

THE BOOK THAT KILLED ANWAR SADAT AND PROVOKED USAMAH BIN-LADEN'S HOLY WAR

by Muhammad Abd al-Salam Faraj

"THE NEGLECTED DUTY" THAT MUHAMMAD FARAJ SPEAKS OF IN THE TITLE OF HIS BOOK IS THE QUR'ANIC OBLIGATION TO TAKE JIHAD AS SERIOUSLY AS THE MEDIEVAL CATHOLIC CHURCH REGARDED THE INQUISITION. THE BATTLE IS TO PRESERVE AND ENHANCE THE RELIGION THROUGH THE REMOVAL AND SUPPRESSION OF THE APOSTATE AND THE HERETICAL.

THE ISLAMIC REVOLUTION OF IRAN INSPIRED FARAJ IN HIS QUEST FOR STRICT AND ABSOLUTE OBSERVANCE OF THE QUR'AN. AND HE WROTE *THE NEGLECTED DUTY* IN 1979, STEAMING WITH FRUSTRATION OVER THE MUSLIM BROTHERHOOD'S RELUCTANCE TO ENGAGE IN ENOUGH CORRECTIVE WARFARE. FARAJ QUIT THE BROTHERHOOD TO BECOME THE IDEOLOGIST OF JAMA AT AL-JIHAD (SOCIETY OF STRUGGLE), AND HE SPENT HIS TIME READING HOLY BOOKS FOR THOSE EXPLICIT DIRECTIVES TO JUSTIFY REMOVING ALL THOSE WITH VIEWS, STATEMENTS OR ACTIONS HE DESPISED.

ANWAR SADAT, KNOWN FOR BRIDGING THE GAP BETWEEN THE NASSERITE NATIONALISTS AND ISLAMICISTS, RELEASED, SOON AFTER HIS INAUGURATION, MEMBERS OF MUSLIM BROTHERHOOD CLAPPED INTO PRISON BY GAMEL NASSER. TO PROVE HIS DEVOTION TO ISLAM, SADAT FAMOUSLY DEVELOPED A LARGE BROWN SPOT ON HIS FOREHEAD AS IF TO PROVE THAT HE WAS OBSESSED WITH THE SEVEREST SORT OF HEAD-BOBBING PRAYER. SPOT OR NOT, SADAT'S PEACE DEAL WITH ISRAEL HELPED TO ONCE SECURE SINAI LAND LOST IN THE 1967 WAR, WAS PROOF ENOUGH TO THE SOCIETY OF STRUGGLE THAT ALLAH DID NOT

APPROVE OF HIS POLITICAL DECISIONS. AFTER TWO YEARS OF SMALLER LOCALIZED ACTS OF VIOLENCE, FARAJ'S COHORTS WAS READY FOR A BIGGER STRIKE. IN OCTOBER 1981 ANWAR SADAT WAS PUMPED FULL OF BULLETS, SHOWING TO ARABS INTERNATIONALLY THAT BUSSING LIPS WITH AMERICAN AND ZIONIST LEADERS WAS NOT CONDUCIVE TO A LONG LIFE.

DURING THE OPENING SESSION OF THE TRIAL, WHEN THE MAIN DEFENDANT, LIEUTENANT KHALID AL-ISAMBULI, SHOUTED, "I KILLED THE PHARAOH," HE EXPRESSED THE TRUE FEELINGS OF ORDINARY EGYPTIANS AND BECAME AN INSTANT HERO. DURING THE TRIAL NO DEFENSE WITNESSES WERE ALLOWED TO BE CALLED; OF THE 24 MEN ACCUSED OF ASSASSINATING, OR PLOTTING TO ASSASSINATE, THE LATE PRESIDENT SADAT, FIVE WERE SENTENCED TO DEATH, FIVE TO 25 YEARS IMPRISONMENT, EIGHT TO 15 YEARS, THREE TO 10 YEARS, ONE TO FIVE YEARS, AND TWO WERE ACQUITTED. THE TRIAL WAS PROMPTLY SHUT DOWN AFTER EGYPTIAN INTELLIGENCE TOLD AUTHORITIES THAT THE TRIALS WERE INCREASING THE POPULARITY OF THE ACCUSED WITH THE MASSES, WHICH MIGHT LEAD TO A REVOLT WHEN THE ACCUSED WERE SENTENCED TO DEATH.

THE KIND OF JIHAD EXPRESSED BY *THE NEGLECTED DUTY* AND THE SADAT ASSASSINATION DIRECTLY INSPIRED THE GUERRILLA ACTIONS OF USAMAH BIN-LADEN. ACCORDING TO ROSALIND GWYNNE, A PROFESSOR OF RELIGIOUS STUDIES AT THE UNIVERSITY OF TENNESSEE, BIN-LADEN WAS SO INFLUENCED BY FARAJ'S PAPER THAT HE HELPED HIMSELF TO PORTIONS OF ITS SOURCE MATERIAL TO COMPOSE HIS LENGTHY 1996 EPISTLE, WHICH CALLS FOR JIHAD AGAINST SAUDI ARABIAN LEADERS (DESCRIBED AS BEING APOSTATES) AS WELL AS THE EXPECTED VILLAINS IN THE WEST.

THE RULERS OF THE MUSLIMS TODAY ARE IN APOSTASY FROM ISLAM

The Rulers of this age are in apostasy from Islam. They were raised at the tables of imperialism, be it Crusaderism, or Communism, or Zionism. They carry nothing from Islam but their names, even though they pray and fast and claim (idda'a) to be Muslim. It is a well-established rule of Islamic Law that the punishment of an apostate will be heavier than the punishment of someone who is by origin an infidel and has never been a Muslim, and this in many respects. For instance, an apostate has to be killed even if he is unable to carry arms and go to war. Someone, however, who is by origin an infidel and who is unable to carry arms and go to war against the Muslims should not be killed, according to leading Muslim scholars like Abu Hanifah and Malik and Ahmad ibn Hanbal. Hence, it is the view of the majority of the jurists that an apostate has to be killed, and this is in accordance with the opinions held in the Schools of Law of Malik, Al-Shafi'i and Ahmad ibn Hanbal. Other examples of this difference are that an apostate cannot inherit, cannot conclude a legally valid marriage, and to eat from the meat of animals which he slaughtered is forbidden. No such rules exist concerning someone who is by origin an infidel and has never been a Muslim. When apostasy from a religion is worse than having always been an infidel, then apostasy from the prescripts of a religion is also worse than having always been an infidel. So, apostasy is worse than rebellion against the prescripts of a religion which comes from someone who has always been outside this religion.

Ibn Taymiyah:
> "It is a well-established rule of Islamic Law that the punishment of an apostate will be heavier than the punishment of someone who is by origin an infidel and who has never been a Muslim, and this in many respects. For instance, an apostate has to be killed in all circumstances, he does not have the right to profess his new religion against the payment of the head tax, and there can be no Covenant of Protection between an ex-Muslim and the Muslim authorities unlike the case with someone who has always been an infidel (non-Muslim, e.g., a Christian or a Jew).

MY STORY
A PROSE "POEM" BY LIEUTENANT KHALID SHAUQI AL-ISLAMBULI, WHO KILLED ANWAR SADAT, AND WAS PUT TO DEATH IN APRIL, 1982. IT WAS RECITED BY ONE OF KHALID'S COLLEAGUES IN JANUARY 1983 DURING A SUMMARY MILITARY TRIAL IN CAIRO:

The judges asked me: What instigated me against you, Sadat, and what had I to do with you? I said: "wait, how can you understand my answer . . ." But, listen, I will relate my story. I have not committed a crime to be confined, in humiliation and disgrace, behind bars. I have performed an act for which I hold my head high, in truth, not in falsehood. Only if my people knew who is the wronged and who was the criminal! Respectable judge, I have known my end and I am content with it. I will meet Muhammad and his companions, and I will meet angels of the Most Merciful. Virgins (hoor) of Paradise will conduct my procession, and all the creatures of the universe will sing the sweetest of songs for me. We have to endure in patience the remaining days of our lives. Everyone here is ephemeral, and will pass away.

Cartoonists from Iran
and Palestine take on
Ronald Reagan,
Jimmy Carter,
George Bush,
Bill Clinton and
Mikhail Gorbachev.

YOU HAVE MADE ME YOUR HUMAN BOMB
By Edna Yaghi

THIS ACCUSATIONAL ESSAY, FROM <WWW.PALESTINE-INFO.ORG>, FEA-
TURES A REMARKABLE TITLE, BUT ITS CONTENTS ARE NOT DISSIMILAR TO
HUNDREDS OF OTHERS ON WEBSITES REGARDING PALESTINE.

I am the product of your tyranny. You have dissected the leftovers of
my country into bits and pieces of shantytowns, ghettoes and concen-
trations camps. You have cut off my water supply and left me thirsty
while you, the Israelis, bathe in cooled pools not far from where I live.
You have uprooted my trees and desecrated my fields making sure I
have no way to sustain myself or those who depend on me. You have
cut off medical supplies that treat the wounded, and at your checkpoints, you detain and humiliate Palestinians and prevent those who
are in dire need of medical assistance to pass through causing my
people, who are your victims, to die at your impromptu borders.

You assassinate my freedom fighters while explaining to the world that
you are merely defending your own squatters. You shoot to kill little
children who in defiance and courage wield small stones in the name
of liberty against you, the fiercely armed enemy.

You torture the children and resistance fighters; you incarcerate and try
to bribe or coerce my people into collaborating against one another.
You bulldoze homes and you prevent me from earning a living. You
kill me by remote control from your U.S.-made Apache helicopters,
and your settlers who squat on what you have left me of my land
throw firebombs into my dwellings and on my passageways, attack my
children and womenfolk with guns and clubs and hate.

You occupy my land and on my bloodstained hills station your tanks
and armored jeeps in order to shoot off one by one little children
playing in the streets.

You take over the Orient House, my one symbol of freedom that was
donated by a man worth all Israelis put together, while at the same
time you starve the orphans just across the street.

You shoot out my water tanks and you kill off Palestinian servicemen even though at the time of your brutal massacres, these servicemen were patrolling their land or simply eating their last supper. You cut off my electricity so you can assassinate me more easily in the dank shadows of your dark treachery.

You are cowards and you are afraid of little Palestinian children with stones. You never kill them single handedly. You roam in groups like packs of wild dogs and you are just as vicious if not more so.

You leave me and my people without hope and when you have driven me into a corner and deprived me of all that is human, I react with anger and bitterness. I strap explosives onto my body and search for a place to detonate myself. Yes, I kill your civilians, but this is the price you have to pay for taking away my inalienable rights, the rights that all men are entitled to, for your demoniacal oppression of my people.

It is really very simple. God created all men equal and no man better than any other. Yet, somehow you have made it your protocol that Jews are better than all others and that you have the right to come to my land committing rape and plunder yet expect me to thank you for doing so.

Just the other day, a young boy was eating lunch. One of your settlers who came from America threw a firebomb into this boy's house. His two brothers were killed immediately. But the one boy survived albeit horribly disfigured. His name is Amar Emeera. His scars have turned a once beautiful child into a grotesque being that does not even look human. What did this child do to go through life so horribly disfigured?

You shoot babies point blank while swaddled in their parent's arms in Palestinian cars going to weddings. You slay Palestinian children going to and from school and you slaughter Palestinian children when they fight your armies with their bare hands. One such child,

Mohammed Abu Arrar was shot down and killed when he protested your occupation of his land. Palestinian relatives of the boy kissed his body laid out in his coffin before he was taken away to be buried in the Gaza Strip.

You kill unarmed Palestinian fathers on their way to buy school supplies and books for their children. You have even run out of excuses for the atrocities you continue to perpetrate. You shell the homes of Palestinian families, instantly killing the occupants and then claim that the action was friendly fire from the Palestinians even though the homes were far removed from the scene of the battle and even though remnants of your American-made shells are scattered about the demolished homes of the innocent.

You collectively punish three million Palestinians, half of whom are children who reside on what is left of their own land though you know full well that their only desire is to free themselves from your barbaric cruelty.

You tell the world that you want peace yet at every corner, at every instance, you are as far from peace as the earth is from a different universe speeding in an opposite direction.

You speak peace with the forked tongues of your warmongers and then pretend shock when finally a Palestinian human bomb blows himself up.

You will only be free of the threat of human bombs when you seek a just and comprehensive peace and when you end your occupation of the indigenous inhabitants of Palestine.

"There is no such thing as a Palestinian people." — Golda Meir.

"There is no other way than to transfer the Arabs from here to neighboring countries . . . all of them; not one village, not one tribe, should be left." — Joseph Weitz, 1967.

"The only good Arab is a dead Arab When we have settled the land, all the Arabs will be able to do about it will be to scurry around like drugged cockroaches." — Rafael Eitan, Likud, 1981.

"It is forbidden to be merciful to them . . . Evil ones, damnable ones. May the Holy Name visit retribution on the Arabs' heads, and cause their seed to be lost, and annihilate them . . ." — Rabbi Ovadia Yosef, Shas, 2001.

Israeli Minister of the Interior Eli Yesha's response to Yosef's remarks: "They reflected the overall state of thinking of the Israeli Jewish society."

EVER INTENT ON NEW MISCHIEF

BUT THEY (EVER) STRIVE
TO DO MISCHIEF ON EARTH

وَيَسْعَوْنَ فِى ٱلْأَرْضِ فَسَادًا

AND ALLAH LOVETH NOT
THOSE WHO DO MISCHIEF*

وَٱللَّهُ لَا يُحِبُّ ٱلْمُفْسِدِينَ ٦٤

Holy Qur'an 5:64

**THEY SPIT ON OUR PRIDE THESE VENEMOUS SNAKES!
A DAILY OCCURENCE IN THE STRUGGLE
OF AN OPPRESSED PEOPLE!**

* NOTE: The argument of the whole verse may be thus stated. The Jews
blaspheme and mock, and because of their jealousy, the more they are taught,
the more obstinate they become in their rebellion. But what good will it do to
them? When they stir up wars, especially against the innocent, Allah's mercy is
poured down like a flood of water to extinguish them. But their wickedness continues to devise ever new mischief. And Allah loves not mischief or those who do
mischief.

32

MEMORIZE THE VERSE AND ITS MEANING

THOSE WHO ARE CLOSEST
TO THEIR LORD

THOSE WHO BELEIVE,

AND SUFFER EXILE AND
STRIVE WITH MIGHT AND
MAIN IN ALLAH'S CAUSE,

WITH THEIR GOODS AND
THEIR LIVES,

THEY HAVE THE
HIGHEST RANK IN
THE SIGHT OF ALLAH: *

الَّذِينَ ءَامَنُواْ

وَهَاجَرُواْ وَجَهَدُواْ فِى سَبِيلِ ٱللَّهِ

بِأَمْوَلِهِمْ وَأَنفُسِهِمْ

أَعْظَمُ دَرَجَةً عِندَ ٱللَّهِ

Holy Qur'an 9:20

O JEWS! WHAT HAVE YOU DONE
TO GENERATE SUCH FURY IN THESE MOTHERS?

* **NOTE:** Here is a good description of Jihad. It may require fighting in Allah's cause, as a form of self-sacrifice. But its essence consists in (1) a true and sincere Faith, which so fixes its gaze on Allah, that all selfish or wordly motives seem paltry and fade away, and (2) an earnest and ceaseless activity, involving the sacrifice (if need be) of life, person, or property, in the service of Allah

33

MEMORIZE THE VERSE AND ITS MEANING

Two pages from a pro-Palestinian booklet, circa 1995.

A FASHIONABLE HIJACK

From *My People Shall Live*, Memoir of the Attractive
Palestinian Revolutionary, Leila Khaled

LEILA KHALED, A SOCIALIST PRIMARILY INSPIRED BY CHE GUEVARA, IS
NOT A MUSLIM, NOR WAS SHE EVER PART OF THE ISLAM REVOLUTION,
THOUGH HER ENERGY AND VIOLENCE WAS CONVEYED THROUGH THE
ARAB PRESS TO OTHER FEMALE WARRIORS OF ALLAH, ONES WHO WEAR A
CHADOR WHILE PARADING AROUND WITH SEMI-AUTOMATICS. TODAY,
KHALED LIVES IN AMMAN, JORDAN AND IS ACTIVE IN PALESTINIAN
FORUMS, BUT SAYS FOR THE BENEFIT OF THE WESTERN PRESSES THAT,
AFTER 9/11/01, HIJACKING PLANES IS NO LONGER THE ANSWER.

I had trained for every conceivable contingency; I had mastered most
operational details of the great Boeing 707. There was something,
however, I did not train for: the human situation. How to deal with
idle or curious conversationalists. How not to arouse their suspicions
or be rude to a seat-mate. I had to improvise and felt very uncomfortable. I imagined that all the Westerners aboard knew about my
mission.

My seat-mate from Beirut to Rome was a clean-cut sociable
American on his way to New York. I knew that Americans, like most
other tourists, like to make casual conversation about everything under
the sun. I didn't realize that they posed personal questions so directly
and so nonchalantly. Mr. Holden must have been bored, and he
wanted to talk. "Where are you going?" he asked to open the conversation. "I am going to Rome," I said. "Why are you going to Rome?" he
continued.

I paused momentarily to fabricate an answer, and said with simu-
lated shyness, "I am going to meet my fiancé who is coming from
London to meet me in Rome in a few days." I suddenly realized I had
made a slip. What if he too were going to Rome, and asked me to
dinner or something while I was waiting for my "fiancé." I swiftly corrected my mistake by adding, "It is quite possible that he might surprise me and be waiting for me at the airport."

Then I asked him, "Where are you going?"

"To New York," he said, much to my relief.

He was determined not to let the conversation lapse. "How on
earth would an Arab girl be going to Rome to meet her fiancé alone
and get married?" he asked. I answered in a superficially self-assured

tone, "I've known him since we were children, and we've been engaged for several years; besides, we are modern, not traditional Arabs." "That's good," he said, and started telling me how he and his wife had

August 1969
Leila Khaled commandeers
TWA Boeing 707 into 7-min
detour over occupied homeland

eloped because her parents had disapproved of him. As I assured him that I was not eloping, the stewardess cheerfully announced that there was a newly-married couple on the plane and they had a huge cake they would like us to share. "Who would like to have some cake?" she said. Everybody, including Mr. Holden and I, chanted in a chorus of "I would." In the midst of this jolly atmosphere, Mr. Holden asked, as if to dampen my enthusiasm for marriage, "How come you're getting married when your fiancé is still a student and without a career?" I smiled. "We're not filthy-rich oil kings, but we're rich enough to afford it while we're young." "Then," he said, "may I suggest that you spend your honeymoon on a yacht by yourselves, on a Mediterranean cruise." I interrupted, protesting "I'd rather be among people." He slyly asked, "Are you going to marry the people?" "No," I said, "but I love being with people."

As I cleared customs and claimed my luggage, I had to face a porter who insisted on helping me, and then asked, "When can I see you — tonight?" I was angered by his forwardness, and firmly said, "I am engaged; I am sorry," resorting to the traditional stewardess's reply. I had to face the same problem with another man on the bus into Rome. By now I was running out of patience, especially as my suitor squeezed close to me and practically tried to hold me in his arms without having spoken to me. I said furiously, "Take your hand off me. You're about to drive me out of the bus with your pushiness." He did, and he didn't dare make any other overtures all the way.

I spent two days at the hotel fending off invitations for personally guided tours of Rome. During these two days, I walked the streets of Rome alone. It is strange, but I had no desire to purchase anything, see Rome's ancient glory, or even go to a film. I only walked and walked, contemplating my mission and reciting its details to myself.

Early on the morning of August 29, I checked out of the hotel and caught a bus to Fiumicino Airport on the outskirts of Rome.

Happily, the only snag was a half-hour flight delay. My associate, whom I recognized only from a photograph, appeared on schedule and we exchanged pre-arranged signals. His name was Salim Issawi; he was a Palestinian from Haifa who had been raised in Syria. Salim sat quietly nearby and we tried to ignore each other.

All was going smoothly when suddenly the human element threatened our careful planning. A few seats away there was a little girl with a button on her dress cheerfully proclaiming "Make Friends". That message brought me up short, forced me to remind myself, as I watched her playing with her little sister, that this child had committed no crime against me or my people. It would be cruel to imperil her life by hijacking a plane, the symbolic meaning of which she had no conception — a plane that could explode during our attempted seizure or be blown up by Israeli anti-aircraft fire when we entered the "Israeli airspace."

While these qualms pricked my conscience, the whole history of Palestine and her children came before my eyes. I saw everything from the first day of my exile. I saw my people homeless, hungry, barefoot. The twice "refugee" children of Bagan camp near Amman seemed to stand, a humiliated multitude, in front of me saying, "We too are children and we are a part of the human race." The scene strengthened me enormously. I said to myself, "What crime did I and my people perpetrate against anyone to deserve the fate we have suffered?" The answer was "None". The operation must be carried out. There can be no doubt or retreat. My children have spoken.

On the bus across the field to the Boeing 707, another unscheduled problem developed. A handsome man in his early 30s came up to me and said "Hello" in a most jovial, enthusiastic manner. "Hello," I replied nonchalantly, as I calmly tried to read *My Friend Che* by Ricardo Rojo. He seemed very eager to talk and asked me who I was and where I was going. I couldn't very well repeat the marriage tale and couldn't invent anything quickly enough. I said, "Guess."

He tried, "Greek, Spanish, Italian?" I asked him where he was from. "I am from Chicago," he answered, and continued his questioning. "You wouldn't be South American, would you?" Now that I knew where he was from, I figured it was safe to say that I was a South American. I thought it might end his questioning, at least. "From Brazil ?" he asked, looking admiringly at me, and ogling my whole body. "You're getting closer," I said.

"Bolivia?" "Yes," I replied, "but how did you know?" "It's your book that gave you away," he declared. I asked him what he thought of Che.

"Good man," he said. "Where are you going?" I countered, trying to change to a less controversial topic. "To Athens, to see my mother. I haven't seen her in 15 years. I bet she's there already, waiting for me at the airport." I was astounded, and almost told him, "You bloody fool, you'd better get off this plane, because it isn't going to Athens." I tried to ignore him and closed my ears to keep his voice from penetrating my inner conscience. I plunged into a nervous reading of *My Friend Che*.

This encounter made me stop and think, because I understood the longing for one's own country. However, I rationalized his plight by making a distinction between his "exile," which was voluntary, and mine, which was forced. But these human encounters made me decide to be extra careful not to jeopardize the lives of the passengers unnecessarily. Their welfare, however, did not and could not cripple my operation. The deed had to be carried out. There was no turning back.

The plane was airborne for only 20 minutes before the hostesses were graciously trying to serve their five first-class passengers. Neither Salim nor I was anxious to eat. The stewardesses were very solicitous. They offered us drinks and peanuts. Anything we wanted. I settled for a coffee, Salim for a beer. But they made us nervous, as they kept returning and asking us if we wanted anything else. I pretended that I had a stomach ache and asked for a blanket. I innocently placed it over my lap, so I could take my hand grenade out of my purse and put my pistol right in the top of my trousers without being noticed. Salim asked for an aspirin tablet. I was afraid the stewardess might suspect something had she realized that two passengers opposite each other in the first row were sick. In any case, I dreaded the prospect of having a companion with a headache, so was relieved when he merely pocketed the aspirin. Seconds after the only other male passenger in the first class section returned from the small lounge, I gestured to Salim to proceed to the cockpit. Just at that moment, another hostess carrying the crew's lunch trays was opening the door of the cockpit. Salim seized the opportunity and leapt in ahead of her. She screamed, "Oh no!" and her trays flew in the air, causing much noise but no injury. I was behind Salim and ordered the stewardess to get out of the way. She did, quivering and watching us over her shoulder. Salim was so huge that he blocked my view, and I couldn't see the reaction of the crew. I could, however, hear him say that the plane had been taken over by the Che Guevara Commando Unit of the PFLP, and announce that the new captain was Shadiah Abu Ghazalah.

In the middle of his speech, my pistol slipped down the leg of my trousers and, as I bent down to pick it up, I saw the bewildered looks on the crew's faces. I suppose all they could see was part of my wide-brimmed chic hat. I felt ridiculous for a moment, laughed at my ineptness, put the pistol away, and entered the cockpit solemnly brandishing my hand grenade and declaring I was the new captain. The crew were completely shocked to see me there, but they showed no fear. To demonstrate my credibility, I immediately offered my predecessor, Captain Carter, the safety pin from the grenade as a souvenir. He respectfully declined it. I dropped it at his feet and made my speech. "If you obey my orders, all will be well; if not, you will be responsible for the safety of passengers and aircraft."

"Go to Lydda," I instructed. "To Lod?" he queried, using the Israeli name. "You understand English, don't you?" I said curtly. "You just listen to my orders and don't ask silly questions." Since I knew the plane carried fuel for almost three hours and 45 minutes, I decided to reaffirm my authority by testing the flight engineer. I turned towards him and asked, "How much fuel do you have, flight engineer?" "For two hours," he promptly replied, without even looking at the fuel gauge. "Liar," I shouted, and told him that I knew just as much as he did about the Boeing, and that if he ever lied to me again I'd break his neck. The pilot tried to calm me down. He thought I was angry, but I was actually overjoyed. He warned the crew not to be obstinate in dealing with their new captain.

Realizing that he was prepared to co-operate, I asked Captain Carter to radio Rome so that I could explain my action to the Italian people. He explained that we were too far away. I insisted that he try. He did. We had no luck. I asked a steward to bring our hand luggage forward, and then ordered him and the other first-class passengers to move to the tourist section. Next I demanded that the intercom system be turned on. All orders were complied with, and I read the following message to the passengers:

> Ladies and gentlemen, your attention please. Kindly fasten your seat belts. This is your new captain speaking. The Che Guevara Commando Unit of the Popular Front for the Liberation of Palestine which has taken over command of this TWA flight demands that all passengers on board adhere to the following instructions.
>
> Remain seated and keep calm.
>
> For your own safety, place your hands behind your head.
>
> Make no move which would endanger the lives of other passengers on this plane.

We will consider all your demands within the safe limits of our plan. Among you is a passenger responsible for the death and misery of a number of Palestinian men, women and children, on behalf of whom we are carrying out this operation to bring this assassin before a revolutionary Palestinian court. The rest of you will be honorable guests of the heroic Palestinian people in a hospitable, friendly country. Every one of you, regardless of religion or nationality, is guaranteed freedom to go wherever he pleases as soon as the plane is safely landed.

Our destination is a friendly country, and friendly people will receive you.

As I completed reading the message, I observed that the plane had swerved off the course I charted for it. I ordered the captain not to play games if he wanted to reach our destination safely and put him on course again. Then Salim reminded me that fifteen minutes had elapsed since the passengers were asked to hold their hands behind their heads. I quickly advised them to relax and to drink champagne if they so desired, and offered an apology for inconveniencing them.

Shortly afterwards, a stewardess came in and explained that most of the passengers didn't understand English, didn't know what we had said, and would like us to repeat the message. She even offered to translate it into French for them. I repeated the message and assured them that everything was normal, that there was only one person on the plane we were after. Later, this was interpreted by the press as indicating that we were after the Israeli ambassador to the US, General Itzhak Rabin of June War fame. We were not, and if we had been, I would not have boarded flight 840 at Rome, since I saw all the passengers and knew that Rabin was not among them. Saleh Al Moualim, an Israeli Arab on board, must have thought that he was the person we meant, because he became very jittery and frightened. The selective terror tactic worked; the passengers' fear diminished and everyone cooperated with us. In explaining the message to the passengers, I told them that we detested the American government's Middle East actions, and held no grudge against any individual person. They were frightened, however, when I announced that we intended to blow up the plane upon arrival in a friendly country. I announced this only an hour before reaching Damascus.

Meanwhile, I resumed radio contact with the ground, sending messages of solidarity to the Greek revolutionaries and to the people of

South Europe. I demanded that the Greek colonels release our imprisoned revolutionaries, and said that the CIA plotters would be toppled by the Greek people. All went according to plan, until we got the Egyptian observation tower on our wavelength. I identified myself to the controller in Arabic and asked him to convey to the Egyptian people the greetings of the Palestinian revolution. I advised him that I was going to Lydda, and his voice crackled: "Allah, to Lydda, what will you do there?" "Visit the fatherland," I said. "Are you sure of that?" "I certainly am," I replied enthusiastically. He tried to tell me that it was too dangerous. I switched him off, then relented momentarily as he screamed, "Oh Front, Oh Popular, Oh Arab Palestine!" but the rest of the appeal was too incoherent and inaudible.

Within minutes, I could see the coast of my Palestine in the haze. As we approached the land of my birth, it seemed that my love and I were racing towards each other for an eternal embrace. I rushed towards my beloved and saw Palestine for the first time since my forced exile in 1948. I was lost in a moment of passion and meditation. Then I remembered the mission and ordered the pilot to descend, and I addressed a message in Arabic to my fellow exiles in occupied Palestine, telling them we shall return and we shall recover the land. I advised them to remain steadfast and promised to smash the Zionist fortress of conceit. I told Lydda tower in Arabic that we were going to land. He didn't understand, the pilot said, and told us we should ask for clearance and wait. I said, "This is my country. I do not need permission from the Zionist vultures to land."

I spoke to the tower in English, saying: "Here we come again. Shadiah Abu Ghaselah has come back to life. There are millions of Shadiahs who will be returning again and again to reclaim the land." The Israeli tower must have been terrified for a while because I said that we intended to blow up the plane right in the airport. In seconds three Israeli Mirages appeared on the horizon and tried to prevent us from landing. I turned the intercom on so that the passengers could hear the exchange.

I declared anew that the pilot and the Israelis were responsible for the safety of the passengers and the plane, and that we intended to do no harm to anyone if our orders were obeyed. The co-pilot asked if he could speak to the Israelis and I let him. He said, "Popular Front, Free Arab Palestine, Armed people have threatened to explode the plane with hand grenades if your Mirages don't clear out." Until this moment the Israeli tower was still addressing us as TWA 840. My patience ran out and I told him to shut up and turned him off, saying that there will be no further communications until he addressed us as Popular Front, Free Arab Palestine.

In seconds he did so as we swung around my beloved Haifa. The pilot asked, "What shall I do now?" I said, "Let's take a seven-minute tour of the fatherland." My father's image appeared before my eyes, and I could hear his voice saying, "When will we return home?" My whole world came together. I was silent. I looked out at the greenery and mountains of Palestine. I could see Tel Aviv below. I wept out of affection and longing, and said softly, "Father, we shall return. We shall redeem your honor and restore your dignity. We shall become the sovereign of the land some day." Suddenly, I remembered that the mission preceded personal emotions. I instructed the pilot, "Go to Lebanon, where my people live as refugees." The Israeli planes continued to pursue us. At the Lebanese border, they zoomed away. I called Cyprus and sent greetings to its heroic anti-imperialist fighters, and sent messages to my people in South Lebanon. The pilot interrupted. "We must ask for clearance from Beirut." "We don't need to ask for clearance," I said. "This is an Arab country." We circled Beirut briefly before I ordered the pilot to go on to Damascus. He objected, "The airport there couldn't accommodate the Boeing 707." "Look, do you think we're so backward that we couldn't handle your damned plane?" I said strongly. He didn't respond. I took the microphone and addressed the passengers for the last time: "Evacuate immediately on landing; have a happy holiday in Syria. I trust we shall have a smooth landing."

The fuel gauge was reading empty; the pilot sought clearance and I ordered him to land immediately on the runway farthest from the air terminal. "Let's have a smooth landing," I said, "because if I fall, the hand grenade could explode and that would be a terrible anticlimax to a happy journey."'He landed smoothly and in less than three minutes the plane was empty. Salim and I tried to tell the passengers to slow down and to take their personal belongings with them. Most ran out barefooted. Even the crew left their jackets behind. As Captain Carter stepped out, I saluted and thanked him for his cooperation. He looked at me in astonishment. The co-pilot said, "You're most welcome."

I checked the plane. All the passengers had left. Salim wired the cockpit and lit the fuse. I slid out on one of the torn emergency chutes and fell to the ground on my rear. Salim followed and landed on my shoulders. The plane did not explode as scheduled. Salim's personal courage made him climb back in and set everything in motion once more. When Syrian soldiers arrived on the scene, I distracted them by saying, "The Israeli officers ran in that direction. Go and get them."

Salim was still in the plane. I feared for his safety, but admired his heroism and selfless devotion. I tried to leap in and couldn't. Suddenly he appeared and waved reassuringly. The Boeing still did not explode. He fired a few shots into the wing of the plane, but there was no fuel left, so it wouldn't readily ignite. When sparks finally fluttered, we took cover 20 yards away. Half a mile away, the passengers in the terminal watched the bonfire and the explosion of the Boeing. The Syrian soldiers returned, astounded. They were even more surprised when Salim and I surrendered to them and turned over our weapons. The Al-Hadaf photographer, who was parachuted by the Front to film our landing and the explosion, was so excited that he forgot to remove the lens cap from his camera.

Our Syrian hosts took us to the air terminal, where I delivered a brief speech to the passengers:

Ladies and gentlemen, thank you for your kind attention and co-operation during the flight. I am captain Shadiah Abu Ghazalah. That's not my name; my name is Khaleda. Shadiah is an immortal woman who wrote: "Heroes are often forgotten, but their legends and memories are the property and heritage of the people." That is something historians and analysts cannot understand. Shadiah will not be forgotten by the Popular Front and by the generation of revolutionaries she helped mould in the path of revolution. I would like you to know that Shadiah was a Palestinian Arab woman from Nablus; that she was a schoolteacher and a member of the Popular Front underground; that she died in an explosion at her own home at the age of 21 on November 21, 1968, while manufacturing hand grenades for the Front. She was the first woman martyr of our revolution. I assumed her name on flight 840 to tell the world about the crimes the Israelis inflict upon our people and to demonstrate to you that they make no distinctions between men, women and children. But for their own propaganda objectives they repeatedly state in your press how we attack their "innocent" women and children and how cruel we are. I want you to know that we love children, too, and we certainly do not aim our guns at them. We diverted flight 840 because TWA is one of the largest American airlines that services the Israeli air routes and, more importantly, because it is an American plane. The American government is Israel's staunchest supporter. It supplies Israel with weapons for our destruction. It gives the Zionists tax-free American dollars. It supports Israel at world conferences. It helps them in every possible way. We are against America because she is an imperialist country. And our unit is called the Che Guevara Commando Unit because we abhor America's assassination of Che and because we are a part of the Third World and the world revolution. Che was an apostle of that revolution. We took the plane to Haifa because Comrade Salim and I come from Haifa. Both of us were evicted in 1948. We took you to Tel Aviv as an act of defiance and challenge to the Israelis and to demonstrate their impotence when the Arabs embark on offensive rather then defensive strategy. We brought you to Damascus because Syria is the pulsating heart of the Arab homeland and because the Syrians are a good and generous people. We hope you will enjoy your stay in Damascus. We hope you will go home and tell your friends not to go to Israel — to the Middle East war zone. Please tell your neighbors that we are a people like you who wish to live in peace and security in our country, governing ourselves. Please tell the Americans that if they hate war and the exploitation of others, they should stop their government from making war on us and helping the Israelis to deprive us of our land. Tell your people that coming to Israel helps her to deny our rights. Revolution and peace. Greetings to all lovers of the oppressed!

It was nearly seven p.m., August 29, 1969. As I concluded my speech, I saw my Greek friend sobbing, and an American woman trying to assuage him. I do not think he recognized me as his bus companion. Salim and I mixed with the passengers and distributed sweets to the children. Two old ladies were consoling each other; one was saying she was "wet" and the other was telling her to thank God for having arrived in Damascus alive. The Syrian authorities cleared the passengers through customs and took them to hotels in Damascus. They released all of them with the exception of six Israelis. One American woman was taken to hospital with a broken ankle. On September 3, four Israelis were released; later the other two were exchanged for two Syrian air force pilots in Israeli custody and a handful of imprisoned fighters. Salim and I were taken to police headquarters.

Although we had arrived at the airport to the cheers of the Syrian crowds, the Syrian officials were not that friendly. An arrogant colonel started his investigation by demanding, "What do you think you are?" "Soldiers, like you," I said. "No," he angrily replied, "you are a terrorist organization." "Hey," I said, "am I in Israel or the Syrian Arab Republic, the advocate of revolutionary warfare?" The colonel didn't like my tone of voice. "This action is not fedayeen-like. It is terrorism," he said. "Look," I explained, "I am a soldier who carried out her assignment. If you wish to debate the validity and legitimacy of our revolutionary strategy, we'll be happy to do it with you, but not in a police station." "Where did you train?" "I will answer no further questions, since I already gave you my name and told you what party I belong to."

The colonel ordered us to be held in dingy little rooms and gave us two blankets each. At about 11:30 p.m., we were taken from our cells to the second floor for further interrogation. I gave my name as Khaleda and they obviously knew it was false. The officer in charge was rather suave and clever. He ordered his assistants to bring us dinner and proceeded to tell us how he strongly identified with the Palestine revolution. I interrupted, "That is not the colonel's view." "What colonel?" he said. "You should know," I answered.

The assistants brought food, and I declined it, declaring, "I won't eat until I am released." "Where will you go if released?" he asked. "To my country, Palestine," I said. The officer enquired about many things, and my answer was an emphatic "No comment" to every question. Late that night, I asked to go to the bathroom, and I was accompanied by a male policeman who was under orders to search me before I went in. I dared him to touch me, and threatened to attack him and scream rape if he did. He ignored the orders and took me back to my windowless cell. I asked the male guard to buy me a packet of cigarettes; he refused, doling out one cigarette at a time for the remainder of the night. Since I was unable to sleep, see anyone or talk, I kept the guard marching me back and forth to the bathroom all night. I do not know who was more exhausted by morning. I continued that strategy for the next four nights.

On the morning of August 31, breakfast was brought in and I declined to eat again, announcing that I was on a hunger strike. By then I hadn't had a good meal in three days and I was smoking very heavily. I was also getting bored being in isolation but knowing full well that my comrades were joyously celebrating my deed. Around noon, I twisted the edge of the rusty iron partition between me and Salim and we started whispering to each other face to face. I told him about the "wet lady" at the airport, and we laughed boisterously about it. The guard heard the noise and ran towards the cell thinking I must have gone mad. He asked me to share the joke with him. I refused to say anything. But when he realized that I was still sane, he looked around my cell, and found the hole. He accused me of being a terrorist, and threatened dire consequences if I widened the hole. I dared him, "Go and tell your superiors."

That afternoon, another colonel came to visit us, but he was in civilian clothes. He was smoother than his predecessors. He introduced himself as a Palestinian pilot with the Syrian air force from Al-Nassera. My name is Azzani," he said, "and I have just returned from the front bringing you the revolutionary greetings of the fighters." I said, "If you recognize us as revolutionaries, why are you holding us in prison?" "Why are you on a hunger strike?" he asked, without answering my question. I said, "Because I am being treated like a criminal, and I protest very strongly against these insulting interrogations of intelligence officers like yourself." He asked if I needed anything or any money. I replied proudly, "I have money and the only thing I want is departure from this Baath prison." He left without comment.

On September 1, I felt very weak and tired. Stomach ache, headache, general fatigue seemed to have overtaken me. I began to feel dizzy, but I still refused to eat. That evening I fainted on my way to the bathroom, and it took them a few minutes to revive me. The Syrians were very disturbed and called in a doctor who tried to persuade me to eat some yogurt or drink something other than coffee. I insisted "No" and passed out again. All I remember after that was a nurse bathing my face, and Salim carrying me to a hospital ambulance. I was not fully conscious until the morning of September 2, when, with a sense of inner peace and self-fulfillment, I sat down in the hospital and wrote a few notes, taking my inspiration from Che's immortal dictum: "We must grow tough, but without ever losing our tenderness."

"I MADE THE RING FROM A BULLET AND THE PIN OF A HAND GRENADE"
When Palestinian liberation fighter Leila Khaled hijacked her first plane in 1969, she became the international pin-up of armed struggle. Then she underwent cosmetic surgery so she could do it again. Thirty years on, she talks to Katharine Viner about being a woman at war. (*The Guardian*, 1/26/01)

The iconic photograph of Leila Khaled, the picture which made her the symbol of Palestinian resistance and female power, is extraordinary in many ways: the gun held in fragile hands, the shiny hair wrapped in a keffiah, the delicate Audrey Hepburn face refusing to meet your eye. But it's the ring, resting delicately on her third finger. To fuse an object of feminine adornment, of frivolity, with a bullet: that is Khaled's story, the reason behind her image's enduring power. Beauty mixed with violence.

And the ring? "I made it from the pin of a hand grenade — from the first grenade I ever used in training," she says. "I just wrapped it around a bullet."

Leila Khaled — international hijacker for the Popular Front for the Liberation of Palestine (PFLP), the papers' favourite '70s "girl terrorist" and "deadly beauty" — is now 57, and sitting with me in the House of Commons for her first ever interview on British soil. Her cheekbones are still like knives; her eyes are gentle but flicker when moved. She has a Rothmans cigarette constantly dangling languorously between her fingers (she once said of a potentially boring time in Kuwait: "I was politically conscious and a chain smoker — I needed no other diversions").

She is, of course, wearing a keffiah, fringed with wool in the Palestinian colors of red, green, black and white, like a shawl. But she looks very different now from the way she did in that famous photo, and not just because of age. Since that picture was taken in 1969, after her first (successful) hijack of a TWA plane, Khaled underwent no fewer than six cosmetic operations on her face, so that no one would ever recognize her again. She refused to wander around with the face of an icon.

"The surgeon just made a few differences to my nose and my chin," she says. "But it worked. No one recognized me." She elected to have surgery without a general anaesthetic; because, as she said in her autobiography: "I have a cause higher and nobler than my own, a cause to which all private interests and concerns must be subordinated."

Such revolutionary-speak is a reminder that Khaled is from a very different time: an age when hijacks were a political tool of the moment, when commitment, extreme risk and sacrifice were admired and often romanticized. Her sexuality was always emphasized; as recently as 1980, a Norwegian newspaper made jokes about her "bombs" (Norwegian slang for breasts) and she is supposed to have been the inspiration for Leela, Dr. Who's foxy sidekick in 1975.

She is the pin-up of armed struggle; like her hero, Che Guevara, Khaled had the glamour as well as the belief. She had a certain disdain for her fellow western revolutionaries, however: "We found it very amusing that they honestly believed they were making a 'revolution' if they undressed in public, seized a university building, or shouted an obscenity at bureaucrats," she says.

The surgery meant that Khaled was able to undertake her second hijack without detection; this time of an El Al jet from Amsterdam. "At Amsterdam airport my comrade Patrick [Arguello, a Nicaraguan] and I were stopped by Israeli officers," she says. "They searched our bags very thoroughly, but they didn't find anything in there. Because the grenades were in my pockets." She takes a deep breath. "We had passports from Honduras. The officer said to me, 'do you speak Spanish?' At once I said, 'Si señor' — I was lucky, because they were the only words I knew."

In mid-flight, Khaled and Arguello tried to storm the cockpit. They banged on the door; Khaled took the pins out of her grenades with her teeth and ordered the captain to let them in. But there were armed guards on the plane and they began to shoot. "Patrick was shot in the back four times, and another man came with a bottle of whisky and banged it over his head," says Khaled. "It was terrible." Why didn't they shoot her? "I had grenades," she says, with a shrug of her shoulders. "Eventually I was hit on the back of my head, and I lost consciousness. When I woke up I was tied up and being kicked.

"Passengers were shouting; I heard a woman scream, 'Stop the bloodshed.' But we had very strict instructions: don't hurt the passengers. Only defend yourselves."

But the grenades would have hurt the passengers, had she released them. "I did not want to blow up the plane," she says, sternly. "It was only to threaten." (While the PFLP was involved in other controversial armed actions in Israel, including some which led to the deaths of civilians, no one died during either of the hijacks in which Khaled was involved.

The plane landed at Heathrow and Khaled was taken to Ealing police station where she was held for 28 days, until the then prime minister, Edward Heath, released her in exchange for western hostages held by the PFLP. Her stay in Britain was pleasant, she says. "People were very nice. They would say to each other: is she the one? They could hardly believe it, this tiny creature sitting on the bench. I was 26 and I was very thin. I had two policewomen with me in my cell, and we were always discussing our cause and our suffering. After I left I sent them books about Palestine; they asked me to. We wrote to each other. One of them had a problem with her boyfriend, and we often discussed this."

It's an intriguing thought: the Palestinian revolutionary and the Ealing policewoman finding common ground by discussing men.

Although it is not, perhaps, so surprising. Women have always related to Khaled. As Eileen Macdonald, in her book *Shoot the Women First*, puts it: "She shattered a million and one taboos overnight and she revolutionized the thinking of hundreds of other angry young women around the world."

She flamboyantly overcame the patriarchal restrictions of Arab society where women are traditionally subservient to their husbands, by taking an equal fighting role with men, by getting divorced and remarried, having children in her late 30s, and rejecting vanity by having her face reconstructed for her cause.

There were difficulties with being both a woman and a fighter, however. "In the beginning, all women had to prove that we could be equal to men in armed struggle," says Khaled. "So we wanted to be like men — even in our appearance." Robin Morgan, in her book, *The Demon Lover: The Sexuality of Terrorism*, writes about how Khaled lost out in two ways.

The men in her organization resented the attention she got, while women were frustrated that she never spoke about women, only about the revolution. (She once said, "I represent Palestinians, not women.") This has echoes of something Mairead Farrell, the IRA volunteer who was shot dead by the SAS in Gibraltar in 1988, once said: "I'm oppressed as a woman, but I'm also oppressed because I'm Irish . . . We can't successfully end our oppression as women until we first end the oppression of our country."

But things seem to have changed for Khaled. "I no longer think it's necessary to prove ourselves as women by imitating men," she says. "I have learned that a woman can be a fighter, a freedom fighter, a political activist, and that she can fall in love, and be loved, she can be married, have children, be a mother.

"You see, at the beginning we were only interested in the revolution. We were not mature enough politically. The question of women is a part of our struggle but not the only part. Revolution must mean life also; every aspect of life." Is she a Palestinian first, or a woman first? "I cannot differentiate, she says. "A woman and a Palestinian at the same time."

Khaled was born in Haifa, now on the Israeli coast, but became a refugee with her family at a camp in Tyre, Lebanon, as a toddler in

1948. (During her 1969 hijacking of the TWA flight she forced the pilot to fly over Haifa, so that she could look at the home town she was not permitted to visit.) She can barely recall a time when she was not politicized: she remembers at the age of four being told by her mother not to pick oranges because they were in Lebanon; the fruit was not theirs, they were not in Haifa now. She committed herself full-time to armed struggle at the age of 15.

Since the time of the hijacks, Khaled has lived in Lebanon, Syria and Jordan, and has brought up two sons who are now 18 and 15. She continued her activism, first as a fighter and then as a politician for the PFLP as a member of the Palestinian National Council. (Her sons offer to be her bodyguards and when they were small really did say: "Tell us stories about the struggle, mum.")

But she is still as radical as ever. "The struggle of the Palestinians has taken many faces. Armed struggle, intifada, and now both. Which means as long as there is occupation in our country, the conflict will continue." She demands the right to self-determination, a state with Jerusalem as its capital, the right to return for refugees and the withdrawal of Israel from all the land it has occupied since 1967. "Otherwise the purpose for conflict will always be there." And now? "Now people are fed up. They are saying: now and forever. Let's do it. This time."

What she says can be difficult for peaceniks, or pacifists, to hear — the unashamed justification for violence. Many ordinary Palestinians share her views, many politicians do not. Similarly, views on Khaled herself are mixed, even among Palestinians: some think she is an inspiring heroine, others believe she reinforces the old '70s image of Palestinians as terrorists.

Is she a terrorist? "Whenever I hear this word I ask another question," she says. "Who planted terrorism in our area? Some came and took our land, forced us to leave, forced us to live in camps. I think this is terrorism. Using means to resist this terrorism and stop its effects — this is called struggle." She recalls in her memoirs thinking of the risk to children she saw on the plane she was hijacking, and telling herself: "We Palestinians are children too and we are a part of the human race."

Would she still die for the Palestinian cause? She draws on her long cigarette, and turns to face me after some silence. "Of course." She shakes her head, smiling, cigarette burning in her hand. "Of course."

"YASSER" MEANS "EASY"
Yasser Arafat's Address to the UN, November 1974
By Yasser Arafat

"I DON'T KNOW ANYONE WHO HAS AS MUCH CIVILIAN JEWISH BLOOD ON HIS HANDS AS ARAFAT SINCE THE NAZIS' TIME," SAYS ARIEL SHARON. ISRAEL'S PRIME MINISTER HAS FAILED TO CONVINCE HAMAS AND HIZBULLAH, OTHER PALESTINIAN TERROR ORGANIZATIONS, OF THE TRUTH OF HIS STATEMENT. THE VERY POPULAR AND ACTIVE HAMAS SAY THAT YASSER ARAFAT HAS NOT ONLY SOLD OUT HIS PEOPLE WITH PEACE TREATIES, BUT THAT HE'S BECOME A HARD-HEADED COP, HAVING THE PALESTINE AUTHORITY ROUND UP AND ARREST THE MOST ACTIVE MEMBERS OF ITS ORGANIZATION. IN THE AMERICAN MEDIA, THE TERRORIST EPITHET HAS ELUDED ARAFAT FOR ABOUT AS LONG AS THE OSLO AGREEMENT. BUT WHEN HE ADDRESSED THE UNITED NATIONS' GENERAL ASSEMBLY IN 1974, GUN ATTACHED, PROTEST WAS LOUD AND LONG, AND AMERICAN NEWSPAPERS HAD NO TROUBLE RUNNING OPINION ARTICLES CALLING FOR HIS MURDER AND EDITORIAL CARTOONS PICTURING ARAFAT AS A RAT —THE SAME SORT OF RACIAL TARRING APPLIED TO JEWS IN THE NAZI FILM, *THE ETERNAL JEW*. WHAT IS ARAFAT TODAY? A TRAITOR, HANDSOMELY AND COVERTLY PAID OFF BY THE UNITED STATES? DOES HE BATHE NIGHTLY IN THE BLOOD OF JEWS, AS MANY LETTER WRITERS STILL MAINTAIN HE LITERALLY DOES IN HEBREW LANGUAGE NEWSPAPERS? OR HAS AGE AND PARKINSONS MELLOWED ARAFAT, AND DOES THE PROMISE OF RUNNING AN ACTUAL GOVERNMENT HAS HIM INHABITING MIDDLE GROUND?

Mr. President, I thank you for having invited the Palestine Liberation Organization to participate in this plenary session of the United Nations General Assembly. I am grateful to all those representatives of States of the United Nations who contributed to the decision to introduce the question of Palestine as a separate item of the agenda of this Assembly. That decision made possible the Assembly's resolution inviting us to address it on the question of Palestine.

The roots of the Palestinian question reach back into the closing years of the 19th century, in other words, to that period which we call the era of colonialism and settlement as we know it today. This is precisely the period during which Zionism as a scheme was born; its aim was the conquest of Palestine by European immigrants, just as settlers colonized, and indeed raided, most of Africa. This is the period during which, pouring forth out of the west, colonialism spread into the further reaches of Africa, Asia, and Latin America, building colonies everywhere, cruelly exploiting, oppressing, plundering the people of those three continents. This period persists into the present. Marked evidence of its totally reprehensible presence can be readily perceived in the racism practiced both in South Africa and in Palestine.

Arafat and Nasser

Just as colonialism and its demagogues dignified their conquests, their plunder and limitless attacks upon the natives of Africa with appeals to a "civilizing and modernizing" mission, so too did waves of Zionist immigrants disguise their purposes as they conquered Palestine. Just as colonialism as a system and colonialists as its instrument used religion, color, race and language to justify the African's exploitation and his cruel subjugation by terror and discrimination, so too were these methods employed as Palestine was usurped and its people hounded from their national homeland.

Just as colonialism heedlessly used the wretched, the poor, the exploited as mere inert matter with which to build and to carry out settler colonialism, so too were destitute, oppressed European Jews employed on behalf of world imperialism and of the Zionist leadership. European Jews were transformed into the instruments of aggression; they became the elements of settler colonialism intimately allied to racial discrimination.

Zionist theology was utilized against our Palestinian people: the purpose was not only the establishment of Western-style settler colonialism but also the severing of Jews from their various homelands and subsequently their estrangement from their nations. Zionism is an ideology that is imperialist, colonialist, racist; it is profoundly reactionary and discriminatory; it is united with anti-Semitism in its retrograde tenets and is, when all is said and done, another side of the same base coin. For when what is proposed is that adherents of the Jewish faith, regardless of their national residence, should neither owe allegiance to their national residence nor live on equal footing with its other, non-Jewish citizens —

when that is proposed we hear anti-Semitism being proposed. When it is proposed that the only solution for the Jewish problem is that Jews must alienate themselves from communities or nations of which they have been a historical part, when it is proposed that Jews solve the Jewish problem by immigrating to and forcibly settling the land of another people — when this occurs exactly the same position is being advocated as the one urged by anti-Semites against Jews.

Thus, for instance, we can understand the close connection between Rhodes, who promoted settler colonialism in southeast Africa, and Herzl, who had settler colonialist designs upon Palestine. Having received a certificate of good settler colonialist conduct from Rhodes, Herzl then turned around and presented this certificate to the British Government, hoping thus to secure a formal resolution supporting Zionist policy. In exchange, the Zionists promised Britain an imperialist base on Palestine soil so that imperial interests could be safeguarded at one of their chief strategic points.

The Jewish invasion of Palestine began in 1881. Before the first large wave of immigrants started arriving, Palestine had a population of half a million; most of the population was either Moslem or Christian, and only 20,000 were Jewish. Every segment of the population enjoyed the religious tolerance characteristic of our civilization.

Palestine was then a verdant land, inhabited mainly by an Arab people in the course of building its life and dynamically enriching its indigenous culture.

Between 1882 and 1917 the Zionist Movement settled approximately 50,000 European Jews in our homeland. To do that it resorted to trickery and deceit in order to implant them in our midst. Its success in getting Britain to issue the Balfour Declaration once again demonstrated the alliance between Zionism and imperialism. Furthermore, by promising to the Zionist movement what was not hers to give, Britain showed how oppressive the rule of imperialism was. As it was constituted then, the League of Nations abandoned our Arab people, and Wilson's pledges and promises came to naught. In the guise of a mandate, British imperialism was cruelly and directly imposed upon us. The mandate document issued by the League of Nations was to enable the Zionist invaders to consolidate their gains in our homeland.

In the wake of the Balfour Declaration and over a period of 30 years, the Zionist movement succeeded, in collaboration with its imperialist ally, in settling more European Jews on the land, thus usurping the properties of Palestine Arabs.

By 1947 the number of Jews had reached 600,000: they owned about six percent of Palestinian arable land. The figure should be compared with the population of Palestine which at that time was 1,250,000.

As a result of the collusion between the mandatory Power and the Zionist movement and with the support of some countries, this General Assembly early in its history approved a recommendation to partition our Palestinian homeland. This took place in an atmosphere poisoned with questionable actions and strong pressure. The General Assembly partitioned what it had no right to divide — an indivisible homeland. When we rejected that decision, our position corresponded to that of the natural mother who refused to permit King Solomon to cut her son in two when the unnatural mother claimed the child for herself and agreed to his dismemberment. Furthermore, even though the partition resolution granted the colonialist settlers 54 percent of the land of Palestine, their dissatisfaction with the decision prompted them to wage a war of terror against the civilian Arab population. They occupied 81 percent of the total area of Palestine, uprooting a million Arabs. Thus, they occupied 524 Arab towns and villages, of which they destroyed 385, completely obliterating them in the process. Having done so, they built their own settlements and colonies on the ruins of our farms and our groves. The roots of the Palestine question lie here. Its causes do not stem from any conflict between two religions or two nationalisms. Neither is it a border conflict between neighboring states. It is the cause of a people deprived of its homeland, dispersed and uprooted, and living mostly in exile and in refugee camps.

With support from imperialist and colonialist powers, it managed to get itself accepted as a United Nations Member. It further succeeded in getting the Palestine Question deleted from the agenda of the United Nations and in deceiving world public opinion by presenting our cause as a problem of refugees in need either of charity from do-gooders, or settlement in a land not theirs.

Not satisfied with all this, the racist entity, founded on the imperialist-colonialist concept, turned itself into a base of imperialism and into an arsenal of weapons. This enabled it to assume its role of subjugating the Arab people and of committing aggression against them, in order to satisfy its ambitions for further expansion on Palestinian and other Arab lands. In addition to the many instances of aggression committed by this entity against the Arab States, it has launched two large-scale wars, in 1956 and 1967, thus endangering world peace and security.

As a result of Zionist aggression in June 1967, the enemy occupied Egyptian Sinai as far as the Suez Canal. The enemy occupied Syria's Golan Heights, in addition to all Palestinian land west of the Jordan. All these developments have led to the creation in our area of what has come to be known as the "Middle East problem." The situation has been rendered more serious by the enemy's persistence in maintaining its unlawful occupation and in further consolidating it, thus establishing a beachhead for world imperialism's thrust against our Arab nation. All Security Council decisions and appeals to world public opinion for withdrawal from the lands occupied in June 1967 have been ignored. Despite all the peaceful efforts on the international level, the enemy has not been deterred from its expansionist policy. The only alternative open before our Arab nations, chiefly Egypt and Syria, was to expend exhaustive efforts in preparing forcefully to resist that barbarous armed invasion and this in order to liberate Arab lands and to restore the rights of the Palestinian people, after all other peaceful means had failed.

Under these circumstances, the fourth war broke out in October 1973, bringing home to the Zionist enemy the bankruptcy of its policy of occupation, expansion and its reliance on the concept of military might. Despite all this, the leaders of the Zionist entity are far from having learned any lesson from their experience. They are making preparations for the fifth war, resorting once more to the language of military superiority, aggression, terrorism, subjugation and, finally, always to war in their dealings with the Arabs.

It pains our people greatly to witness the propagation of the myth that its homeland was a desert until it was made to bloom by the toil of foreign settlers, that it was a land without a people, and that the colonialist entity caused no harm to any human being. No: such lies must be exposed from this rostrum, for the world must know that Palestine was the cradle of the most ancient cultures and civilizations. Its Arab people were engaged in farming and building, spreading culture throughout the land for thousands of years, setting an example in the practice of freedom of worship, acting as faithful guardians of the holy places of all religions. As a son of Jerusalem, I treasure for myself and my people beautiful memories and vivid images of the religious brotherhood that was the hallmark of our Holy City before it succumbed to catastrophe. Our people continued to pursue this enlightened policy until the establishment of the State of Israel and their dispersion. This did not deter our people from pursuing their humanitarian role on Palestinian soil. Nor will they permit their land to become a launching pad for aggression or a racist camp predicated on the destruction of civilization, cultures, progress and peace. Our people cannot but maintain the heritage of their ancestors in resisting the invaders, in assuming the privileged task of defending their native land, their Arab nationhood, their culture and civilization, and in safeguarding the cradle of monotheistic religion.

By contrast, we need only mention briefly some Israeli stands: its support of the Secret Organization in Algeria, its bolstering of the settler-colonialists in Africa — whether in the Congo, Angola, Mozambique, Zimbabwe, Azania or South Africa — and its backing of South Vietnam against the Vietnamese revolution. In addition, one can mention Israel's continuing support of imperialists and racists everywhere, its obstructionist stand in the Committee of 24, its refusal to cast its vote in support of independence for the African States, and its opposition to the demands of many Asian, African and Latin American nations, and several other States in the Conferences on raw materials, population, the Law of the Sea, and food. All these facts offer further proof of the character of the enemy which has usurped our land. They justify the honorable struggle which we are waging against it. As we defend a vision of the future, our enemy upholds the myths of the past.

The enemy we face has a long record of hostility even towards the Jews themselves, for there is within the Zionist entity a built-in racism against Oriental Jews. While we were vociferously condemning the massacres of Jews under Nazi rule, Zionist leadership appeared more interested at that time in exploiting them as best it could in order to realize its goal of immigration into Palestine.

If the immigration of Jews to Palestine had had as its objective the goal of enabling them to live side by side with us, enjoying the same rights and assuming the same duties, we would have opened our doors to them, as far as our homeland's capacity for absorption permitted. Such was the case with the thousands of Armenians and Circassians who still live among us in equality as brethren and citizens. But that the goal of this immigration should be to usurp our homeland, disperse our people, and turn us into second-class citizens — this is what no one can conceivably demand that we acquiesce in or submit to. Therefore, since its inception, our revolution has not been motivated by racial or religious factors. Its target has never been the Jew, as a person, but racist Zionism and undisguised aggression. In this sense, ours is also a revolution for the Jew, as a human being, as well. We are struggling so that Jews, Christians and Moslems may live in equality enjoying the same rights and assuming the same duties, free from racial or religious discrimination.

We do distinguish between Judaism and Zionism. While we maintain our opposition to the colonialist Zionist movement, we respect the Jewish faith. Today, almost one century after the rise of the Zionist movement, we wish to warn of its increasing danger to the Jews of the world, to our Arab people and to world peace and security. For Zionism encourages the Jew to emigrate out of his homeland and grants him an artificially-created nationality. The Zionists proceed with their terrorist activities even though these have proved ineffective. The phenomenon of constant emigration from Israel, which is bound to grow as the bastions of colonialism and racism in the world fall, is an example of the inevitability of the failure of such activities.

We urge the people and governments of the world to stand firm against Zionist attempts at encouraging world Jewry to emigrate from their countries and to usurp our land. We urge them as well firmly to oppose any discrimination against any human being, as to religion, race, or color.

Why should our Arab Palestinian people pay the price of such discrimination in the world? Why should our people be responsible for the problems of Jewish immigration, if such problems exist in the minds of some people? Why do not the supporters of these problems open their own countries, which can absorb and help these immigrants?

Those who call us terrorists wish to prevent world public opinion from discovering the truth about us and from seeing the justice on our faces. They seek to hide the terrorism and tyranny of their acts, and our own posture of self-defense.

The difference between the revolutionary and the terrorist lies in the reason for which each fights. For whoever stands by a just cause and fights for the freedom and liberation of his land from the invaders, the settlers and the colonialists, cannot possibly be called terrorist; otherwise the American people in their struggle for liberation from the British colonialists would have been terrorists, the European resistance against the Nazis would be terrorism, the struggle of the Asian, African and Latin American peoples would also be terrorism, and many of you who are in this Assembly Hall were considered terrorists. This is actually a just and proper struggle consecrated by the United Nations Charter and by the Universal Declaration of Human Rights. As to those who fight against the just causes, those who wage war to occupy, colonize and oppress other people — those are the terrorists, those are the people whose actions should be condemned, who should be called war criminals: for the justice of the cause determines the right to struggle.

Zionist terrorism which was waged against the Palestinian people to evict it from its country and usurp its land is registered in our official documents. Thousands of our people were assassinated in their villages and towns, tens of thousands of others were forced at gun-point to leave their homes and the lands of their fathers. Time and time again our children, women and aged were evicted and had to wander in the deserts and climb mountains without any food or water. No one who in 1948 witnessed the catastrophe that befell the inhabitants of hundreds of villages and towns — in Jaffa, Lydda, Ramle and Galilee — no one who has been a witness to that catastrophe will ever forget the experience, even though the mass blackout has succeeded in hiding these horrors as it had hidden the traces of 385 Palestinian villages and towns destroyed at the time and erased from the map. The destruction of 19,000 houses during the past seven years, which is equivalent to the complete destruction of 200 more Palestinian villages, and the great number of maimed as a result of the treatment they were subjected to in Israeli prisons, cannot be hidden by any blackout.

Their terrorism fed on hatred and this hatred was even directed against the olive tree in my country, which has been a proud symbol and which reminded them of the indigenous inhabitants of the land, a living reminder that the land is Palestinian. Thus they sought to destroy it. How can one describe the statement by Golda Meir which expressed her disquiet about "the Palestinian children born every day"? They see in the Palestinian child, in the Palestinian tree, an enemy that should be exterminated. For tens of years Zionists have been harassing our people's cultural, political, social and artistic leaders, terrorizing them and assassinating them. They have stolen our cultural heritage, our popular folklore and have claimed it as theirs. Their terrorism even reached our sacred places in our beloved and peaceful Jerusalem. They have endeavored to de-Arabize it and make it lose its Moslem and Christian character by evicting its inhabitants and annexing it.

I must mention the fire of the Aqsa Mosque and the disfiguration of many of the monuments, which are both historic and religious in character. Jerusalem, with its religious history and its spiritual values, bears witness to the future. It is proof of our eternal presence, of our civilization, of our human values. It is therefore not surprising that under its skies the three religions were born and that under that sky these three religions shine in order to enlighten mankind so that it might express the tribulations and hopes of humanity, and that it might mark out the road of the future with its hopes.

The small number of Palestinian Arabs who were not uprooted by the Zionists in 1948 are at present refugees in their own homeland.

Israeli law treats them as second-class citizens — and even as third-class citizens since Oriental Jews are second-class citizens and they have been subject to all forms of racial discrimination and terrorism after confiscation of their land and property. The have been victims to bloody massacres such as that of Kfar Kassim; they have been expelled from their villages and denied the right to return, as in the case of the inhabitants of Ikrit and Kfar-Birim. For 26 years, our population has been living under martial law and has been denied the freedom of movement without prior permission from the Israeli military governor — this at a time when an Israeli law was promulgated granting citizenship to any Jew anywhere who wanted to emigrate to our homeland. Moreover, another Israeli law stipulated that Palestinians who were not present in their villages or towns at the time of the occupation were not entitled to Israeli citizenship.

The record of Israeli rulers is replete with acts of terror perpetrated on those of our people who remained under occupation in Sinai and the Golan Heights. The criminal bombardment of the Bahr-al-Bakar School and the Abou Zaabal factory are but two such unforgettable acts of terrorism. The total destruction of the Syrian city of Kuneitra is yet another tangible instance of systematic terrorism. If a record of Zionist terrorism in South Lebanon were to be compiled, the enormity of its acts would shock even the most hardened: piracy, bombardments, scorched earth, destruction of hundreds of homes, eviction of civilians and the kidnapping of Lebanese citizens. This clearly constitutes a violation of Lebanese sovereignty and is in preparation for the diversion of the Litani River waters.

Need one remind this Assembly of the numerous resolutions adopted by it condemning Israeli aggressions committed against Arab countries, Israeli violations of human rights and the articles of the Geneva Conventions, as well as the resolutions pertaining to the annexation of the city of Jerusalem and its restoration to its former status?

The only description for these acts is that they are acts of barbarism and terrorism. And yet, the Zionist racists and colonialists have the temerity to describe the just struggle of our people as terror. Could there be a more flagrant distortion of truth than this? We ask those who usurped our land, who are committing murderous acts of terrorism against our people and are practicing racial discrimination more extensively than the racists of South Africa, we ask them to keep in mind the United Nations General Assembly resolution that called for the one-year suspension of the membership of the Government of

South Africa from the United Nations. Such is the inevitable fate of every racist country that adopts the law of the jungle, usurps the homeland of others and persists in oppression.

For the past 30 years, our people have had to struggle against British occupation and Zionist invasion, both of which had one intention, namely the usurpation of our land. Six major revolts and tens of popular uprisings were staged to foil these attempts, so that our homeland might remain ours. Over 30,000 martyrs, the equivalent in comparative terms of 6 million Americans, died in the process.

When the majority of the Palestinian people was uprooted from its homeland in 1948, the Palestinian struggle for self-determination continued under the most difficult conditions. We tried every possible means to continue our political struggle to attain our national rights, but to no avail. Meanwhile, we had to struggle for sheer existence. Even in exile we educated our children. This was all a part of trying to survive.

The Palestinian people produced thousands of physicians, lawyers, teachers and scientists who actively participated in the development of the Arab countries bordering on their usurped homeland. They utilized their income to assist the young and aged amongst their people who remained in the refugee camps. They educated their younger sisters and brothers, supported their parents and cared for their children. All along the Palestinian dreamed of return. Neither the Palestinian's allegiance to Palestine nor his determination to return waned; nothing could persuade him to relinquish his Palestinian identity or to forsake his homeland. The passage of time did not make him forget, as some hoped he would. When our people lost faith in the international community which persisted in ignoring its rights and when it became obvious that the Palestinians would not recuperate one inch of Palestine through exclusively political means, our people had no choice but to resort to armed struggle. Into that struggle it poured its material and human resources. We bravely faced the most vicious acts of Israeli terrorism which were aimed at diverting our struggle and arresting it.

In the past 10 years of our struggle, thousands of martyrs and twice as many wounded, maimed and imprisoned were offered in sacrifice, all in an effort to resist the imminent threat of liquidation, to regain our right to self-determination and our undisputed right to return to our homeland. With the utmost dignity and the most admirable revolutionary spirit, our Palestinian people has not lost its spirit in Israeli prisons and concentration camps or when faced with all forms of harassment and intimidation. It struggles for sheer existence and it continues to strive to preserve the Arab character of its land. Thus it resists oppression, tyranny and terrorism in their ugliest forms.

It is through our popular armed struggle that our political leadership and our national institutions finally crystallized and a national liberation movement, comprising all the Palestinian factions, organizations, and capabilities, materialized in the Palestine Liberation Organization.

Through our militant Palestine national liberation movement, our people's struggle matured and grew enough to accommodate political and social struggle in addition to armed struggle. The Palestine Liberation Organization was a major factor in creating a new Palestinian individual, qualified to shape the future of our Palestine, not merely content with mobilizing the Palestinians for the challenges of the present. The Palestine Liberation Organization can be proud of having a large number of cultural and educational activities, even while engaged in armed struggle, and at a time when it faced the increasingly vicious blows of Zionist terrorism. We established institutes for scientific research, agricultural development and social welfare, as well as centers for the revival of our cultural heritage and the preservation of our folklore. Many Palestinian poets, artists and writers have enriched Arab culture in particular, and world culture generally. Their profoundly humane works have won the admiration of all those familiar with them. In contrast to that, our enemy has been systematically destroying our culture and disseminating racist, imperialist ideologies; in short, everything that impedes progress, justice, democracy and peace.

The Palestine Liberation Organization has earned its legitimacy because of the sacrifice inherent in its pioneering role, and also because of its dedicated leadership of the struggle. It has also been granted this legitimacy by the Palestinian masses, which in harmony with it have chosen it to lead the struggle according to its directives. The Palestine Liberation Organization has also gained its legitimacy by representing every faction, union or group as well as every Palestinian talent, either in the National Council or in people's institutions. This legitimacy was further strengthened by the support of the entire Arab nation, and it was consecrated during the last Arab Summit Conference which reiterated the right of the Palestine Liberation Organization, in its capacity as the sole representative of the Palestinian people, to establish an independent national State on all liberated Palestinian territory.

Moreover, the Palestine Liberation Organization's legitimacy was intensified as a result of fraternal support given by other liberation movements and by friendly, like-minded nations that stood by our side, encouraging and aiding us in our struggle to secure our national rights.

Here I must also warmly convey the gratitude of our revolutionary fighters and that of our people to the nonaligned countries, the socialist countries, the Islamic countries, the African countries and friendly European countries, as well as all our other friends in Asia, Africa and Latin America.

The Palestine Liberation Organization represents the Palestinian people, legitimately and uniquely. Because of this, the Palestine Liberation Organization expresses the wishes and hopes of its people. Because of this, too, it brings these very wishes and hopes before you, urging you not to shirk a momentous historic responsibility towards our just cause.

For many years now, our people has been exposed to the ravages of war, destruction and dispersion. It has paid in the blood of its sons that which cannot ever be compensated. It has borne the burdens of occupation, dispersion, eviction and terror more uninterruptedly than any other people. And yet all this has made our people neither vindictive nor vengeful. Nor has it caused us to resort to the racism of our enemies. Nor have we lost the true method by which friend and foe are distinguished.

For we deplore all those crimes committed against the Jews, we also deplore all the real discrimination suffered by them because of their faith.

I am a rebel and freedom is my cause. I know well that many of you present here today once stood in exactly the same resistance position as I now occupy and from which I must fight. You once had to convert dreams into reality by your struggle. Therefore you must now share my dream. I think this is exactly why I can ask you now to help, as together we bring out our dream into a bright reality, our common dream for a peaceful future in Palestine's sacred land.

As he stood in an Israeli military court, the Jewish revolutionary, Ahud Adif, said: "I am no terrorist; I believe that a democratic State should exist on this land." Adif now languishes in a Zionist prison among his co-believers. To him and his colleagues I send my heartfelt good wishes.

And before those same courts there stands today a brave prince of the church, Bishop Capucci. Lifting his fingers to form the same victory sign used by our freedom-fighters, he said: "What I have done, I have done that all men may live on this land of peace in peace." This princely priest will doubtless share Adif's grim fate. To him we send our salutations and greetings.

Why therefore should I not dream and hope? For is not revolution the making real of dreams and hopes? So let us work together that my dream may be fulfilled, that I may return with my people out of exile, there in Palestine to live with this Jewish freedom-fighter and his partners, with this Arab priest and his brothers, in one democratic State where Christian, Jew and Moslem live in justice, equality, fraternity and progress.

Is this not a noble dream worthy of my struggle alongside all lovers of freedom everywhere? For the most admirable dimension of this dream is that it is Palestinian, a dream from out of the land of peace, the land of martyrdom and heroism, and the land of history, too.

Let us remember that the Jews of Europe and the United States have been known to lead the struggles for secularism and the separation of Church and State. They have also been known to fight against discrimination on religious grounds. How can they continue to support the most fanatic, discriminatory and closed of nations in its policy?

In my formal capacity as Chairman of the Palestine Liberation Organization and leader of the Palestinian revolution I proclaim before you that when we speak of our common hopes for the Palestine of tomorrow we include in our perspective all Jews now living in Palestine who choose to live with us there in peace and without discrimination.

In my formal capacity as Chairman of the Palestine Liberation Organization and leader of the Palestinian revolution I call upon Jews to turn away one by one from the illusory promises made to them by Zionist ideology and Israeli leadership. They are offering Jews perpetual bloodshed, endless war and continuous thrall.

We invite them to emerge from their moral isolation into a more open realm of free choice, far from their present leadership's efforts to implant in them a Masada complex.

We offer them the most generous solution, that we might live together in a framework of just peace in our democratic Palestine.

In my formal capacity as Chairman of the Palestine Liberation Organization, I announce here that we do not wish one drop of either Arab or Jewish blood to be shed; neither do we delight in the continuation of killing, which would end once a just peace, based on our people's rights, hopes and aspirations had been finally established.

In my formal capacity as Chairman of the Palestine Liberation Organization and leader of the Palestinian revolution I appeal to you to accompany our people in its struggle to attain its right to self-determination. This right is consecrated in the United Nations Charter and has been repeatedly confirmed in resolutions adopted by this august body since the drafting of the Charter. I appeal to you, further; to aid our people's return to its homeland from an involuntary exile imposed upon it by force of arms, by tyranny, by oppression, so that we may regain our property, our land, and thereafter live in our national homeland, free and sovereign, enjoying all the privileges of nationhood. Only then can Palestinian creativity be concentrated on the service of humanity. Only then will our Jerusalem resume its historic role as a peaceful shrine for all religions.

I appeal to you to enable our people to establish national independent sovereignty over its own land.

Today I have come bearing an olive branch and a freedom fighter's gun. Do not let the olive branch fall from my hand. I repeat: do not let the olive branch fall from my hand.

War flares up in Palestine, and yet it is in Palestine that peace will be born.

GUSH EMUNIM'S VIEW OF ZIONISM
By Yosef Hermoni

GUSH EMUNIM IS ZIONISM IN ITS MOST RADICAL AND MILITANT FORM. MEMBERS WERE ACCUSED IN THE EARLY '80S OF KILLING SEVERAL ARAB MAYORS OF THE WEST BANK, AND THEIR 1984 PLAN TO BLOW UP FIVE ARAB BUSES IN EAST JERUSALEM IN 1984 WAS FOILED BY SHIN BET, ISRAEL'S VERSION OF THE FBI. BUT THEIR MOST AMBITIOUS PLAN BY FAR WAS TO DYNAMITE THE HOLY AL-AQSA MOSQUE, THE THIRD MOST HOLY ISLAMIC SHRINE ON EARTH. THEIR PLANS WERE TEMPORARILY HALTED BY ISRAELI POLICE. YOSEF HERMONI'S ARTICLE ATTEMPTS TO COME TO THE RESCUE OF GUSH EMUNIM'S REPUTATION IN ISRAEL SINCE THEY ARE SEEN AS BEING AN UNSTABLE BUNCH OF KOOKS, BUT IT DOES NOT SEEM VERY CONVINCING.

The tendency to despise the devotion of Gush Emunim to some particular piece of Eretz Yisrael, the facile way some of our sober people use the term "holy madness" to describe those screechy, pesky Levingers, the frothing hatred that is bent on annihilating this "barrier to peace" — all these are reactions and forms of discourse whose significance goes far beyond Gush Emunim per se. They go to the very heart of the meaning of our presence here between the Jordan and the Mediterranean.

The attempt to present the irrational aspect of our affinity to Eretz Yisrael (call it religious, spiritual, mystical, or whatever you like) as devoid of significance or even dangerous is one that knows no green lines. Those who jeer at sentiments roused by rockhills in Samaria are jeering at the act of Jews kissing the ground upon landing at Lod Airport. No intellectual acrobatics can stop Zionism from withering away once it has been cut off from its mystical, Messianic dimension, the very root of its existence. The profound affinity to Eretz Yisrael, this holy madness with which the Jewish People has been sick these 20-odd centuries, is something the only logic of which is illogic. Any attempt to understand the Zionist phenomenon without taking into account the "holy madness" of it is a sterile one.

Zionism is mysticism. It is a secular expression of Judaism and the religion of the secularists among us. To be sure, it has additional, mundane meanings (a safe haven for a persecuted people, etc.), but it has no meaning when it is cut off from the sanctity of rocky hills in Samaria, sandy dunes in the Coastal Plain, and other things beyond the chemical composition of polluted Kinneret waters.

Mysticism is not the wellspring from which the roots of Zionism draw their nourishment. It is more: Zionism is mysticism. I think that even our sensible people will agree that "the State of Israel is a vision fulfilled." And what is a vision? Not a historical forecast, the sum of a calculation of social, economic and climatic factors. Not an assessment of the prospects, trends and probabilities of measurable developments. "Vision" is a concept from the world of the very-inexact sciences. The same goes for Zionism. The vision of the Jewish People returning to its land never knew any green or any other lines. The vision of the Jews returning to the Samarian rockhills and the Judean mountains is of the very stuff of the Zionist vision. Whoever derides and mocks this vision is mocking the entire Zionist vision and deriding the Jewish People's undertaking in Eretz Yisrael.

A Jew for whom the Western Wall is no more than a heap of large stones possesses a castrated Jewishness. A Jew whose skin did not tingle when Jerusalem was liberated either has no skin or no Jewishness. Jewish history and its young offspring, Zionism, are a history of sanctified symbols without which they have no future. Stripping Zionism of its ability to experience mystical emotions means the strangulation of Zionism.

And here lies the importance of Gush Emunim: in guarding and fanning the embers of the pure, abstract vision and putting fashionable sobriety in its place. (Sane realism is a vital commodity which should be kept within reach. But it is meaningless unless somewhere above it flies the flag of vision.) Gush Emunim, described as the standard-bearer of "insane Zionism" is indeed carrying that standard. A good thing too, for there is no such thing as "sane Zionism."

"Come on now, be realistic!" say the sane ones in our midst when you try to tell them that one day there will be five, six, seven, eight million Jews living here. And they add: "Who's going to come here? They're happy in the affluent countries, and those in the Soviet Union aren't being permitted to come. That's the way things are."

This sober realism is umbilically linked to the almost physical revulsion that the sober ones feel towards Judea and Samaria. The demographic bookkeeping and the scorn felt towards the people clinging to the Samarian rocks somewhere at Kaddum are Siamese twins. It is no oversight that the population calculators do not take the factor of aliya (immigration — also "going up," in a physical and symbolic sense) into consideration. It is an expression of their view of Zionism as an instrument whose job is done.

Those who declare categorically that the slender trickle of aliya cannot reshape a statistical reality and shows no prospect of turning into a stream, are passing the death sentence on Zionism. The demo-graphic-bookkeeping theories are positive proof that "realistic Zionism" is a dewinged, sane, impossible Zionism.

What is this near physical disgust that our sober ones feel towards the passionate yearning and mysticism of Zionism? It seems to me that this is a natural, human expression of fatigue. Hikers climbing a mountain sometimes start grumbling about the long way remaining till they reach top. Breath comes short, feet turn heavy and long for level ground. Zionism, too, is getting tired of climbing — and the level meadows are a long way off. We all know this. But too many of us are wont to sink into a Nirvana of pipe dreams of peach and lush plains. The razor-edged, cliff-like truth is eagerly and consistently being pushed behind curtains of Western affluence and of the lifestyles of satiated societies.

There is no explaining the shock of the Yom Kippur War and the cult of weeping that followed, the trauma caused by the death of several thousand youngsters — about one third of Auschwitz's daily toll — except against the background of this sinking into a national Nirvana, this national pipe dream of comfort-just-around-the-corner, this frightening "sobriety." And the hatred of Gush Emunim is nothing less than hatred of the need to look behind the curtain of sen-sible euphoria.

Gush Emunim with its demands on us is not the center of Zionism today or its only standard-bearer. It would be more accurate to describe it as a shaft of light shattering our Nirvana-befuddlement. Gush Emunim — that band of people dancing like a band of savages — how easy it is to sic the satire-bounds on them. With satire and scorn we try to stop the tears, the dreams, the longings of dynamic, constructive Zionism that have infiltrated into our oh-so-measured lives, for — it is said — they are endangering democracy. Is this a real concern about any real threat to democracy? Or can this nail-biting about democracy be no more than a cover for our fear lest someone comes along and explode our pipe dreams?

Anthrax Should Be Put in US Water Supply Says Hamas Columnist

The following piece is from the website of the Middle East Media Research Institute, who was responsible for its translation. Daniel Pipes, who runs the Institute, says online that sympathizes with Likud, the most hawk-like Israeli political party, who would like to see members of the Hamas organization imprisoned or killed.

Atallah Abu Al-Subh, a columnist for the Hamas weekly *Al-Risala* based in Gaza, writes open letters to prominent figures, ideologies, and events. His most recent letter, No. 163, was titled "To Anthrax":

The truth is that I wondered how to begin! Should I greet you [i.e. anthrax], or should I curse you? Should I hold my tongue? . . . I will begin by saying: Oh Anthrax, despite your wretchedness, you have sown horror in the heart of the lady of arrogance, of tyranny, of boastfulness! Your gentle touch has made the US's life rough and pointless . . .

You have entered the most fortified of places; [you have entered] the White House and they left it like horrified mice . . . The Pentagon was a monster before you entered its corridors . . . And behold, it now transpires that its men are of paper and its commanders are of cardboard, and they hasten to flee as soon as they see — only see — chalk dust!

Nevertheless, you have found your way to only eight American breasts so far . . . May you continue to advance, to permeate, and to spread. If I may give you a word of advice, enter the air . . . the water faucets from which they drink, and the pens with which they draft their traps and conspiracies against the wretched peoples.

MONTHLY REPORT ON THE ISRAELI Colonization Activities in the West Bank August 2001

MONTHLY REPORTS, SHOWING THE DEPRESSINGLY AMBITIOUS DAY-TO-DAY TAKEOVER OF WEST BANK LAND BY ISRAELI COLONISTS BACKED BY THE ARMY, ARE FOUND ON THE WEBSITE <WWW.POICA.ORG/ARIJ/ARIJ.HTM> OF THE APPLIED RESEARCH INSTITUTE OF JERUSALEM (ARIJ), A "NON-PROFIT ORGANIZATION DEDICATED TO PROMOTING SUSTAINABLE DEVELOPMENT IN THE OCCUPIED PALESTINIAN TERRITORIES AND THE SELF-RELIANCE OF THE PALESTINIAN PEOPLE THROUGH GREATER CONTROL OVER THEIR NATURAL RESOURCES."

8/1/01: The occupied Jerusalem municipality confiscate more than 100 dunums of land in Jabal Al-Mukaber neighborhood to the southeastern of the old city in order to build a colony bypass road linking eastern colony outposts including Maale Adummim within the city center and Jabal Abu Ghnaim (Har Homa) to the south. Israeli authorities continue the construction of a tunnel under French Hill colony to separate Israeli communities and roads from Palestinian ones.

8/2/01: A group of Jewish colonists seize a Palestinian building located near Tel Al Rumeida neighborhood in Hebron District. The colonists say that the mobile homes they live in are not safe, and for that reason they decided to move to solid buildings. They say they would stay there until permanent housing is built for them. Israeli forces demolish a part of Beit Einun girls' school, located near a colony bypass road in Sa'ir Village of Hebron District; the demolition occurs without notification order.

8/3/01: Occupied Jerusalem municipality delivers demolishing orders to seven families in allegation of building without permits, in Shu'fat neighborhood. A group of Jewish colonists seize a plot of land lying in Al Baq'a Area near the #60 bypass road that lead to Qiryat Arba colony; this land belongs to Sultan Al Tamimi family. According to eyewitnesses, the colonists erect a tent on this land, which is cultivated with olive, almond trees and grapevine attempting to install fencing wall around it for preparation of building a new colony.

8/4/01: In Nablus District between Zawata and Ijnisinya villages the Israeli forces burn more than 200 olive trees, preventing firemen from reaching the area for firefighting. Jewish colonists of Shaare Tikva, which is near Azzun Atma village in Qalqiliya District, damage and burn agricultural properties of Palestinian villagers such as green houses and a wide area of land cultivated with tomatoes. The Israeli occupation army bulldoze an agricultural land located next to a bypass road in east Jericho. In addition they bulldoze a farm of bananas belonging to Yaser, Isam Ibrahim Asied, Munir, and Mazen Yunis Asied, as well as destroying the water network which is irrigated the fields in the area. Israeli bulldozers, protected by Jewish colonies and occupation army, construct a new colony bypass road linking Karmel colony with Maon colony which are established on confiscated land to the east of Yatta village in Hebron District. The new road is 1.2 km long and will affect more than 300 dunums of land and damage another hundred dunums of land belonging to Palestinian families.

8/5/01: Israeli occupation bulldozers destroy a wide area of a hundred dunums on Surif and Al Jab'a villages land, northwest of Hebron, aiming to erect a new colony outpost.

8/6/01: In Qalqiliya District Scores of Jewish colonists, backed with Israeli army, set fire to more than 300 olive trees from Jit village land and these trees belonged to Elayan Sedah, Muhammed Khader, Muhammed Yamin, Rashad Sedah. Tens of Jewish colonists attacked Palestinian villagers and their properties in Hebron old town; they also blocked a road leading to the Ibrahimi Mosque, and threw stones at the Palestinian cars.

8/7/01: The Israeli occupation forces demolished Palestinian house that is located to the west of the tunnel in Beit Jala neighborhood without any reason or notification, the house belongs to Ibrahim Qanis.

8/8/01: Israeli forces place six more six caravans, totaling 25 caravans, to Negohot colony, established on confiscated land of Fuqeiqis village in west Hebron. Colonists have expanded this colony on Palestinian village land since it was transformed from military colony to civilian colony. Israeli Interior Ministry releases figures showing that the Jewish colonists of the West Bank and Gaza was 203,067 in December and 208,015 in June, an increase of 2.43%.

8/9/01: In Nablus District, the Jewish colonists of Elon Moreh bulldoze a wide area of land in Yanun village to establish a new colony outpost. Israeli bulldozers, accompanied by a large number of Israeli army, destroy a hundreds dunums of agricultural land cultivated with olive, almond and forestry trees in Yatta village, Hebron District. Karmel Jewish colonists expand their colony after seizing new agricultural land in Yatta village in Hebron District, in addition to burning a Palestinian house that belongs to Fadel Abu Mayalah inside Al Luban Market in Hebron.

8/10/01: Scores of Jewish colonists from Hashmonaim set fire to olive trees in Al Midya village of Ramallah District. And the Israeli army prevent villagers from extinguishing the fire. Ya'bad Palestinian villagers confirm that Israeli authorities continue to confiscate lands surrounding Mevo Dotan 2 outpost. Eighteen new caravans are established, after confiscated hundred of dunums of Ya'bad land in Jenin District.

8/11/01: In Hebron District a group of Jewish colonists attack a Palestinian building (between Avraham Avino colony and Ibrahimi mosque), throwing stones and glass bottles and harassing residents who enter or exit from the building. Manager Salah Al Natsheh said that the Jewish colonists saw the main doors of the building to seize it. The Israeli occupation army storms Beit Qad agricultural station and transforms it into a military barrack in Jenin District.

8/12/01: A group of Jewish colonists burn land planted with olives and almond trees that belong to Mustafa Barqawi from Shufa village in Tulkarem District.

8/13/01: Installation of a new colony outpost in Jenin District by the Jewish colonists of Mirag (located on Jalbou' mountain) after alleging that a woman colonist had been killed in that location. In Qalqiliya District the Jewish colonists continue assaulting Palestinian land in Azzun village where they chop down 300 fruitful olive trees that belong to Ahmad Yousef Majed and Mohammed Suidan.

8/14/01: The Israeli occupation army seize a Palestinian house belonging to Jamal Al Jawarish, transforming it into a military barracks in Beit Jala neighborhood, Bethlehem District.

8/16/01: The Jewish colonists of Shilo and Rahel, under the protection of the Israeli soldier, confiscate wide areas of Palestinian land in Jalud village, preventing the villagers from reaching their land. According to eyewitnesses, Israeli bulldozers destroy wide areas of land in Aqraba and Yanun villages, aiming to expanding Itamar colony that is established on the villagers' land. Itamar Jewish colonists attack five Palestinian shepherds while they are grazing their sheep near Yanun village southeast Nablus city. In Nablus District, Jewish colonists attack a Palestinian car, throwing stones and shooting bullets; the driver loses control of the car causing the death the of taxi driver Kamal Saed Muslem, 50 years old from Talfit village near Nablus District. Six passengers are injured.

8/18/01: In Hebron District the Israeli occupation forces capture two Palestinian houses and transform them into military barracks and watchtower points; the first one belongs to Adnan Hamdan Henhin and the second one is owned by Ali Abed Alah Shetat.

8/19/01: Ten armed Jewish colonists storm a Palestinian shepherd from Aqraba village, south Nablus city and poison and exterminate 128 heads of sheep. Villager Abedel Ghani (65 years old) says that Jewish colonists open fire against him and another group of shepherds while they were tending to their sheep near the main road between Aqraba and Yanun villages. The day before, the same group of colonists spread grazing land in the area with poisonous substances, causing the death of many cows, sheep and goats.

8/20/01: August 20, 2001: Israeli bulldozers belonging to occupied Jerusalem municipality, guarded by police and soldiers forces, demolish two Palestinian buildings under the pretext of not being legal buildings in Beit Hanina neighborhood, north of Jerusalem. The first structure (four story) belongs to Ibrahim Al Julani, and the second one belongs to Fahmi Ahmad al Najar. The occupied Jerusalem municipality deliver demolished houses tenders for scores of Palestinian families in allegation of building without permits. In Tulkarem District, Israeli military bulldozers, guarded by Israeli soldiers, dig and destroy road, in addition to closing Ras Al Shomer road with rocks and blocks. In Hebron District, Israeli bulldozers accompanied by armored vehicle demolish a stone factory that located in Al Fahs area without prior notification despite the owner Rateb Abu Hamdiya having permit documents for 20 years. The factory is the only income source of 150 people. Four Jewish colonists shoot Palestinian farmer Reyad Bani Hasan from Arabbuna village in Jenin District when he was working his land.

8/22/01: Israeli bulldozers destroy a hundred dunums of land cultivated with olive and almond trees belong to the villagers west of Jenin, aiming to execute the separation plan between the Palestinian land and the green line along separate boundaries. Villagers say that Israeli bulldozers dug a trench, its height about 2 m. and its width about 2.5 m. along tens of kilometers. The villager Mohamad Jaradat confirm that the bulldozers, under the protection of occupied Israeli soldiers, swallow scores of kilometers of agricultural village land without notice to their owners. In Yatta village of Hebron District, two Israeli bulldozers accompanied by Karmel colonists storm land belonging to Mohamad Al Hazalin and commence wide bulldozing work. The bulldozer constructs a new bypass road linking Karmel and Maon colonies. Villager Mohamad and family try to defend their land but Israeli soldiers and Jewish colonists attack them. In Jericho District, a large number of Israeli army storm Fasayil village giving eviction notices to a number of villagers. Israeli bulldozers, under the protection of Israeli police and army, dig a trench along the road near military checkpoints erected on the Jerusalem District to forbid cars and lorries and even walkers from passing the region. In addition the bulldozers dig a deep trench on roads separating "Nisabeh" buildings from the northern area and other Palestinian houses.

8/23/01: A group of Homesh Jewish colonists block the road leading to Sabastiya village west of Nablus with burning tires.

8/24/01: In Jenin District Jewish colonists place a large quantity of poisonous substances near road edges between Al Araqa and Anin villages beside the colonies established on the villagers' land. In Tulkarem District, the Israeli Bulldozer, under protection Israeli forces, destroy lemon trees and another citrus trees farm owned by a farmer from Illar village.

8/25/01: An Israeli decision to demolish 12 commercial shops in Masha village market in allegation of not possessing permits. These commercial shops belong to: Abu Safia, Mohamad Abu Shhadeh, Talal Odeh, Abed Al Aziz Ibrahim, Nemer Abed Al Rahman, Saleh Abu Safia, Jamal Alqarem, Zaher Rashedeh, Daoud Abed Al Haq, Sami Al

Aqra, Jamal Abu Safia. In addition to a house owned by Mouhamed Issa. In Hebron District Jewish colonists continue their harassment of Palestinian people. In Wadi Al Tufah the colonists of Tal Al Rumeida fire shots at Palestinians, injuring one. Israeli forces transformed Palestinian houses into military barracks in Beit Furik village in Nablus District. In Tulkarem District Israeli bulldozers uproot more than 200 olive trees from the land of Khaled and Majed Khresha, and construct a road through villagers' land leading to Izbat Abu Khameish and towards a military base near Avne Hefets colony.

8/26/01: Israeli Authorities deliver demolition orders to three houses and a kindergarten under the pretext of building without permits, in Dhaher Al Abed village of Jenin. In Qalqiliya District, the Israeli Authorities impose a curfew in Azun village, and blocked the northern entrance of the village, which is the main entrance linking it to the District. Colonists of Tekoa poison heads of sheep after spraying poisonous substances into the grazing area located between the colony and Al Qab village south. The sheep belonged to Farhan Hasan Al Salahat.

8/28/01: Villagers from Beit Furik say that tens of Jewish colonists attack villagers' properties, and burn scores of dunums of agricultural land. Israeli bulldozers destroy villagers' land cultivated with citrus trees and vegetable in Sufeen east of Qalqiliya. Israeli soldiers fire at a livestock pen, causing the death of more than 15 heads of sheep in Rakhme village, Bethlehem District. Israeli forces storm Abu Nujeim village in Bethlehem District, destroying the water network as well as damaging part of Abu Nujeim school in addition uprooting more than 20 olive trees that belonged to the school.

8/29/01: A group of Jewish colonists fire shots into a Palestinian car at Hizma-Jericho road, causing the death of a 25-year-old young man named Hedar Jadou' Kanan from Hizma village while he was traveling to his work; also his father and brother were injured. Kanan's father and brother reported that three Jewish colonists riding in a car opened fire at the Palestinian car and ran away toward Maale Adummim colony. o The Israeli army occupy a Palestinian house owned by Ibrahim Qasem Salim, located near by the main road in Beit Ur at Tahta, west of Ramalllah city, which has been placed under curfew for four days consecutively.

8/30/01: In Jenin District Israeli bulldozers uproot scores of olive trees belonging to the villager Hamza Abu Al Rub (45 years old) from Jalbun village without prior notification. And also closed his land by blocks to prevent him entry. In Jerusalem District, Israeli forces set up new four military posts in Palestinian villages overlooking the Givat Zeev colony and Modin colony west of Jerusalem. Several villagers said that military posts were established on houses in Tera, Beit Ur At Tehta and Kharbatha Al Misbah villages.

The monthly report is an overview of events that have been reported by field workers and/or by one or more of the following sources: Al-Ayyam, Al-Quds, Alhayat Al Jadeeda, Ha'aretz, Jerusalem Post, Ministry of Information (MOI) and Palestinian Information Center (PIC). The text is not quoted directly from the sources but is edited for size and clarity.

"The Hebrew State will End in 2027"
Sheikh Ahmed Yassin, Founder of Hamas, Interviewed

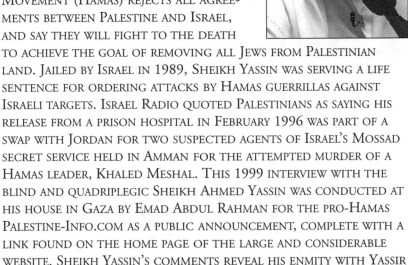

HAMAS, FOUNDED BY MUSLIM
BROTHERHOOD SUPPORTER SHEIKH YASSIN,
IS CONSIDERED MORE FUNDAMENTAL, AND
THEREFORE MORE EXTREME, THAN YASSIR
ARAFAT'S FATEH OR THE PALESTINIAN
AUTHORITY. THE ISLAMIC RESISTANCE
MOVEMENT (HAMAS) REJECTS ALL AGREE-
MENTS BETWEEN PALESTINE AND ISRAEL,
AND SAY THEY WILL FIGHT TO THE DEATH
TO ACHIEVE THE GOAL OF REMOVING ALL JEWS FROM PALESTINIAN
LAND. JAILED BY ISRAEL IN 1989, SHEIKH YASSIN WAS SERVING A LIFE
SENTENCE FOR ORDERING ATTACKS BY HAMAS GUERRILLAS AGAINST
ISRAELI TARGETS. ISRAEL RADIO QUOTED PALESTINIANS AS SAYING HIS
RELEASE FROM A PRISON HOSPITAL IN FEBRUARY 1996 WAS PART OF A
SWAP WITH JORDAN FOR TWO SUSPECTED AGENTS OF ISRAEL'S MOSSAD
SECRET SERVICE HELD IN AMMAN FOR THE ATTEMPTED MURDER OF A
HAMAS LEADER, KHALED MESHAL. THIS 1999 INTERVIEW WITH THE
BLIND AND QUADRIPLEGIC SHEIKH AHMED YASSIN WAS CONDUCTED AT
HIS HOUSE IN GAZA BY EMAD ABDUL RAHMAN FOR THE PRO-HAMAS
PALESTINE-INFO.COM AS A PUBLIC ANNOUNCEMENT, COMPLETE WITH A
LINK FOUND ON THE HOME PAGE OF THE LARGE AND CONSIDERABLE
WEBSITE. SHEIKH YASSIN'S COMMENTS REVEAL HIS ENMITY WITH YASSIR
ARAFAT'S PALESTINIAN AUTHORITY, WHICH IS SEEN BY HAMAS AND
OTHER MILITANT PALESTINIAN GROUPS AS PRACTICING VILLAINOUS
TREACHERY. THE INTERVIEW IS PRESENTED HERE IN EXCERPTED FORM.

Q: In the light of the Arab and Islamic popular interaction with the
intifada, what are in your opinion the effective tools to employ such
sympathy in practice to support this intifada?
A: In the name of Allah the most Gracious the most Merciful. The
truth is that our Palestinian people are proud of the Arab and Islamic
peoples' supportive stands in backing of the Aqsa Intifada. Our people
believe that the popular demonstrations reflected those people's
backing of the intifada and reflected their readiness for Jihad in
Palestine to liberate Al-Quds (Jerusalem) and holy shrines. This is a
big advantage in the Arab and Islamic region but the Palestinian
people do not wish that it would remain at this limit. What is required

is first: moral support to the Palestinian people, second: political and informational support so as to clarify the truth before the hostile part of the world and not only to explain it to the Arab and Islamic worlds but rather to the hostile world that is siding with our enemy . . . to expose to that world the enemy's myths that the Palestinians were the aggressors and the Jews were the victims. . . . Third: economic support because the Palestinian people are besieged and could be starved or killed. They need financial support to be able to remain steadfast in their homeland and so as not to immigrate or flee the battlefield. . . . Fourth: we need military support, which would be left to each country to determine each according to its capability. Military support means providing suitable arms to the Palestinian fighters for the current battle and in preparation for the final and decisive battle: opening the borders before Arab and Islamic fighters to join the (Palestinian) fighters and terminate the Zionist presence, which, God willing, will take place in the near future. . . .

Q: Don't you think that such sympathy has decreased a little and what is the reason for that?
A: . . . When the Arabs and Muslims watch on TV scores of martyrs and wounded and rallies they would react more than when they do not view any martyrs . . . All such events spur them into action but they think that the intifada will remain using stones, which used to start marches . . . our intifada now is turning into an armed intifada.

Q: But don't you think that the (Palestinian) Authority's resumption of negotiations had a negative impact on that sympathy?
A: Our battle with the Zionist enemy had moved from the stones to the bombs and machine guns. It will further develop in future to live up to the challenge with the Zionist enemy because it will only agree to submit concessions when it suffers big losses. It is true that the Palestinian people are at pains when they view duplicity of the Authority when it insists on negotiations and races along the road of a failed settlement process that could never serve the Palestinian cause. All the Palestinian people view such negotiations with disrespect and consider it as bad omen that should be stopped along with all dealings with the Zionist entity, viewing resistance as the only feasible option with Israel. I believe that the Palestinian people are saying instead of dying while throwing a stone why not die while throwing a bomb so that I would be killing before getting killed . . .

Q: People are wondering about the validity of confronting Israeli tanks and cannons with stones, is there any hope of turning that intifada in future into armed Jihad with all kinds of weapons?

A: The Palestinian people want to expose the ugly image of the Zionist enemy before the world so that it would witness how the Zionists do not differentiate between children, women, the elderly or between civilians and the military and that the Palestinians should develop their means of confrontation using force the only language understood by that enemy. The world would then understand why the Palestinians are using weapons though not the same level of that used by the enemy but the important thing is that they inflict casualties in enemy ranks. The Palestinians have offered 450 martyrs while the enemy lost between 60 to 70 persons killed, which is not a simple number over a period of four to five months . . . The enemy has lost over four months what it had lost in Lebanon in three years. On the other hand, we die and rejoice but the enemy dies while fearing the next. The soldier is afraid in spite of being equipped with tanks, missiles and bombs, the Israelis are afraid while walking in the markets and streets or going to schools. This is the first evidence of the coming victory *Insha'allah*.

Q: Many Jihad liberation movements were established in several parts in the world such as in Afghanistan, Chechnya and Kashmir and many have overcome the problem of obtaining arms and training areas to realize their goals, so what is the reason for failure of the Islamic movements in Palestine to reach that level?

A: . . . We are facing a difficult situation . . . an occupying enemy. I cannot establish arms factories. . . . We should not forget that the Palestinian Authority played a role in disarming the Islamic movements for the sake of preserving Israeli security in addition to arresting *Mujahideen*. Over the past seven years, resistance in Palestine faced an Authority that refuses resistance and chases resistance members and imprisons them. You know that resistance members are also chased in the Arab borders surrounding Palestine, resistance from Egyptian and Jordanian borders is barred and resistance from Lebanon is banned unless for certain considerations. Hence the Palestinian fighter is left working on the Palestinian land only. . . . Look at the past five months when the PA stood by the people and stopped its persecution of fighters, many creative resistance operations were made. . . .

Q: Islamists have watched with admiration your great role in preventing the outbreak of a civil war among the Palestinians due to the suspicious role played by PA elements against Hamas and other Islamic movements. Is it possible to continue in the light of the continued provocative acts against you or are there any red lines?

A: We are facing a difficult equation. The Zionist enemy similar to any other colonialist force in the world wishing to divide and rule. It signed the Oslo agreement to bring the PA to power with the sole aim of preserving Zionist security in face of resistance represented by the Islamic forces. It put part of the Palestinian people along its side against the whole of the Palestinian people, in the event of which the Zionists will be the winners. We, in Hamas, understood that equation and asked ourselves will we proceed along the same policy? [The Palestinian Authority] are pursuing us for the sake of Israeli security but if we resisted we would enter a civil war the only winner in which would be the Zionist entity. Our people will be the loser similar to what was going on in Algeria, massacres in the name of Islam and Muslims while in fact they are the brainchild of foreign intelligence and enemies of Islam to smear the Islamic image. Thus we chose the option of pain, patience and sacrifice to that of colliding with the Authority and shedding Palestinian blood. For this reason leaders from both the Qassam Brigades and Hamas were thrown into prisons. Thousands of our brothers were thrown into PA jails and faced severe torture worse than in Zionist dungeons . . .

Q: No doubt each act carries right and wrong, what are the most prominent successes of Islamic work in Palestine in the past half-century? And what are its most prominent mistakes?

A: There are two prominent successes for Islamic work in Palestine. The first raising Muslim propagators, the human factor that served the Palestinian people in the form of institutes and societies. The other was the Jihad success. You know that we as Palestinian Islamists started as a Muslim Brotherhood group and we had a role in resistance in the years 1935–36 until 1948. Muslim Brothers from Egypt and other Arab countries entered Palestine to fight Jewish invasion in 1948. Muslim groups were formed in the Palestinian lands occupied in 1948 such as Qufr Qassem, Teiba and others and they were imprisoned in the '70s. Finally our intifada broke out in 1987 through which the Islamic movements entered with all its Jihad and resistant weight and persisted until the present moment. In short we chose both raising the true Muslim to expand the Islamic foundation in Palestine and forming the real Mujahid and fighter against the enemy.

As for the mistakes, no doubt there were some but if compared to the successes they would not be worth mentioning. At a certain stage there was internal fighting that led to the fall of a number of dead but we overcame that stage. In another incident interrogation of collaborators went wrong and maybe some were not 100% proven guilty. . . .

Q: How do you explain the rarity of Hamas' qualitative Jihad operations in the first days of the intifada compared to what happened before especially during the reign of Rabin?
A: . . . I remember the first soldier killed by the brothers in Hamas and they told me of the incident. I told them to bury him without telling anyone and they killed a second one and I told them the same thing because we do not want any propaganda. However, Allah's will was overwhelming and the operations were uncovered. We have launched huge qualitative operations in the past five months but those asking such questions should know that our fighters over seven meager years were being pursued and imprisoned. The PA confiscated all our potentials and arms. Now suddenly after those years of persecution while our hands are empty of any arms, our sons in prisons, others martyred . . . you want us to launch qualitative operations! We need time; it is true that there was no good work at start of the intifada because there were no capabilities. However, the Movement within two months was able to launch qualitative operations that shook the world. For the first time a Palestinian launches a huge marine martyrdom operation. You have watched the qualitative operations against army tanks on TV. We are proud of such operations and the next days will witness better and bigger ones.

Q: How do you view the relations between the Islamic factions on the one hand and the secular factions within and outside Palestine on the other?
A: Our policy in Hamas is that of amicability and against clashing with any faction, not even the Authority, which detains and tortures. We support mobilizing all potentials against the one enemy and we pursue the policy of not clashing with the regimes even in the Arab countries. We advocate directing all forces against the Zionist entity because victory of Islam in Palestine means its victory in the Arab and Islamic world as a whole. Hence, our relationship with the Islamic factions is that of fraternity and cooperation. Our relations with secular factions remain amiable with a certain degree of cooperation but not in the field but on the level of coordinating popular activities and marches. There is coordination with all Islamic and secular factions but on the military level each has its own action . . .

Q: Is there any possibility for moving the Hamas work from the regional to the international framework turning Hamas into an international organization for instance?

A: . . . It should be known that Islam's battle is a lengthy and large one and arrows are directed against Islam and Muslims from everywhere. We as Mujahideen live in a country whose holy places are occupied. The loss of this country represents a humiliation to the Arab and Islamic Nation. Its liberation would be a source of pride for the Arab and Islamic Nation . . . I am in need of an Islamic organization and Islamic conferences only to back the Palestine cause and the Palestinian fighters. I agree for this purpose on establishment of an international organization but not on the basis of transferring the conflict to an arena outside the country. The fighting and resistance will persist on the Palestinian lands until we reach our goal. I do not want to incite an Arab, European or eastern regime against me, I want to win sympathy of those peoples or at least to neutralize them.

Q: How do you think we can disengage the bond between the Zionist entity and the allied international forces topped by America?

A: This question calls for Arab-Islamic-Palestinian cooperation to reach that goal at first. The western world that is backing the Zionist entity only respects force and the strong. It practices its pressures on the weak to exploit and humiliate them. Hence I believe that we should invoke renaissance in the Arab and Islamic Nation to support the Palestinian people through the means that I spoke about previously and to confront the terrorist enemy that is backing the Zionist entity through peaceful means that is economic and commercial boycott. . . . Such means could pressure those countries into submitting to Arab and Islamic potentials. Furthermore, the Palestinian people with the help of their modest means and backing of Arab and Islamic peoples are capable of forcing that enemy to kneel down. And when the enemy falls down it will not find anyone to back it because the supporters will suffer big losses. I give you a simple example: America landed its forces in Lebanon to practice its hegemony, but with two operations against the marines Americans fled that country. America also tried to do the same thing in Somalia but an armed operation forced them to pack up and leave. Those people only understand the language of force. There is an armed resistance draining the Zionist enemy from within while Arab and Islamic peoples can share in draining that enemy through boycotting its goods. Experience in Saudi Arabia and the Gulf proved that boycotting American goods and restaurants led to the bankruptcy of those shop owners. They will come running begging us because we are quarter of the world population we are one and a quarter billion Muslims. We can boycott their arms and manufacture them in our countries . . . .

Q: That means that you do not support attacking western interests who are allied with the Zionist entity?
A: If I fought those people would that serve my interest or damage it? Will it increase or lessen the enemy's strength? I want to keep those forces away from my enemy and I do not want to open side battles with others and increase my enemy's force. I need to decrease the number of my enemies and supporters of my enemy. Consequently, I should limit my battle to my direct enemy even if it was permissible to fight others. . . .

Q: Many analysts believe that there is no way to embark on an effective Jihad against the enemy except through establishment of resistance fronts similar to the national resistance in Lebanon taking into consideration the differences between the two cases. Is there any hope of establishing such fronts so that they would launch armed resistance in Palestine?
A: Armed resistance in Palestine is shouldering a big role similar to the resistance in Lebanon and experiencing much bigger difficulties. The Lebanese moves from Beirut and other areas in Lebanon to the Israeli borders knowing that his back is protected and that the authority and people support him in addition to availability of military supplies. But here I fight the Jewish enemy while the PA is arresting me and confiscating my weapons. My back is not safeguarded in addition to the fact that the Israeli enemy controls the lands. In Lebanon they own anti-aircraft guns but if I brought such weapons under occupation where would I hide or protect them? I only own weapons that I can hide and I cannot bring bigger means such as Scud missiles or others; where would I put them and if I managed to hide one or ten missiles . . . what next? You should not forget that we are besieged and our borders are closed and that the Arab borders are not open for us to bring what we like. The Israeli enemy is besieging us from all directions. Thus our situation here is very difficult but when there is some kind of freedom here on the part of the Authority similar to Lebanon the world will witness that our people will make miracles never witnessed before.
Q: If we say, for the sake of argument, that the Authority won a recognized state and given part of Al-Quds as its capital, what will be the nature of the relationship between you and the Authority?

A: We view the issue from two aspects: what did the Authority gain from that enemy and second what did the Authority lose from the Palestinian people's rights? We believe that the land of Palestine is a Waqf land that no one has the right to surrender. We reject any concession in this matter. It is good to win our lands and holy places from the enemy along with sovereignty over the lands and borders but we refuse to accept that in return for giving up lands occupied in 1948. Does sovereignty mean a mere a self-rule under Israeli security or full sovereignty over crossings, borders and entrances coupled with an end to occupation, settlements and army, or a mere redeployment of the Israeli army, from Nablus mountain to Jenin (nearby) mountain, or moved from the Ramallah borders to the Jordan River borders to the east? The concessions will determine the relationship. Surrendering any right in Palestine is rejected and we will continue to struggle.

Q: Is there any probability that the Jews would carry out their criminal schemes against the Aqsa Mosque and the Dome of the Rock in the present circumstances?
A: There is a big probability and a serious conspiracy. The Zionist creed backed by a Zionist Christian creed is seeking to build the temple in place of the Aqsa Mosque or near to it. Zionists and Jews all over the world believe in such a creed along with Christians who support Jews. As long as the Zionist entity was in control of things we should expect any day attempts to blow up or burn the Mosque or destroy it using explosives put in tunnels dug under its foundations. This is very likely unless the Arab and Islamic Nation adopts a solid stance against all those supporting the Zionist entity and unless that Nation strongly supports the Palestinian people in their resistance of that enemy. I believe that if the Israelis sense any slackness on the part of the Arab and Islamic Nation, they would immediately launch their plots and conspiracies and build the temple, which they consider would herald the return of the Messiah and their ultimate victory over Muslims in the Armageddon battle. However, I say that the final battle will result in our victory and that this land will reject this enemy similar to its predecessors.

Q: You have previously pinpointed a specific date for the end of the Jewish state as published in some papers, what are the basis of your expectation or was it merely optimism in the future?
A: In fact that was based on readings in the holy Qur'an and historic calculations. Almighty Allah changes generations and features of

peoples each 40 years. That was evident in history of the Jews. They could not enter the land for forty years because they refused to fight alongside prophet Mousa (Moses). So the cowardly generation perished and a new generation was born capable of fighting. In another historic incident, the Islamic Nation bowed for 40 years before the crusaders and for another 40 years Muslims started resisting and clashes until end of the crusade. Hence the 40/40 is a correct historic/Quranic equation. The Palestinians in 1948 lost the battle; we were chased and expelled out of our lands. The Palestinians in the occupied homeland were submissive while the resistance was from abroad from Jordan and Lebanon. The period from 1948 to 1987 was the first forty years and ended with the Palestinian people's revolt in their first intifada. The world did not recognize the presence of the Palestinian people nor the Palestinian cause, it absolutely denied them and the question was shelved at the UN. However, the intifada turned things upside down, initiatives were made, rights were acknowledged, people were recognized and the ugly Zionist image was unveiled before the whole world. Our people who were afraid and fled their homes in 1948 after a couple of massacres and Zionist propaganda, today started to fight the enemy with stones. Hence the Palestinian people after forty years changed and we believe that after another forty years the Zionist entity would be defeated and eliminated God willing.

Q: That means their elimination will take place in 2027 approximately?
A: Approximately. It is not a must that it would be in 2027 for it could be five years earlier or ten years later. The important thing is that the equation revolves round 2027 and the Hebrew state would end *Insha'allah*.

THE LEGACY: ON THE DEATH OF A MOTHER OF PALESTINE

By Fathi Hussein

She faces the blinding light
body dilapidated
memories engulfed by flames
as the thread of childhood, lost virginity and children born
is bulldozed aside
the final portals of her survival
close.

With borderless love
she leaves me the sword and shield of Ayn Gazhal:
"remember.
Lest the sun sets on who we are
Lest the voids of history obscure
the Arab melody still whistling through the trees.
Fight, fight, the fading of the light."

Ghazala, Ghazala, I came inside you
as the cup of grief spilt over
I anointed your foundations.
My love, me golden love,
a delicate ruin
welcoming me
home

I am blind to the whores of Zion
their vulgar forms
available for a price
I turn my face from their makeshift cities
My little Ghazala,
I have eyes only for you.

There is ash in the wind
The golden rubble of Ghazala is exposed
and between the olive trees of my ancestors
I ache for the final consummation.

[Poetry section continues after color section]

The assassination
of King Faisal. On
25 March 1975,
Faisal, King of
Saudi Arabia, was
shot and killed with
a pistol fired by a
member of his own
family. The print
shows the incident
in a series of
episodes, ending
with the beheading
of the assassin.

Below:
Anti-American
graffiti in Tehran.
(From *L'Islam Nelle
Stampe* by Sergio
Stocchi)

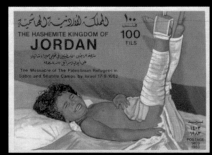

The battle of Karbala as reflected in the Arab-Israeli war. (From *L'Islam Nelle Stampe* by Sergio Stocchi)

An Iranian student soldier battles American "Den of Spies."

THE AMERICAN GOVERNMENT MUST RETURN THE CRIMINAL SHAH TO THE IRANIAN PEOPLE FOR TRIAL.

The Shah is choked out of Jimmy Carter's mouth.

The snake fills the gas tank.

Satanic allies, Menachem Begin
and America.

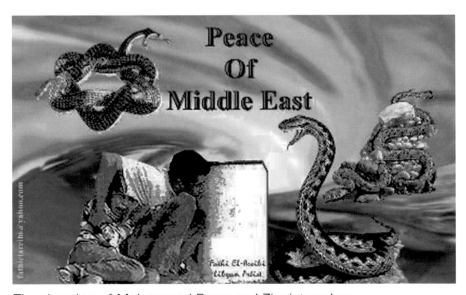

The shooting of Mohammed Durra and Zionist snakes.

Poster, circa 1980, of American Swinehundt.

Thunder and lightning strikes from the Imam rip apart the United
States of Barbed Zion.

Top: Iran banknote showing revolt for Islam.
Middle: Saddam Hussein's Ba'ath Regime. Ties, not turbans.
Bottom: Islam Republic banknote reveres Ka'bal.

FIGHT FOR OUR RIGHT
By M.V. Ahmad

If we have to fight,
For our right,
We will hold on tight,
To our gun,
We won't run
Our help comes from high above the sky,
Even higher than fighter jets can fly,
It only takes a nod,
From our God,
The super powers will grumble,
When they see them selves crumble,
Like we have seen in the past,
Worldly super powers don't last,
Then you will see God's power,
He, his love will shower,
All will live in ease,
All will live in peace,
Please don't fear,
Inshallah the time is near,
Just keep praying to God,
For that one nod.

I AM WITH TERRORISM
by Nizar Qabbani

Amerika
Against the cultures of the peoples
with no culture
Against the civilizations of the civilized
with no civilization
Amerika
a mighty edifice
with no walls!

We are accused of terrorism:
if we refused an era
Amerika became
the foolish, the rich, the mighty
translated, sworn
in Ivri.

We are accused of terrorism:
if we throw a rose
to Jerusalem
to al-Khalil
to Ghazza
to an-Nasirah
if we took bread and water
to beleaguered Troy.

We are accused of terrorism:
if we raised our voices against
the regionalists of our leaders.
All changed their rides:
from Unionists
to Brokers.

We are accused of terrorism
if we defended land
and the honor of dust
if we revolted against the rape of people
and our rape
if we defended the last palm trees in our desert
the last stars in our sky
the last syllabi of our names
the last milk in our mothers' bosoms
if this was our sin
how beautiful is terrorism.

I am with terrorism
if it is able to save me
from the immigrants from Russia
Romania, Hungaria, and Poland

They settled in Palestine
set foot on our shoulders
to steal the minarets of al-Quds
and the door of Aqsa
to steal the arabesques
and the domes.

I am with terrorism
if it will free the Messiah, Jesus of Nazareth,
and the virgin, Meriam Betula
and the holy city
from the ambassadors of death and desolation

Yesteryear
The nationalist street was fervent
like a wild horse.
The rivers were abundant with the spirit of youth.

But after Oslo,
we no longer had teeth:
we are now a blind and lost people.

We are accused of terrorism:
if we defended with full-force
our poetic heritage
our national wall
our rosy civilization
the culture of flutes in our mountains
and the mirrors displaying blackened eyes.

We are accused of terrorism:
if we defended what we wrote
El azure of our sea
and the aroma of ink
if we defended the freedom of the word
and the holiness of books

I am with terrorism
if it is able to free a people
from tyrants and tyranny
if it is able to save man from the cruelty of man
to return lemon, olive tree, and bird to the South of Lebanon
and the smile back to Golan

I am with terrorism
if it will save me
from the Caesar of Yehuda
and the Caesar of Rome

I am with terrorism
as long as this new world order
is shared
between Amerika and Israel
half-half

I am with terrorism
with all my poetry
with all my words
and all my teeth
as long as this new world
is in the hands of a butcher.

I am with terrorism
if the U.S. Senate
enacts judgement
decrees reward and punishment

I am with Irhab [terrorism]
as long this new world order
hates the smell of A`rab.

I am with terrorism
as long as the new world order
wants to slaughter my offspring.
and send them to dogs.

For all this
I raise my voice high:
I am with terrorism
I am with terrorism
I am with terrorism . . .

DEFIANCE
by Mahmud Darwish

Tighten my fetters.
Confiscate my papers
and cigarettes.
Fill my mouth with dust.
Poetry is blood in the heart,
salt in bread,
moisture in eyes.
It is written with fingernails,
with eyes,
with daggers.
I shall proclaim in my detention cell,
in the bathroom,
in the stable,
under the lash,
manacled,
in the violence of chains,
that a million birds
on the branches of my heart,
are singing fighting songs.

IDENTITY CARD
by Mahmud Darwish

RECORD!!
I am an Arab
and my identity is number fifty thousand
I have eight children

and the ninth
is coming in midsummer
Will you be angry?
RECORD!!
I am an Arab
employed with fellow workers
at a quarry
I have eight children
to get them bread
garments
and books
from the rocks
I do not supplicate
at your doors
Nor do I belittle myself
at the footsteps of your chamber
So will you be angry?

RECORD!!
I am an Arab
without a name — without a title
in a patient country
with people enraged
My roots
were entrenched before the birth of time
and before the opening of the eras
before the olive trees, and the pines, and grass

My father
descends from the family of the plow
not from a privileged class
And my grandfather
was a farmer
neither well-bred, nor well-born
And my house
is like a watchman's hut
made of branches and cane
This is my status
Does it satisfy you?
I have a name but no title

RECORD!!
I am an Arab
The color of my hair is black
The color of my eyes is brown
And my distinctive features
The headdress hatta wi'gal
And the hand is solid like a rock
My favorite meal
is olive oil and thyme
And my address

A village isolated and deserted
where the streets have no names
and the men work in the fields and quarries
They like socialism
Will you be angry?

RECORD!!
I am an Arab
You have stolen the orchards
of my ancestors
and the land
which I cultivated
Along with my children
And you left us with those rocks
so will the State take them
as it has been said?

Therefore!
Record on the top of the first page:
I do not hate man
Nor do I encroach
But if I become hungry
The usurper's flesh will be my food

Beware, beware of my hunger
and my anger!!

POEMS AGAINST THE WEST
by Allama Iqbal

THE POET/PHILOSOPHER ALLAMA IQBAL (1877–1938) IS CONSIDERED
BY MANY TO BE THE MUSE FOR THE CREATION OF THE MUSLIM STATE
OF PAKISTAN. THOSE WHO HAVE A STRICT IDEA OF THE ISLAMIC STATE
ARE UNCOMFORTABLE WITH IQBAL'S SUFIC MYSTICISM AND NATION-
ALISTIC IMPULSES. THE POEMS BELOW WARN OF THE SOULLESS NATURE
OF MATERIALIST CULTURE AND THE REACTIONARY ACTIONS OF BOTH
WEST AND EAST COMMUNISM.

THE MATERIALISTIC CULTURE
Of this civilizations of ungodliness beware
At war which is with men of truth;
The mischief-monger nothing but mischief breeds,
In the Harem it reinstalls the idols of Lat and Uzza.
By its sorcery the eye of the heart is sightless,
The soul thirsty with its barrenness;
The joy of eagerness it kills in the heart,
Nay the heart itself it destroys.
The depredations of the old thief are for all to see,
Even the tulip cries, "What have they done to my scar?"

COMMUNISM AND IMPERIALISM
The soul of both of them is impatient and restless,
Both of them know not God, and deceive mankind.
One lives by production, the other by taxation,
And man is a glass caught between two stones.
The one puts to rout science, religion, art,
The other robs the body of soul, the hand of bread.
I have perceived both drowned in water and clay,
Both bodily burnished, but utterly dark of heart.
Life means a passionate burning, an urge to make,
To cast in the dead clay the seed of heart.

THE APPROACHING BATTLE FOR JERUSALEM and the War of Gog and Magog

By TempleMountFaithful.org

TEMPLEMOUNTFAITHFUL.ORG IS THE WEBSITE FOR ALL ZIONISTS AND ZIONIST CHRISTIANS WHO WISH TO DEMOLISH DOME OF THE ROCK, THE THIRD HOLIEST ISLAMIC SHRINE, FOR THE SAKE OF RAISING AND REBUILDING THE TEMPLE OF SOLOMON, THOUGHT TO BE BENEATH THE HOLY MUSLIM SITE. KEYWORDS: WORLD WAR III, END TIMES, APOCALYPSE, ARMAGEDDON.

As we have previously stated, Israel is now living in the most critical time in her history. On the one hand Israel is in the midst of her godly end-time redemption while on the other hand she is in the midst of the political and violent attacks of he Arab enemies in the Middle East together with their backing of many Islamic nations as well as their supporters all over the world led by the UN and the President of the United States, Bill Clinton.

Using the false and evil Oslo so-called "Peace" agreements, they cut off piece after piece from the body of the land of Israel and give them to the so-called "Palestinian Authority" which was planted by them in the midst of the land of Israel and which grows like a cancer in the midst of the body of the Holy Land of Israel. These agreements were signed by the weak and secular government of Israel under the pressure of the above powers. Now these powers are putting pressure on Israel to give away more parts of the land and the main pressure is now on Jerusalem, the capital of the G-d and people of Israel.

The terrorist and murderer, Yasser Arafat, has stated that there will never be peace and that he will renew the Intifada, the battle against Israel, unless Israel agrees to give him Jerusalem as the capital of a "Palestinian" state and give up her sovereignty over Jerusalem. More than this, he is demanding all the area of Judea, Samaria and Gaza to be immediately given to him and that on 13 September, or earlier, he will declare a "Palestinian" state in those areas with Jerusalem as its capital which he knows that the UN and all the nations will recognize. President Clinton is now acting to hold a summit in Washington DC together with the Prime Minister Barak and Yasser Arafat and there to put further pressure on Barak and force him to agree to Arafat's demands.

The agents of Arafat on the Temple Mount are now in the midst of an intensive, violent campaign to destroy and remove all the remains of the First and Second Temples and to change the identity of the Temple Mount into an Islamic site. They realize that, whether they want it or not, the Third Temple is going to be built on the Temple Mount as a major event in G-d's end-time prophetic plans. By this barbaric violence against the G-d and people of Israel they try to prevent this even through such a terrible revolt and violence against G-d and His holy house. As we have stated, they bitter illusions if they think that they can succeed in doing so but it is a terrible sin and a shame for them and that the weak Israeli Government and everyone in the world allows them to do this.

In a speech which Arafat gave in Ramallah (the Biblical city of the Hill of G-d, Givat Elohim, and was a Jewish city settled by Jews but occupied by the Arabs in 630 CE) he stated that he is ready for a war and that he is not afraid of the Israeli tanks and aircraft. The same threats of war are coming closer and closer to Israel from the north from the Hizbullah terrorist organization in Lebanon which has stated that their battle will not stop until they have occupied Jerusalem. The same spirit of war is coming form Syria, Iraq, Iran and Egypt, all enemies of Israel who are preparing their nuclear, biological and chemical warheads to destroy Israel. The UN and the European Union have stated on more than one occasion and made resolutions that Jerusalem is not the capital of Israel but occupied territory, and that Israel should withdraw from Judea, Samaria, Gaza and the Golan Heights.

All of this brings Israelis to the conclusion that the time is very critical and that the prophecies of the prophet Ezekiel about the War of Gog and Magog against Israel and Zechariah's and other prophets' prophecies about the war of all the nations against the land of Israel and Jerusalem are soon to be fulfilled. Never since the foundation of the State of Israel in 1948 has Israel felt that the black clouds of this terrible war were so close to Jerusalem. This war will not be a simple war and Israel will pay a high price because of the sinful weakness over her leadership in signing false agreements with the agents of the devil and not with the G-d of Israel. Zechariah states that half of the population of Jerusalem will go into exile. However, the Israelis, after great disappointment in the behavior of their leadership, are coming closer to the G-d of Israel and understanding that they can only trust in their One Father, the G-d of Israel, Who has repeatedly saved them over the last

4000 years and Who will save them again from all those powers and nations who will attack them and that He will severely judge all these enemies as He promised in His Word. "Son of man, set your face against Gog, the land of Magog, the chief prince of Meshech and Tubal, and prophesy against him, And say, Thus says the Lord God: Behold, I am against you, O Gog, the chief prince of Meshech and Tubal; . . . After many days you shall be called upon; in the latter years you shall come against the land that is brought back from the sword, and is gathered from many peoples, against the mountains of Israel, which have been always waste; but it is brought out from the nations, and they shall dwell safely all of them. You shall ascend and come like a storm, you shall be like a cloud to cover the land, you, and all your bands, and many people with you . . . And you shall come up against my people of Israel, like a cloud to cover the land; it shall be in the latter days, and I will bring you against my land, that the nations may know me, when I shall be sanctified in you, O Gog, before their eyes . . .

The prophet Zechariah states that the weapons (the nuclear, chemical and biological weapons) used against Israel will backfire and will hurt the enemies of Israel and not Israel: "And this shall be the plague with which the Lord will strike all the people who fought against Jerusalem; Their flesh shall consume away while they stand upon their feet, and their eyes shall consume away in their sockets, and their tongue shall consume away in their mouth. And it shall come to pass on that day, that a great panic from the Lord shall be among them; and they shall lay hold everyone on the hand of his neighbor, and his hand shall rise up against the hand of his neighbor." (Zechariah 14:12,13)

We know that the coming time will not be an easy time in Israel. This will be the climax of all the end-time troubles which Israel through which Israel is now passing. Israel must trust in G-d and be strong and, together with the G-d of Israel, we will overcome these terrible events. The G-d of Israel is determined to accomplish the redemption of Israel and all the universe and nothing can or will prevent Him.

The Temple Mount and Land of Israel Faithful Movement and all the others in Israel who are with the G-d of Israel and who are in His army to serve and fight with all their devotion and dedication for Him and His end-time plans are ready to face these events and their challenges as they have been up to this time. We do not fear the enemies of the G-d and people of Israel but only G-d and we trust and love

Him and we shall continue to serve Him and His prophetic plans with all the strength which He gave us.

We warn all the enemies of Israel and their allies all over the world that G-d will severely judge and punish them because of their violence and their battles to destroy Israel.

To all the wonderful friends of Israel all over the world who decided to be with the G-d and people of Israel at this great and critical time we send our sincerest thanks and love and the deep appreciation of the G-d and people of Israel. Exactly as the prophets prophesied, you will be redeemed together with the people of Israel whom you love and support with such devotion. It is so good to know that, together with the G-d of Israel, we have righteous friends and brothers and sisters like you who have placed themselves together with Israel at a time when it is so needed. You are an important sign, example and a great hope for this prophetic, godly time in which we are now living. Continue to be strong with the G-d and people of Israel and the G-d of Israel and the Universe will continue to bless you richly.

Holy War Ground Zero

As the navel is set in the centre of the human body,
so is the land of Israel the navel of the world . . .
situated in the centre of the world,
and Jerusalem in the centre of the land of Israel,
and the sanctuary in the centre of Jerusalem,
and the holy place in the centre of the sanctuary,
and the ark in the centre of the holy place,
and the foundation stone before the holy place,
because from it the world was founded.
Midrash Tanchuma, Qedoshim.

— From TempleMount.org,
an apocalyptic Christian pro-Zionist website

Al-Haram al-Sharif (or Al-Aqsa), located atop Jerusalem's Mount Moriah, or what Jews and Zionist Christians call Temple Mount, is Ground Zero of all holy wars: Christian, Jewish, Islamic.

The Prophet Muhammad took off to visit heaven from the rock from which Al-Aqsa shelters and celebrates.

Messianic Orthodox Jews believe that two holy Jewish temples are located directly beneath the third holiest Islamic mosque, and that the messiah will come once the mosque is destroyed, the area purified by the sacrifice of animals, and the temple rebuilt.

Fundamentalists Christians view the Jewish conquest of Temple Mount as the fuse lighting Armageddon, the horrible end time scenario to which Jesus Christ will return to impose his thousand year dominion. The "left behind" genre of Tim LaHaye sells millions of copies of dispensational premillennialist beliefs through novelized sermons, which promotes the idea of Temple Mount as ground zero for the apocalypse.

"Zionist Christians," who have raised hundreds of millions of dollars for the most warlike elements of Israel, actually share an apocalyptic belief with Muslims. The devil coming these impending end days is a Jew. Jerry Falwell, a "close friend" of Israel, particularly financially, said in January 1999 that the antichrist was probably alive and "must be male and Jewish." Muslims also believe in Jesus Christ, but alter his role as a prophet who will return to destroy the Jews for Islam. In his best-selling Arabic book, *Al-Masih al-Dajjal*, Sa'id Ayyub writes that the antichrist will come in the form of the Jewish Prophet who will live at "the Temple in Jerusalem. For this reason they sometimes try to burn Al-Aqsa, and try to conduct archeological excavations, and even try to buy the ground through the Masons of America."

Ayyub's seemingly bizarre accusation that American Masons attempted to purchase Temple Mount is not without historical credibility. Freemasonry, the decaying fraternal society linked to American and British power structures, and to which most American presidents have belonged — including Harry Truman, who pressured allies to support the United Nations' creation of the Jewish state — offered the amount of one hundred million dollars to purchase the Islamic shrine in 1968. Why? "Freemasonry is blended indestructibly with the rites, cere-monies, and traditions of Hebrew worship," writes Robert W. Bowers in his Masonically-sanctioned 1899 book, *Freemasonry and the Tabernacle and Temple of the Jews.*

The fundamentalists pray that their struggle for the possession of Temple Mount will bring on the final war that will at last sort out whose belief comes out on top.

Messianic Jews, with support from the state of Israel, are already laying the cornerstone for the new temple, predicated on the destruction of Islam's holy spot. The article about the cornerstone, and the following historical piece by "Guy Le Strange," are both from the Christian Zionist website, <templemountfaithful.org>:

A Cornerstone for the Third Temple at Sukkoth
On the third day of the festival of Sukkoth this year (7th October 1998) at 9:30 AM, The Temple Mount and Land of Israel Faithful Movement will lay the cornerstone for the Third Temple. We trust that this time it will be on the Temple Mount on the location of the First and Second Temples.

This date was chosen because during the festival of Sukkoth King David brought the Ark of the Covenant from the city of David to the Temple Mount in a special exciting ceremony.

It will be a very special and exciting event. The cornerstone of 4.5 tons in weight is very similar to the stones of the First and Second Temples. It is a marble stone brought from the desert of Israel not far from the desert where the children of Israel walked in the time of Moses from Egypt to the Promised Land during the time of the first redemption of Israel. It also is not so far from the Mt.Sinai where G-d gave the Torah to the children of Israel. This stone was brought from this area because of the special significance of this place and the similarity to the stones of the First and Second Temples. The stone as found in this area as it is with no need to cut it with any metal or iron instrument as the G-d of Israel ordered the people of Israel not to beat a stone for His House with iron or any other metal and to respect the special significance and holiness of the Temple and its stones. In Biblical times the stones were cut with Shamir, a stronger stone brought from Lebanon. In this way they could cut and polish the stones for the Temple and keep G-d's law. It was so special that the stone was found as it is and we immediately felt that the Hand of G-d as in these special circumstances. The stone is currently located in the middle of a traffic circle which was especially built by the Municipality of Jerusalem for this stone. The circle is not far from the Damascus Gate of the Old City, near the third wall of the Second temple era, near to the special monument for the soldiers who died for the liberation of Jerusalem in the Six-Day War and near to the American Consulate.

The cornerstone will be transported on a big truck painted with Israeli flags and the Star of David and the stone will be covered with a Tallith (prayer shawl). The stone will be carried in a special ceremony. Levites will play from the Psalms of Ascent and a high priest will anoint the stone. He will be dressed in white priestly garments recreated in Jerusalem over the last years according to Biblical Law. Temple vessels which have been recreated in Jerusalem exactly according to the Torah will be carried by the members of the Movement who will march with the stone and shofars will be blown along the way. The stone will be taken to the City of David and in the place where King David anointed and blessed the ark of the Covenant, we shall say special blessings and prayers and read the prayers of King David and the special prayers when he dedicated the First Temple. It will be a very special and exciting moment. The stone will then be taken to the Pool of Shiloah where a special ceremony of Nisuch HaMaiim will be performed. This ceremony is a renewal of the ceremony which was performed in the First and Second Temple eras during the feast of

Sukkoth when the high priest and all the other priests and the pilgrims who had come to celebrate the feast at the Temple marched to the Pool of Shiloh in a very exciting ceremony with the Levites playing music to draw the holy water of the Shiloah with special blessings and prayers and then carry the water back to the temple where it was poured out on the altar. The High priest prayed to the G-d of Israel for a blessed year with lots of rain. In the Mishna it is written that those who did not experience this exciting ceremony never saw a real special celebration with such joy and thankfulness to G-d. At Sukkoth we shall perform the same ceremony at the Pool of Shiloah. We want to renew everything which belongs to the Temple and Biblical tradition. The water that we draw from the Pool will be poured on the cornerstone with special blessings and prayers and, at the same time, we shall anoint it. When the Third Temple is built this water will again be poured on the altar. We know that this will be soon.

From the City of David, we shall march with the stone to the Temple Mount. The truck with the stone will circle the walls of the Temple Mount seven times exactly as Joshua ben Nun did at Jericho with shofars being blown. With the cornerstone there will be a very old Torah Scroll. The cornerstone will stand for a while before the Eastern Gate of the Temple Mount (the Golden Gate) for a special prayer that the gate will soon be opened and Mashiach ben David will enter through it to the Temple.

We pray and believe and do everything that we can that this time the gates of the Temple Mount will be open to the cornerstone this time and that it will be laid on the same location of the cornerstones of the First and Second Temples which were built by King Solomon and Zerubbabel. We trust in the G-d of Israel. We know that we are living in a special exciting time of the redemption of the people an the land of Israel, the Temple Mount and Jerusalem. We feel and live the special significance of this time. The members of the Temple Mount and Land of Israel Faithful Movement dedicated themselves to fulfill the wish of the G-d of Israel and the prophecies of the prophets of Israel for the end-times.

We are doing and shall continue to do everything that the Third Temple will soon be built in our lifetime for the honor of the G-d of Israel and to fulfill His prophetic wishes. For this goal we have completely dedicated our lives, we left everything and we are acting full-time for this godly prophetic purpose. We shall do everything to save the Temple Mount from the terrible abomination which is done today by foreigners and enemies and to purify the Temple Mount for the G-d of Israel and the universe exactly as our forefathers did when they liberated the Temple Mount from foreign occupation and abomination. We shall do everything to open the Eastern Gate for Mashiach ben David and he will be the king of Israel and of all the world. We want to see the fulfillment of the godly prophecy of Isaiah that many nations will come up to the House of G-d in Jerusalem to give Him glory and to thank Him and to learn His Laws and ways and to give Him thanks that He gave them the privilege to worship Him.

We trust in G-d that this godly end-time vision will soon be a reality in our lifetime and our activities will be accomplished. We feel the presence of G-d in our activities and He is with us. It is such a privilege to serve Him in these exciting times, to be a part of His army and his prophetic end-time plans and to live in such a generation. A lot of thanks to the G-d of Israel.

History of Jerusalem Under the Muslims,

(From A.D. 650 to 1500) By Guy Le Strange, 1890

The great mosque of Jerusalem, Al Masjid al Aqsa, derives its name from the traditional Night Journey of Muhammad, to which allusion is made in the words of the Qur'an (xvii. 1): "I declare the glory of Him who transported His servant by night from the Masjid al Haram (the Mosque at Mecca) to the Masjid al Aqsa (the Further Mosque) at Jerusalem" — the term "Mosque" being here taken to denote the whole area of the Noble Sanctuary, and not the main building of the Aqsa only, which, in the Prophet's days, did not exist.

According to the received account, Muhammad was on this occasion mounted on the winged steed called Al Burak "the Lightning" and, with the angel Gabriel for escort, was carried from Makkah (Mecca), first to Sinai, and then to Bethlehem, after which they came to Jerusalem. "And when we reached Bait al Makdis, the Holy City," so runs the tradition, "we came to the gate of the mosque (which is the Haram Area), and here Jibrail (Gabriel) caused me to dismount. And he tied up Al Burak to a ring, to which the prophets of old had also tied their steeds." (Ibn al Athir's Chronicle, ii. 37.) Entering the Haram Area by the gateway, afterwards known as the Gate of the

Prophet, Muhammad and Gabriel went up to the Sacred Rock, which of old times had stood in the center of Solomon's Temple; and in its neighborhood meeting the company of the prophets, Muhammad proceeded to perform his prayer-prostrations in the assembly of his predecessors in the prophetic office Abraham, Moses, Jesus, and others of God's ancient apostles.

From the Sacred Rock Muhammad, accompanied by Gabriel, next ascended, by a ladder of light, up into heaven; and, in anticipation, was vouchsafed the sight of the delights of Paradise. Passing through the seven heavens, Muhammad ultimately stood in the presence of Allah, from whom he received injunctions as to the prayers his followers were to perform. Thence, after a while, he descended again to earth; and, alighting at the foot of the ladder of light, stood again on the Sacred Rock at Jerusalem. The return journey homeward was made after the same fashion — on the back of the steed Al Burak and the Prophet reached Makkah again before the night had waned. Such, in outline, is the tradition of the Prophet's Night Journey, which especially sanctifies the Rock and the Haram Area in the sight of all true believers.

After the capitulation of Jerusalem to Omar in 635 (A.H. 14), that Khalif caused a mosque to be built on what was considered to be the ancient site of the Temple (or Masjid) of David. The traditional position of this site, Omar (as it is stated) verified, by the rediscovery of the Rock concealed under a dunghill from the description that had been given to him, Omar, by the Prophet, of the place where he had made his prayer prostrations in Jerusalem on the occasion of his Night-Journey.

A Chronology of Important Events concerning Jerusalem and the Temple Mount
from *The Coming Temple: Center Stage for the Final Countdown* by Don Stewart and Chuck Missler, Dart Press, 1991

1967
June 7 — The Old City of Jerusalem falls into Israeli hands. Israeli paratrooper commander Mordehai Gur, mounted on a half track. takes the Temple Mount on the third day of the Six Day War. The Temple Mount is regained but authority is turned back over to the Moslems.

June 28 — Prime Minister Levi Eshkol meets Moslem and Christian leaders from both side of the pre-war border and pledges free access to all holy places and the government's intention to place the internal administration for the holy places in the hands of the respective religious leaders. The same day the barriers came down between east and west Jerusalem.

August 1 — Jerusalem police take on the maintenance of public order at the holy places in the Old City at the request of Moslem and Christian authorities who claim of improper behavior by visitors at the Church of the Holy Sepulchre and the Temple Mount.

August 8 — A committee headed by the ministry of religious affairs Zerah Warhaftig is given cabinet responsibility for the Holy places in Jerusalem and the West Bank.

August 15 — IDF Chief Chaplain Aluf Shlomo Goren, and fifty followers including other army chaplains hold a service on the Temple Mount. Goren contends that some parts of the compound are not part of the Temple Mount and therefore the ban against Jews stepping on the Mount until the Temple is rebuilt does not apply. He said his measurements were based upon Josephus, Maimonides, Sa'adia Gaon and archaeological evidence. He also declared that the Dome of the Rock is not the site of the Holy of Holies. The defense ministry criticizes Goren noting that be is a senior army officer. Goren claims he first met with Warhaftig and that the Moslem authorities consented to his prayers.

August 17 — An Israeli Defense Forces spokesman reveals that the arms cache was found during the fighting in the Al Aksa Mosque.

August 22 — The Chief Rabbinate puts up signs outside the Compound noting the religious ban on visiting the Temple Mount area.

Sept. 9 — Moslems protest against the abolition of fees to enter the Temple Mount area. The Defense Ministry says that the Waqf can only charge fees to enter the Mosques.

1968

July 15 — The President of the Moslem Court of Appeals turns down a request by an American Masonic Temple Order who asked permission to build a $100 Million "Solomon" temple on the Temple Mount.

Dec. 19 — Hanukka prayers are offered by a group of nationalistic Jews on the Temple Mount.

1969

April 15 — State Attorney Zvi Bar Niv, responding to an order against the Police Minister Shlomo Hillel. explains that Jews should not be allowed to pray on the Temple Mount because "premature prayer" by Jews on the Temple Mount would raise grave security and international political problems. The plaintiff is the Faithful of the Temple Mount.

August 21 — A fire at the Al Aqsa Mosque guts the southeastern wing. Brigades from West and East Jerusalem fight the blaze together for four hours while an angry Moslem crowd chants "Allah Akbar" and "Down with Israel." A curfew is imposed on the Old City. The president of the Moslem Council claims arson and charges deliberately slow response on the part of the fire brigades. Arab states blame Israel.

August 23 — A non-Jewish Australian tourist, Dennis Michael Rohan, identifying himself as a member of the "Church of God" is arrested as a suspect in the arson. East Jerusalem and major West Bank towns go on general strike as an expression of grief and sorrow over the fire. Police use force to break up a demonstration at the compound exit. Angry demonstrations break out in Arab capitals.

August 27 — Rohan tells the court he acted as the "Lord's emissary" in accordance with the Book of Zechariah. The Temple Mount is closed to non-Moslems for two months.

Dec. 30 — Court convicts Rohan but declares him not criminally liable by reason of insanity.

1970

Sept. 9 — High Court of Justice decides it has no jurisdiction in matters connected with the right and claims of different religious groups. Therefore it won't interfere with the position of the government prohibiting Jewish prayer on the Mount.

1971

March 11 — Altercation on Temple Mount occurs when students led by Gershon Salomon, a leader of the Faithful of the Temple Mount, try to hold prayers on the site.

1973

August 8 — Despite police warnings, Rabbi Louis Rabinowitz and Knesset Member Binyamin Halevi pray on the Mount. They are removed.

October — The Yom Kippur War. Israel is attacked by four nations. Israel gains territory in the Sinai and Golan Heights. Temple Mount is not affected.

1976

Jan. 30 — Magistrate Court Judge Ruth Or rules that Jews are permitted to pray on the Temple Mount. She acquits eight youths who were accused of disturbing public order by holding prayers on the site against police orders. Police Minister Shlomo Hillel says he will continue to bar prayers.

Feb. 1 — Yitzhak Raphael, Minister of Religious Affairs, says praying on the Temple Mount is a religious law question and not in his jurisdiction.

Feb. 9 — East Jerusalem high schools protest the court decision. The protests continue nearly two week with over 100 arrests. Shopkeepers strike and riots occur in West Bank towns. Security services impose inter-city travel ban.

Feb. 11 — The January Magistrate Court decision of January 30th is appealed.

March 4 — Kurt Waldheim, ex-Nazi and UN Secretary General, pledges to take up Islamic complaints about Israel interference with Moslem holy places and worshippers in Jerusalem.

March 8 — A group of young People — many non-religious — led by Rabinowitz and Salomon are barred from the Temple Mount by police. The police say they are acting in accordance with the High Court decision of September 9, 1970 decision.

March 11 — Ramallah Birzeit and El Birch councils join Nablus in resigning to protest against police action against Arab demonstrations protesting Judge Ruth Or's Temple Mount decision.

March 17 — Magistrate Or's ruling is overturned by Jerusalem District Court. The Court rules that eight Betar youths who attempted to pray "demonstratively" on the Temple Mount were guilty of behavior "likely to cause a breach of the peace." The court also rules that Jews have an unquestionable historical and legal right to pray on the Temple Mount, but that these rights could not be exercised until the authorities had adopted regulations fixing the time and place for such prayers. Such regulations were necessary, said the court, in order to maintain public order. The court notes that the Religious Affairs Ministry had "good reason" for not yet setting the rules.

Aug. 10 — The attorney general appeals to the Supreme Court on its Temple Mount ruling. Religious Affairs Minister Yitzhak Raphael will not rule on district Court jurisdiction until there's a Supreme Court decision.

1977
June 28 — Interior Minister Joseph Burg, given the police is a part of his purview, notes that those trying to pray on the Mount are "not exactly from the God-fearing sector." He states "the law will be kept." That is taken to mean that the Jews would continue to be barred from attempting to pray on the Temple Mount on the coming Tisha B'Av.
August 14 — (Tisha B'Av) An attempt by 30 members of the El Har Hashem (To the Mount of God) to pray on the Temple Mount is foiled by the General Security Services. At a press conference, the group led by Gershon Salomon, emphasizes the ties of the Jewish people to the site and claims it is "absurd" that Jews were forbidden from entering the compound.

1979
March 25 — Rumors that followers of Meir Kahane and Yeshiva students would attempt Temple Mount prayers cause a general West Bank strike and bring 2,000 Arab youths with staves and rocks to the compound. They disperse after police intervention.
August 3 — Land of Israel movement "Banai" and other nationalists are prevented from praying on the Temple Mount.

1980
August 6 — The High Court is asked to revoke ban on prayer on the Temple Mount, in light of clause three of the new Jerusalem Law, which guarantees freedom of access.
August 10 — 300 members of Gush Emunim try to force their way onto the Temple Mount and are dispersed by police.

1981
August 28 — Religious Affairs Ministry workers are found digging a tunnel under the Temple Mount. The work began secretly a month earlier when water began leaking from a cistern under the Temple Mount and had to be drained. Chief Rabbi Shlomo Goren closes the dig because of the issue's sensitivity.
August 30 — Former Deputy Prime Minister Yigael Yadin protests quasi-archaeological activities of Religious Affairs Ministry north of the Western Wall.

Sept. 2 — Jews and Arabs clash with stones and fists in a tunnel north of the Western Wall. The Arabs had attempted to seal the cistern. A group of Yeshiva students under orders from Rabbi Getz, rabbi of the Western Wall knocked down the wall. The two groups were separated by police after a scuffle. Police Inspector-General Arye Ivtzan says the cistern will be sealed to restore the previous situation — until there is a legal ruling. Ivtzan is praised by Mayor Teddy Kollek, and condemned by Goren, who says the cistern was part of the Second Temple and had nothing to do with Islam. The next day the cistern is sealed. Goren is quoted as saying the cistern was a tunnel that could lead to temple treasures including the lost ark.

Sept. 4 — A strike by the Supreme Moslem Council closes shops and schools in East Jerusalem to "protest against excavation under the Temple Mount."

Sept. 10 — The Waqf seals the cistern from the other side to prevent Jewish penetration. Meanwhile archaeologist Dan Bahat discounts theories the cistern was connected with the Temple.

Sept. 15 — Attempt by the Temple Mount Faithful to pray in compound thwarted by Moslem opposition. The High Court decides that the right of the Jew to pray on the Mount is a political issue upon which the government must decide. The Jerusalem Law doesn't cover the issue, rules the court.

1982

April 11 — Israeli soldier Alan Harry Goodman, a U.S. immigrant goes on a shooting rampage on the Temple Mount. He kills one and wounds three. The incident sets off a week of rioting in Jerusalem, the West Bank, and Gaza and angry reaction internationally against Israel. At his trial Goodman told the court that by "liberating the spot holy to the Jews," he expected to become King of the Jews. A year after the incident Goodman is convicted and sentenced to life plus two terms of 20 years.

July 25 — Yoel Lerner, member of Meir Kahane's Kach Party, is arrested for planning to sabotage one of the mosques on the Temple Mount.

Oct. 26 — Lerner convicted of planning to blow up the Dome of the Rock. Previously he had served a three year sentence for heading a group that plotted to overthrow the government and establish a state based upon religious law. He was sentenced to two and one half years in prison.

Dec. 9 — Knesset Member Geula Cohen charges that the Arabs have arm caches on the Mount.

1983

March 10 — Police arrest more than 40 people suspected of planning to penetrate the Temple Mount. Police had found four armed youths trying to break into the underground passage known as Solomon's Stables. Working on the basis of intelligence reports, the police surround the home of Rabbi Yisrael Ariel, former head of the Yamit Yeshiva. There, the others are arrested and a search of his apartment and others reveals several weapons and diagrams of the Temple Mount.
May 11 — High Court allows Faithful of the Temple Mount to hold prayers at the Mograbi Gate on Jerusalem Day, after police had earlier denied them a license. A similar decision is handed down for Tiasha B'Av.
May 22 — SRI's seven man team was thwarted from performing the first scientific study of the Rabbinical Tunnel. Moslems called the Israeli police to stop scientific expedition.
Sept. 17 — On Yom Kippur the police try to prevent former chief Rabbi Shlomo Goren from holding prayers in a room beneath the Temple Mount. Goren claimed he had the consent of IDF chief of staff Rav-Aluf Moshe Levy. Levy showed up for the prayers. Police then allowed the prayer to take place.
Sept. 21 — The Temple Mount 29 are acquitted of all charges against them. The police are reprimanded by District Court Judge Ya'acov Bazak and describes the 29 as "amateurish." But he does not rule on the legality of prayer on the Mount.

1990

Oct. 8 — On Jerusalem Day, Temple Mount Faithful unfurls banner on Temple Mount. A riot breaks out leaving over twenty Palestinians dead. United Nations censures Israel for this act but says nothing as to those who started the riot. Press erroneously report that group was about to lay a foundation stone on the Temple Mount.

Fundamentalists Ache for Armageddon
By Allan C. Brownfeld (Chairman, American Council for Judaism)
May 19, 1987, *The Orange County Register*
The ties between Christian fundamentalism in the United States and Jewish fundamentalism in Israel are growing rapidly, with potentially serious consequences for U.S.-Middle East policy and for the people of that troubled region.

In 1978, Jerry Falwell traveled to Israel on a trip sponsored and paid for by the Israeli government. In 1979, the Israelis extended another free trip, during a period when Prime Minister Menachem Begin was in a rush to build Jewish settlements throughout the West Bank. The Rev. Falwell traveled the road toward the Palestinian town of Nablus and turned off the highway and stood at a cluster of prefabricated houses built by Jewish settlers. At that time, Falwell declared that God was kind to America only because "America has been kind to the Jews."

At a gala dinner in New York in 1980, Prime Minister Begin bestowed upon Falwell a medal named for Vladimir Jabotinsky, the right-wing Zionist leader. In 1981, when Israel bombed the nuclear reactor in Iraq, Begin immediately called Jerry Falwell for support.

Few Americans understood the real reasons for the alliance between Christian fundamentalism and the most extreme segments of Israel political life. In an important new book, *Prophecy and Politics* by Grace Halsell (Lawrence Hill and Co.). She worked as a White House speechwriter during the administration of Lyndon Johnson and explores this growing relationship.

During two of Jerry Falwell's Holy Land tours, the author interviewed fundamentalist members of the Moral Majority, all of whom believed that the biblical prophecy of fighting World War III must be fulfilled preparatory of the Second Coming of Christ.

The strain of fundamentalism known as "dispensationalism," Halsell writes, argues that the world will soon be destroyed: "God knows it will happen. He knew it from the beginning. But, God kept His plan secret from all the billions of people who lived before us. But now . . . He has revealed the plan . . . we must move through seven time periods, or dispensations — one of which includes the terrible battle of Armageddon, where new and totally destructive nuclear weapons will be unleashed and blood will flow like mighty rivers. . . ."

Dispensationalism spread throughout the U.S. largely through the efforts of Cyrus Ingerson Scofield, born in 1843. His belief system was not original with him but goes back to John Nelson Darby, a 19th-century Irishman and one-time priest in the Church of England.

On one occasion, Scofield reminded his audience that year after year he had sounded the same warning: our world will end "in disaster, in ruin, in the great, final world-catastrophe." But, he said, born-again Christians should welcome such a catastrophe because once the final battle began, Christ will lift them up into the clouds.

Grace Halsell became a participant in two Jerry Falwell-sponsored journeys to Israel where she mingled with many dispensationalists. One of them, Owen, explained his belief system, which entailed the need to destroy Jerusalem's most hold Islamic shrine, and the necessity of waging a nuclear Armageddon to destroy the world.

Christian fundamentalists who donate generously to Jewish terrorism include oil and gas tycoon Terry Reisenhoover, a frequent White House visitor, Mission to America Chairman Dr. Hilton Sutton and Dr. James DeLoach, pastor of Houston's Second Baptist Church who visited me . . . and boasted that he and others had formed a Jerusalem Temple Foundation specifically to aid those intent on destroying the mosque and building a temple.

Dr. John Walvoord, who teaches at Southwestern School of Bible in Dallas, explained the dispensationalist beliefs to Halsell: "God does not look on all of His children the same way. He sees us divided into categories, the Jews and the Gentiles. God has one plan, an earthly plan, for the Jews. And He has a second plan, a heavenly plan, for the born-again Christians. The other peoples of the world — Muslims, Buddhists, and those of other faiths as well as those Christians not born again – do not concern Him. As for destroying planet earth, we can do nothing. Peace, for us, is not in God's book. . . ."

At a meeting of Christian Zionists in Basel, Switzerland, the group adopted resolutions calling for all Jews living outside of Israel to leave the countries where they are now residing and move to the Jewish State. The Christians also urged Israel to annex the West Bank. When an Israeli in the audience urged more moderate language, pointing out that an Israeli poll showed that one-third of Israelis would be willing to trade territory seized in 1967 for peace with the Palestinians, one of the Christian leaders, van der Hoeven of Holland, replied, "We don't care what the Israelis vote! We care what God says! And God gave that land to the Jews!"

The discussion in this book of the alliance between Christian and Jewish fundamentalists — whose theological differences have been shelved for the political goal of strengthening Israel — is instructive. Jews in Israel and the U.S., it seems, do not realize that the Christian fundamentalists urge such a policy because they believe it will usher in the Battle of Armageddon and the end of the world — not because they are concerned with Israel's long-run security.

Army chiefs dismayed at decision to open tunnel
By Anton La Guardia, September 30, 1996 (*The Electronic Telegraph*)
Israeli defense chiefs are reported to be dismayed at the government's decision to reopen the archaeological tunnel in Jerusalem that started the conflict with the Palestinians.

Lt. Gen. Amnon Shahak, the Chief-of-Staff, was never consulted about the decision. Ami Ayalon, head of the Shin Bet security service, recommended opening the tunnel only if there was progress in political negotiations over the fate of Hebron, and as part of a deal allowing Palestinians to build an extension to the al-Aqsa mosque.

Zeev Schiff, Israel's foremost defense analyst, said there was unease in the army about the way in which ministers took decisions. But he dismissed suggestions that Lt. Gen. Shahak was about to resign in protest. Mr Schiff said: "The ministers don't have to accept the army's advice, but they should ask. The tunnel was not a minor issue such as how to deal with traffic in Tel Aviv."

The army, which the previous government involved in the talks on the redeployment from the West Bank town of Hebron, has also been kept out of the new administration's plans to re-negotiate the agreement with the Palestinians.

It is ready to re-enter Palestinian areas, if necessary. But instead of dealing with stone-throwers, it would now face 30,000 armed Palestinians fighting for their homeland. As in Lebanon, Israel would be fighting a war while the country is divided.

Shlomo Gazit, former head of military intelligence, said the West Bank and Gaza Strip could be retaken in a few days. He was confident that officers would follow orders. But he doubted that such drastic action would be necessary. Instead he suggested that the army should concentrate on more limited objectives, perhaps strategic terrain to improve its ability to defend isolated Jewish communities.

Mr Gazit was concerned that Mr Netanyahu, with no experience of high office, was isolating himself from the best security advice.

Jews Hail Birth of Red Cow as Sign to Start Third Temple
By Con Coughlin, March 16 1997 (*The Electronic Telegraph*)
The birth of a red heifer in Israel is being hailed by religious Jews as a sign from God that work can soon begin on building the Third Temple in Jerusalem.

A team of rabbinical experts last week confirmed that the animal, born six months ago on a religious kibbutz near the north Israeli port of Haifa, meets the correct Biblical criteria for a genuine holy cow. According to the Book of Numbers (XIX: 2–7), the animal is needed for an ancient Jewish purification ritual.

"The Lord hath commanded saying: Speak unto the children of Israel that they bring thee a red heifer without spot, wherein is no blemish, and upon which never came yoke," says the fourth book of the Old Testament, also part of Jewish holy scripture, the Torah.

The heifer will be slaughtered and burned, and its ashes made into a liquid paste and used in a ceremony which religious Jews believe they must undergo before they can enter the old Temple site in Jerusalem to start building a new structure. Since Herod's Temple was destroyed by the Roman emperor Titus in AD 70, no flawless red heifer has been born within the biblical land of Israel, according to rabbinical teaching.

The birth of the animal, to a black-and-white mother and a dun-coloured bull, is being hailed as a "miracle" by activists who want to rebuild the Third Temple and prepare the way for the Jewish messiah's entry to Jerusalem. The faithful will need to wait until the heifer is at least three before it can be used in a ritual sacrifice. That would enable religious Jews to start the new millennium (a Christian event, but still regarded as portentous) in a state of purity.

News of the red heifer's appearance, however, will not be well received by Muslims. The site of the old Jewish temples in the Holy City is

Pictured here are Rabbi Chaim Richman, Clyde Lott, the Mississippi cattleman, and the "miraculous" red heifer (from *Mystery of the Red Heifer: Divine Promise of Purity*), whose sacrifice and ashes would provide appropriate groundwork for the destruction of Dome of the Rock and the rebuilding of the Temple of Solomon. According to Gershom Gorenberg in *The End of Days*, the biblical verse that moved Clyde Lott to help Rabbi Richman was simply misunderstood. "In Hebrew, the [Genesis] verse says nothing of cows. It refers, unmistakably, to the offspring of sheep and goats — as any Orthodox Israeli schoolchild who was awake in second grade class knows. In the English of King James' time, 'cattle' meant any livestock, not specifically bovines." In December 1998, Rabbi Richman broke off his friendship with the American cattleman, over a financial dispute.

now occupied by one of Islam's holiest shrines, the Dome of the Rock. Jewish extremists want to destroy the Dome and the adjoining Al-Aqsa mosque to make way for a new temple. In 1985 a group of Jewish terrorists were jailed in Israel for planning to destroy the Dome with high explosives.

But Jewish activists regard it as their divine mission to build a new Temple. "We have been waiting 2,000 years for a sign from God, and now he has provided us with a red heifer," said Yehudah Etzion, the ringleader of the Eighties' plot to blow up the Dome, who was present at last week's inspection of the red heifer at Kfar Hassidim. "There were a couple of little white hairs which worried us, but the rabbis are satisfied that it is the red heifer referred to in the Bible," said Mr. Etzion.

Ariel Sharon visits Temple Mount
September 28, 2000 Jerusalem (CNN) — A visit by Likud Party
leader Ariel Sharon to the site known as the Temple Mount by Jews
sparked a clash on Thursday between stone-throwing Palestinians and
Israeli troops, who fired tear gas and rubber bullets into the crowd,
resulting in the death of four Palestinians.

October 2000 – A second Palestinian Intifada (the first one lasted
between 1988 and 1992) is called the Al Aqsa Intifada.

How did Ariel Sharon's tour of Temple Mount inspire a radical escalation of protest and terror? Sharon is known by Palestinians as a "pig"
and "butcher," responsible for Israel's 1982 invasion of Lebanon,
which was designed to remove all Palestinians within bombing distance of Northern Israel. The invasion that helped bring on the
"Beirut massacre," in which 800 Palestinian civilians were brutally
murdered in the Sabra and Shatilla refugee camps. It wasn't Sharon
who did the murdering, not even Israeli soldiers, but Christian
Phalangist allies. The Kahan Commission, formed by the Israeli government to investigate the massacre, found Sharon to be "personally
responsible," and recommended his removal from the government. In
his resignation speech Sharon spoke of his detractors' "blood libel" and
"self-hatred." Those who elected Sharon Prime Minister in February
2001 now wish he would be personally responsible for butchering
every potential suicide bomber.

November 11, 2001 — *New York Times* review of the book, *Sacred
Geography: A Tale of Murder and Archeology in the Holy Land* by
Edward Fox, Metropolitan/Holt, $25. "In the Middle East, Fox points
out, archaeological discoveries have long been used to bolster political
and religious claims. In an atmosphere in which archaeologists sometimes carried guns, and entire layers of history — often related to the
region's Islamic past — were literally bulldozed away, [American arche-
ologist Albert] Glock, a scholarly Lutheran, inspired admiration
among his students, suspicion and vandalism among the Palestinians
who lived near his excavations and suspicion, too, among some Israeli
authorities, who viewed him as a 'troublesome intellectual.' Was Glock
the target of an undercover Israeli operation? Or was a Palestinian
group incensed that an American led what should have been a
Palestinian endeavor?"

From *There's A War On, Folks* — The Coming Tribulation
By Lambert Dolphin

MR. DOLPHIN, A CHRISTIAN ZIONIST WHOSE FUNDAMENTALIST BELIEFS HAVE TAKEN HIM, TIME AND AGAIN, TO JERUSALEM, PRAYS FOR THE REBUILDING OF THE TEMPLE OF SOLOMON BY TAKING DOWN THE THIRD HOLIEST ISLAMIC MOSQUE, THE DOME OF THE ROCK. HERE HE GIVES US THE STANDARD PRETRIBULATION, PREMILLENNIAL VIEW OF CHRISTIAN FUNDAMENTALIST APOCALYPSE.

The Rapture of the church will be accompanied by the removal from earth of much of God's restraint of evil (which presently comes by the Holy Spirit through the salt and light functions of the church). This is described in 2 Thessalonians 2. Meanwhile the Church will (supposedly) be caught up into heaven and there experience (a) the Judgment Seat of Christ, and (b) the Marriage Supper of the Lamb. Meanwhile down on earth, the "man of sin" (the final Antichrist) will rise to power in Europe in cahoots with a false Messiah in Israel. Together they will negotiate a phony peace settlement in the Middle East (Isaiah calls this faulty treaty Israel's "Covenant with Death"). A world-wide false (harlot) church will rise to temporary power in this time frame — and enjoy the support of a united Western-world coalition whose power center is in Europe. The Jews will build and put into service their long-awaited Third Temple with a functioning priesthood and sacrifices. The removal of the church from the earth marks the end of a long interval of history following the death of Christ, ("the great parenthesis"), between the 69th and 70th weeks of Daniel. Thus Israel will return to the center stage of world history once again, and the God of Israel will at last fulfill His unconditional covenants with the patriarchs of Israel.

The tribulation period, seven years total, will change radically in character after 3.5 years of apparent world peace — especially in the Middle East. At that time a false Messiah in Israel will appear on the scene of history (he is the Second Beast of Revelation 13 fulfilling the warning of Jesus, John 5:43, "I have come in my Father's name, and you do not receive me; if another comes in his own name, him you will receive.") This "man of sin" will enter the Holy of Holies of that Third Temple and declare to the world that He is God. He erects an image of the "First Beast" who heads up the political, military and commercial power of Europe. This awful desecration of the temple was predicted by Jesus and is compared by Jesus (Mt. 24:15) to a similar, earlier desecration of the Second Temple by Antiochus Epiphanies (175–163 BC). The mid-trib point is the time for true believers in Jesus who are living in Judea at that time to flee for safety to nearby Jordan where they will be safely guarded by the Lord — while all hell breaks loose back in Israel.

"For then there will be great tribulation, such as has not been from the beginning of the world until now, no, and never will be. And if those days had not been shortened, no human being would be saved; but for the sake of the elect those days will be shortened." (Matthew 24:21–22)

A great and final war will break out in the Middle East in the second half of the tribulation period. Many details are given in the Bible. The principal powers involved are Egypt and allies, Iran, Iraq, Syria, Russia and armies from both the West and the East. It is quite likely that nuclear, biological and chemical weapons will be unloosed. In fact, at mid-trib, the God of Israel will personally intervene decisively in human affairs bringing great and terrible judgment on the nations of the world — including Israel. The second half of the tribulation period is variously called "the GREAT tribulation," "the Day of the Lord," and "the time of Jacob's trouble." (The term "the last days" refers to the entire time period between the First and Second Advents of our Lord). The period of history we live in now could be called "man's day," since to a large extent God allows man to have his own way. Apart from common grace to all men, and much restraint of evil, God now rules the universe but does not yet reign on earth — but this will soon change drastically.

Yet at this approaching darkest-of-all times in history, God (in mercy and grace) will place into service 144,000 trained Jewish evangelists who will have the zeal and vitality of the Apostle Paul. They will travel around the world, preaching the gospel of the kingdom to those who have never heard the good news — with the result that many millions will come to Christ. Animosity against God will, however, be so high that these new converts (the "tribulation saints") will be quickly put to death (martyred). The judgments of God in the second half of the tribulation period will be a combination of horrendous man-made, and terrible natural disasters, cascading in rapid succession — with the end result that the planet will be totally laid waste and devastated. The majority of people on earth will be killed.

Near the end of the seven year tribulation period, while World War III is raging out of control in the Middle East, Jesus Christ will return in power and glory to the Mount of Olives in Jerusalem from whence He departed 40 days after His resurrection in AD 33. Jesus will bring with Him at His epiphaneia "the armies of heaven" — which includes all of us, i.e., his saints. Together with Jesus we Christians will participate in the establishment of world-wide righteous government on earth. Thus the devastated planet will be rebuilt and repopulated under the Kingly rule of Jesus. Our Lord will sit on the throne of David in Jerusalem and reign on earth 1000 years. The believing Jews of the Old Testament will be resurrected at the end of the tribulation (Daniel 12, Hebrews 11:39–40) and God will at long last fulfill His literal promises to the nation Israel, promises made to Abraham, Isaac, Jacob, Moses, David, and to Jesus.

"Lest you be wise in your own conceits, I want you to understand this mystery, brethren: a hardening has come upon part of Israel, until the full number of the Gentiles come in, and so all Israel will be saved; as it is written, 'The Deliverer will come from Zion, he will banish ungodliness from Jacob'; and this will be my covenant with them when I take away their sins." As regards the gospel they are enemies of God, for your sake; but as regards election they are beloved for the sake of their forefathers. For the gifts and the call of God are irrevocable. Just as you were once disobedient to God but now have received mercy because of their disobedience, so they have now been disobedient in order that by the mercy shown to you they also may receive mercy. For God has consigned all men to disobedience, that he may have mercy upon all. O the depth of the riches and wisdom and knowledge of God! How unsearchable are his judgments and how inscrutable his ways! "For who has known the mind of the Lord, or who has been his counselor?" "Or who has given a gift to him that he might be repaid?" For from him and through him and to him are all things. To him be glory for ever. Amen." (Romans 11:25–36)

As mentioned, during the thousand-year reign of Christ in earth, Christians will work together with the believers who survive World War III (Mt. 25:31–46) to rebuild the earth. Then the judgment of all the wicked dead (the "Great White Throne" judgment) will occur (Rev. 20:11–15). Finally, God will renovate the heavens and the earth, by fire, (2 Peter 3:10–12, Rev. 21:1ff) removing all sources of evil sin permanently from both the heavens and the earth.

Breaking of Ties with the Great Satan, America

THIS SPEECH BY AYATOLLAH KHOMEINI WAS PRINTED IN *THE DAWN OF THE ISLAMIC REVOLUTION*, A BOOK OF POSTERS, SPEECHES AND BOOSTER MATERIAL, ALL TRANSLATED INTO ENGLISH AND PRINTED — RATHER SHABBILY — IN IRAN, 1983.

In the Name of God, the Merciful, the Compassionate

Honorable nation of Iran; I have received the news of the severing of relations between the U.S. and Iran. If Carter has ever in his life done a good thing for the oppressed, it is this very severing of relations. Relations between a world-devouring looter and a nation that has risen up to liberate itself from the claws of the international looters, will always be to the loss of the oppressed nation and in the interest of the looter. We consider this severing of relations as a good omen; it shows that the U.S. government has given up all its hopes for Iran. The militant nation of Iran is correct in celebrating this dawn of the final victory in which she has forced a tyrant superpower to cut its ties, to end all its lootings.

We hope for the quick destruction of such puppets as Sadat and Saddam Hussein. The honorable Islamic nations should deal with these treacherous parasites as the Iranian nation dealt with the treacherous Muhammad Reza. Then, later, in order to live freely and to achieve complete independence, they should sever their relations with the superpowers, especially America.

I have repeatedly mentioned that our relations with the likes of the U.S. are like the relations of an oppressed nation with the world plunderers. You, dear nation overcame the enemy with slogans of Allahu-Akbar for the satisfaction of God, the Supreme, and attained freedom and independence. By relying on the Supreme Lord and by preserving unity of expression, be prepared to face the enemies of Islam and the oppressed. You are victorious by the will of Almighty God and will overcome all problems.

Saddam Hussein, who like the deposed Shah, has shown his non-Islamic and inhumane character and has decided to destroy Islam and theological school at Najaf for Carter's satisfaction. He has done to the oppressed Muslims what the Mongols did. He is doing as Reza Khan and Muhammad Reza Pahlavi did to the *Ulema* — such as Ayatollah Seyyed Muhammad Baqir Sadr and the clergy and other social classes. Saddam should know that by these anti-Islamic actions, he is digging his own grave and that of the self-imposed, inhumane and illegal Baathist regime.

Oh, honorable nation of Iraq, you are the descendants of those who drove Britain out of Iraq. Rise up and before this corrupt regime destroys all your values, rid your country of this criminal. Oh, tribes of the Euphrates and the Tigris, unite with the whole nation in order to eradicate this corruption before the opportunity is lost. And for God's sake depend on your Islamic country and Holy Islam and know that God is with you.

Oh, Iraqi army, do not obey him [Saddam] who is against Islam and the Quran. Join the nation and cut the interests of America which Saddam implements. Know that obeying this tyrant is opposing the Supreme Lord and the punishment for this is disgrace and the fire of hell.

I ask Almighty God for the grandeur of Islam and the Muslims and the country of Iran.

> May the Peace and Mercy of God be upon You.
> — Ruhullah al-Musavi al-Khomeini

> This severing of relations shows that the U.S. government has given up all its hopes for Iran.
> — Imam Khomeini

THE DEN OF SPIES FROM THE IMAM'S POINT OF VIEW

FROM THE IMAM'S SPEECH DELIVERED IN A MEETING OF A GROUP OF STAFF MEMBERS OF THE IRAN CENTRAL INSURANCE COMPANY, NOVEMBER 5, 1979.

THE "DEN OF SPIES" REFERS TO THE 52 AMERICANS HELD HOSTAGE HELD FOR 444 DAYS BY IRAN, AND RELEASED THE VERY DAY OF RONALD REAGAN'S INAUGURATION. THE SO-CALLED "THE OCTOBER SURPRISE" AFFAIR HAD PRESIDENTIAL HOPEFUL RONALD REAGAN, THROUGH EX-CIA DIRECTOR AND VICE-PRESIDENTIAL CANDIDATE GEORGE BUSH, AND WILLIAM CASEY, ALSO OF THE CIA, ENGINEER THE RELEASE OF THE HOSTAGES IN SECRET DEALS BEHIND THE BACK OF PRESIDENT JIMMY CARTER IN ORDER TO ASSURE THE ELECTION OF REAGAN AS PRESIDENT. IRAN MADE MUCH OF THE HOSTAGE SITUATION, INSISTING THAT THEY WERE SENT BY "THE GREAT SATAN" TO PLOT A COUP D'ETAT AGAINST KHOMEINI. THE ISLAMIC REVOLUTION PLAYED THE 52 HOSTAGES AS THEY WERE ALL ACES IN HAND. THE "DEN OF SPIES" BECAME A HUGE PROPAGANDA VICTORY THAT EXPOSED THE UNITED STATES AS A BULLY WHOSE STRENGTH WAS MERE ILLUSION; IT COULD BE EASILY BEATEN BACK AND KICKED AGAIN AND AGAIN. THE MATERIAL BELOW WAS PRINTED IN *ECHO OF ISLAM*, IRAN'S ENGLISH LANGUAGE MAGAZINE IN CHARGE OF PROPAGATING REVOLUTIONARY ISLAM.

The center that our youths have seized, as they have announced, has been the center of espionage and plotting.

Our youth have paid full attention to these plots, in order to thwart them.

Today is a day for us to sit and watch. Today hidden treason is at work which is engineered in this same Embassy, most of which are from the Great Satan, the U.S.

They should realize that once again there is a Revolution in Iran, a Revolution greater than the first one.

They should not think that we fear, that we sit and watch them do any damn thing they want. No, this is not the case.

We should advance with force. If we speak of weakness, or if they feel that we are weakened . . . they would become bold and would be encouraged to attack. Do not feel you are weakened.

As it has been reported, Carter's special envoys are on their way to Iran and have decided to come to Qum to meet me. Therefore, I deem it necessary to mention that the U.S. government, by taking care of the Shah, has made clear its opposition to Iran. On the other hand, it has been said that the U.S. Embassy in Iran is a place of espionage of our enemies against the sacred Islamic movement. Therefore, not under any circumstances it is possible for the special envoys to meet me nor are the members of the Revolutionary Council or the responsible authorities allowed to meet them. — from the Imam's message on the occasion of the tour of Carter's special envoys to Iran, November 7, 1979.

You know that at present the center of corruption the U.S. Embassy has been occupied by our youth. You youth remain confident that the U.S. cannot do a damn thing.

It is wrong to even mention "What would we do if the U.S. embarks on a military intervention?" Can the U.S. militarily intervene in this country?

Right now the whole world's attention is focused on Iran. Is the U.S. able to stand against the whole world and to intervene militarily? She errs if she makes a military intervention.

If they intend to embark on a military intervention, I myself will act and your beloved nation will move as well.

The U.S. is more decrepit than to intervene militarily in Iran.

The U.S. always interferes through engineering plots. If they want to do something, they would plot among the youths.

These people who call themselves Fedayeen-e Khalq have not supported the Muslims youth occupying the U.S. Embassy while all others have announced their support. If they are not pro-U.S., why have they not supported [them]? If they are pro-Soviet, they should be the enemy of the U.S. and if they are nationalists, they should be the enemy of the United States like other strata of the nation.

Our nation considers the U.S. as her enemy since the U.S. has sheltered our number one enemy, the toppled Shah. — from the Imam's speech in the gathering of a group of students from the Faculty of Economics of Isfahan University, November 7, 1979.

Embassies don't have the legal right to spy and the U.S. Embassy, as the experts have recognized so far, has been a center of espionage and plotting. How has the reverend Pope at this time thought that they should be released for sake of humanity?

During this period we wanted to recognize the kindness of one of the religious personalities abroad, especially the great Christian leader, towards this oppressed nation.

While Islam has supported Jesus Christ and Christian scholars, we want to hear that those like the Pope would ask, "Why has this nation been living in such a situation?"

Why doesn't the Pope intercede for an oppressed nation who intends to discover parts of the oppression imposed on it and wants to inform the people and the oppressed of the extent of such an oppression?

We do not have any unjust word to say. Our word is acceptable wherever in the world it is taken, except to Carter.

The Pope should think of Christian people and all the oppressed nations, he should think of the honor of Christians.

Since we are oppressed we appeal to you to save the Christian nation.

I tell you, Pope, that if Jesus Christ was living today, he would have impeached Carter. If Jesus Christ was present he would have saved us from the claws of this enemy of the masses and humanity. And you, who are his representative, should do what Christ would have done.

We are neither afraid of military measures nor economic sanctions since we are Muslims following the Imams who welcome martyrdom. Our nation as well welcomes martyrdom today.

We are men of war, we are men of struggle. Our youths have fought and battled against tanks, cannons and machine guns.

Mr. Carter should not try to frighten us from struggle. We are men of struggle even if we may not have the means for it.

We are a nation used to hunger. For 35 or 50 years we have been entangled with these problems and are used to hunger and we fast. If they could impose an economic embargo we would not have meat once a week. Eating a lot of meat is not such a good thing. We could even have one meal a day. Do not frighten us with these things. If it is destined for us to either have a full stomach or to preserve our honor, we would prefer to save our honor and have our stomach empty. — from the Imam's speech to the gathering of a group of students from the Faculty of Economics of Isfahan University, November 7, 1979.

Imam Khomeini's Message on the Occasion of the Day of Quds, 1981

As printed in *The Dawn of the Islamic Revolution*, translated into English and printed, in Iran, 1983.

THIS ADDRESS WAS DELIVERED BY SEYYED AHMAD KHOMEINI ON BEHALF OF THE IMAM ON THE DAY OF QUDS, JULY 31, 1981 AT TEHRAN'S FRIDAY CONGREGATIONAL PRAYER.

In the Name of God, the Merciful, the Compassionate

The last Friday of the month of Ramadhan is Quds Day. In all likelihood the Night of Qadr occurs sometime in the last ten days of the month. This is a night whose memory has been kept alive as a Divine Tradition since it falls in a month which is worth more than a thousand months of the hypocrites. This month is one in which the fate of the people is determined.

It is necessary that the observance of Quds Day, which neighbors Laylati-I-Qadr (Night of Qadr) be revived among the Muslims. They must base their vigilance and alertness on Quds Day so that they can rid themselves of the trap of age-long neglect which has struck them, especially in recent centuries. In this way, the day of their vigilance and wakefulness could well surpass tens of years of the superpowers and the hypocrites of the world, and the world's Muslim will determine their own fate themselves.

On Laylati-I-Qadr, the world's Muslims rid themselves of the bond of worshipping other than the Almighty God — the *Jinn* and human devils — and worship only God. On Quds Day which is one of the last days of the great "Shahru-I-lah" month of God (Ramadan), it behooves the world's Muslims to rid themselves of the shackles of bondage to the Great Satan and superpowers, and to join the eternal power of God, cutting off the hands of the greatest criminals in history from the oppressed nations and to wither the roots of their greed.

O you Muslims of the world! You oppressed masses! Rise up and take your destiny into your hands. How long do you intend to sit quietly while your fate is determined in Washington or Moscow? Until when should your Quds be trampled under the boots of the residue of the United States, the usurper Israel? How long should Quds, Palestine,

Lebanon, and the oppressed Muslims be under the domination of criminals while you remain onlookers, while some of your treacherous rulers aid them? How long should almost one billion Muslims and one hundred million Arabs, with vast lands and endless resources, continue to suffer plundering by the East and the West and oppressions and inhumane massacres by them and their residue? How long do you intend to put up with the savage crimes committed against our brothers (in faith) in Afghanistan, and Lebanon, and remain silent before their pleas? How long do you intend to resort to such tactics as political action and compromise with the superpowers, and giving uninterrupted opportunities to Israel to massacre, and you being a mere onlooker? Why don't you stand against the enemies of Islam and use firearms and military might and a God-inspired power?

Don't the heads of the Muslim countries yet know that negotiations with powerful statesmen and the criminals of history will not end in the liberation of Quds, or Lebanon, or Palestine, but will result in the increase of their crimes and oppressive acts?

To liberate Quds, the Muslims should use "faith dependent machine guns" and the power of Islam and keep away from political games which reek of compromise and the guarantee of satisfaction of the superpowers. The Muslim nations, especially the Palestinian and the Lebanese nations, should punish those who waste time indulging in political maneuvers, and not be influenced by such games which bear no results for the oppressed nation except their loss. For how long should the powerful Muslims be enchanted by the false myths of the East and West and feel intimidated at the sounding of their empty propaganda horns? How long will the Muslims neglect the power of the great Islam — Muslims, who in the course of a half-century, achieved those great and wondrous victories with bare hands and with hearts full of faith and with tongues saying Allahu Akbar (God is Greater) and set the foundations of Islam in the powerful world of those days? If those victories which are recorded in history, are a little far from the sight of Muslims, then the combatant nation of Iran with motives like those of the soldiers at the beginning of Islam whose arms were faith, still stands before their eyes.

The world and the Muslim people in the world saw, with bare hands, the patriotic nation of Iran stand against the accoutrements of the superpowers and against their internal and external dependents and suddenly brought to triumph the Islamic Revolution in Iran. The nation cut the interests of all criminals of history from their dear country, thwarting the U.S. inspired plots and those of the leftist and rightist groups, one after another with hearts full of faith. Men and women, the youth and the elderly are now present on the scene, and control the fate of their own country.

Today, with the blessing of the Almighty God, the foundations of the Islamic Republic have been set by the hands of people who have faith in Islam and in the Islamic Republic. They have expelled troublemakers and conspirators from the scene. Today, despite the sounding of horns against us abroad, and the efforts of the propaganda machinery of the United States, and the Zionists, and the people who have been slapped in the face by the Revolution, the Islamic Revolution of Iran resolutely continues in its path forward towards self-development. This has been a lesson for the Muslim nations and the oppressed of the world. By it, they may find their own Islamic potential and forever throw away their fear of the growls of the East and West and of their dependents and residue, and let it be an example to them to rise up with faith in the Supreme Lord, and reliance on the power of Islam, cutting the criminal interests (of the enemies of Islam) from their own countries, and focusing on the liberation of our noble Quds and Palestine as their principal aim. In this way the disgrace of the domination of Zionism, this outgrowth of the United States, can be wiped out and the memory of Quds Day can be kept alive.

It is hoped that all symptoms of indifference and neglect will end by keeping alive the memory of this Day. It is hoped that by the noble nations' uprisings, certain treacherous leaders who rule over Muslims and Islam, and are hand-in-hand with Israel and act upon the orders of the U.S. in opposition to the interests of Muslims, will be cast from the scene and buried in the grave of history: the usurper rulers who are siding with the unbelievers in the war of unbelievers and apostates such as Israel and Saddam against the Muslims and are raining blows on Muslims and Islam, should be pushed from the scene of Islam. They should be deposed from their rule over Muslims.

The noble people of Egypt and Iraq and other countries who are under the domination of hypocrites should rise up and not listen to the corrupt loudspeakers of the criminal pseudo-Muslims, and fear not the fragile power of these treacherous people.

Muslims and people of the world noted how Saddam Aflaq, [reference to the founder of the Baathist political party], lackey, attacked Iran, a nation which thinks of nothing but Islam and the interests of Muslims, and they have noted how his head was knocked in the dust. He is now stretching an imploring hand to the Arab leaders and Israel so that they might somehow rescue him from his undisputed fall. The Iranian nation and the brave Armed Forces struck him and his criminal supporters such a blow that it has pushed him to either submission or fall. His stupid tricks and the sounding of propaganda horns of the Zionists will be of no avail to him. The nation, government, Majlis, and the Armed Forces of Iran with an Islamic solidarity, compose one single people by Divine Unity and are determined to stand against any satanic power which is encroaching upon the rights of human beings, and defend the oppressed masses and support dear Quds and Lebanon until Quds and Palestine have been returned to the Muslims.

The world's Muslims should consider Quds Day as a special day to Muslims, or rather to the entire oppressed masses of the world, and they should stand against the superciliously arrogant powers and the world devourers, and not sit passively until the liberation of the oppressed from the oppression of the powerful. The oppressed masses, which compromise the absolute majority of the people of the world, should feel assured that the promise of the Supreme Lord is near, and that the star of the oppressors is setting.

The Iranian nation, the sisters and brothers know fully well that the great Revolution of Iran has few or perhaps no precedents and boasts of lofty values. Among its great values are its religious and Islamic content: the same values our exalted Prophets rose up for. It is hoped that this Revolution will serve as a divine spark for creating a great explosion among the oppressed masses and that it will lead to the dawn of the Revolution of the Imam of Time (the Absent Imam), may all souls be sacrificed before him. The noble nation which brought about such a great Revolution should strive ever more to perpetuate it and in order to prove its presence most conspicuously in the arena for enacting Divine justice.

My beloved people! You should remember that the more our Revolution is valued the more necessary will be our acts of self-sacrifice for promoting this Revolution. A revolution in the Path of God and one for establishing the Rule of God, was precisely that for which our

Prophets sacrificed themselves, and the exalted Prophet of Islam devoted his whole lifetime to this path with all his might, and spared no act of self-abnegation in promoting this end. The noble Imams of Islam sacrificed whatever they had in this path and so we too who call ourselves their followers and the Ummah of the Prophet Muhammad, may God's blessing and praise be upon him and his family, should copy their acts, and have revolutionary patience as we confront hardships in the path of righteousness. We should not feel intimidated by the subversive acts of hypocrites and saboteurs which show the symptoms of their misery and defeat, and we should continue to sacrifice ourselves for promoting righteousness and Islam as did our exalted Prophets. The Blessed and Supreme Lord is the supporter of righteous strugglers and the friend of the oppressed.

Salutations to our beloved Islam. Greetings to the crusaders in the path of righteousness. Greetings to the martyrs in the way of God in all history. Greetings be upon the martyrs of Iran, Palestine, Lebanon and Afghanistan, and greetings be upon our combatants in the war against falsehood.

Ruhullah al-Musavi al-Khomeini
July 31, 1981

THE SHAH AND SAVAK ARE OVERTHROWN
But Terror is Here to Stay

THE BOOK COMPILING COMPLAINTS AGAINST ALLAH'S POLICE FORCE, *THE CRIMES OF KHOMEINI'S REGIME: A REPORT ON THE VIOLATIONS OF CIVIL AND POLITICAL RIGHTS BY THE ISLAMIC REPUBLIC OF IRAN*, WAS ISSUED IN 1983 BY A SOCIALIST GROUP KNOWN AS INTERNATIONAL SOLIDARITY FRONT FOR THE DEFENSE OF THE IRANIAN PEOPLE'S DEMOCRATIC RIGHTS (ISF-IRAN).

The Shah as pictured by the Islamic Revolution.

The Iranian people paid a high price in the lives of our children to overthrow the dictatorial rule of the Shah. We paid it gladly, hoping for a future of decency and respect for human dignity.

The economic accomplishments of the Islamic Republic Regime are not discussed here. Their record in human dignity has been disastrous. The Islamic regime has executed its opponents, instituted complete censorship of the mass media; bombed Kurdistan and massacred the Kurdish and Turkoman peoples; violated the right of assembly by breaking up public meetings with armed thugs; suppressed women; shut down universities and smashed the students' resistance; raided bookstores and printshops; kidnapped and assassinated their opponents.

In recent weeks, since the dismissal of President Bani Sadr, their former favorite, a new wave of terror has begun. Youngsters between the ages of 11 and 22, especially girls, are the target of mass arrests and executions without even the show trials that used to be staged. People are killed on fabricated and ridiculous charges or for no reason at all. Children are not identified before they are shot. Charges include: carrying razor blades and knives, giving financial support to opposition organizations, organizing protests against the regime, misleading the innocent by giving them false information about the regime, talking to foreign reporters — in sum, armed revolt and "corruption on earth." Absolute censorship, house-to-house search and public search on the streets, without warrants, extensive telephone eavesdropping, body searches of employees at government buildings and factories, the arrest of doctors and nurses for treating injured anti-regime elements: all this is part of our everyday life.

Opposition figures are kidnapped and beaten by the regime's thugs; prisoners are deprived of legal assistance and family visits. When they are executed, they are made to die slowly; their bodies are not returned to their families; they are denied burial in public graveyards because they are atheists; mourning ceremonies for them are disrupted. This is but a partial list of the crimes of the Islamic Republic.

Because the regime holds particularly reactionary notions about women, they are especially mistreated. These are a few examples:

Undressing them in public, and beating and injuring them. Pulling them by the breasts and other sexual humiliations, both in prison and on the street. Kidnapping opposition women and subjecting them to gang rapes. Numerous cases of prison rape have been reported. Many are raped on the eve of their execution. Examining young girls manually, in public at the time of their arrest, to prove that they are not decent girls. Executing pregnant women. For example, a woman who was eight months pregnant faced a firing squad. Executing teenagers. There have been reports of the executions of girls as young as thirteen.

Tehran's public prosecutor, Ayatollah Mohamadi Gilani, said in an official interview that the execution of a nine-year-old girl is justified by Moslem teachings, because this is the age of puberty and so a nine-year-old is considered a responsible adult. He said, "There is no difference for us between a nine-year-old girl and a 40-year-old man."

We, the National Union of Iranian Women, appeal to all international human rights organizations and all freedom-loving people to hear the voices of our people as we fight for democracy and human dignity.

✧ ✧ ✧

The Mojahed Zahra Mohammed Zadeh was executed in the city of Mashhad. She was six months pregnant. Her only crime was to give refuge to the 87-year-old father and 75-year-old mother of Massoud Rajavi.

Afsaneh Rahimi is 17 years old, a recent high school graduate. She was released from prison two weeks ago and told us the following:

She was beaten several times with 100 strokes of cable and whip, each time 50 strokes to the soles of the feet. In between strokes, they poured water on her feet and then continued, sometimes for four and a half hours.

Hojatollislam Lajevardi has said that beating women's feet is not torture; in fact it purifies their souls. (*Iranshahr*, December 11, 1982)

Hojatollislam Morteza Hosseini, the newly appointed judge responsible for fighting impious acts, has said that women who do not wear the chador will have to face the anger of God and the people. (*The Times*, January 11, 1982)

We have received numerous reports of imprisoned women and girls being raped by the Pasdaran. According to a religious decree issued by Khomeini, women militants are spoils of war and may be used as slaves by Khomeini's followers. This allows all the torturers to rape them. Hadi Ghaffari, a parliamentary deputy, is a notorious rapist. (Office of Massoud Rajavi, Paris; January 13, 1982)

A Pasdar by the name of Jamshid Mehri was injured and taken to the Sorayah Hospital in Tehran. With the help of a member of the hospital Islamic Association, he raped a woman patient while she was ill and unconscious. The Pasdar was arrested but was released four days later and sent to the Iraqi front. (Peykar; July 6, 1981)

Midnight, Tehran. A woman is returning home from a wedding with her husband. They are ordered to halt by a group of Pasdaran. The guards question them about their identities, their destination and so forth, while staring at the woman all the while. The husband answers the questions, hoping to go home soon.

Suddenly the guards become angry and accuse the man of drinking, which he denies. The guards don't argue, but decide to take the couple to the local Committee headquarters. At this point, the wife interrupts, saying that her husband had been forced by his friends to take a few drops, and then urging the guards to forgive him and let them go.

Her well-intentioned lie only aggravates the situation. The couple is taken to headquarters.

As soon as they arrive, the mullah in charge orders them separated and rules that the husband's crime should be punished by 80 lashes. The sentence is immediately carried out, while next door the wife is raped by five guards and officials. When they finish, they tell her to carry the unconscious body of her husband home.

She brings him home and puts him to bed. A few hours later, he awakens and begins to search for her, still suffering from the beating. Eventually he finds her, dead, in the bathroom. She has left a note, saying:

While the guards were whipping you savagely and your cries were echoing throughout the building, five of them came to my cell and raped me, one after the other. I could not live any longer with the shame and misery of this. Please forgive me.

(The weekly publication of the *Moslem Students Society-Britain*, #3; January 20, 1982)

Blood of the Shahid is the Candlelight Which Gives Vision

By Dr. Ali Shariati

ALI SHARIATI IS A CRUCIAL FIGURE IN REVOLUTIONARY ISLAM; HIS WORK CONTINUES TO BE LIONIZED IN IRAN AS THE PRIMARY MUSLIM INTELLECTUAL FORCE FOR KHOMEINI'S IRAN. IT DIDN'T HURT THAT HE DIED IN JUNE 1977 AS THE RESULT OF A SAVAK OPERATION, A MARTYR FOR THE CAUSE. A MEMORIALIZING WEBSITE <WWW.SHARIATI.COM> CONTAINS BIOGRAPHICAL INFO, AS WELL OF ADOBE ACROBAT FILES OF HIS WRITING. SHARIATI PROMOTED THE IDEA OF EMBRACING A MARTYR'S DEATH BEFORE FACING HIS OWN, AND THE FOLLOWING EXCERPT IS FROM AN ESSAY PRINTED IN THE BOOK *JIHAD AND SHAHADAT: STRUGGLE AND MARTYRDOM IN ISLAM*.

Having nothing else to sacrifice, the warrior sacrifices his own life. Because he sacrifices his life for that purpose, he transmits the sacredness of that cause to himself. . . .

The philosophy of the rise of the mujahid is not the same as that of the shahid. The *mujahid* is a sincere warrior who, for the sake of defending his belief and community or spreading and glorifying his faith and community, rises so that he may break, devastate, and conquer the enemy who blocks or endangers his path; thus the difference between attack and defense is *jihad*. He may be killed in this way. Since he dies in this way, we entitle him "*shahid.*" The kind of *shahadat* symbolized by Hamzah is a tragedy suffered by a mujahid in his attempt to conquer and kill the enemy. Thus the type of *shahid* symbolized by Hamzah refers to the one who gets killed as a man who had decided to kill the enemy. He is a *mujahid*. The type of *shahid* symbolized by Husayn is a man who arises for his own death. In the first case, *shahadat* is a negative incident. In the latter case, it is a decisive goal, chosen consciously. In the former, *shahadat* is an accident along the way; in the latter, it is the destination. There death is a tragedy; here death is an ideal. It is an ideology. There the *mujahid*, who had decided to kill the enemy, gets killed. He is to be wailed and eulogized. Here there is no grief, for shahadat is a sublime degree, a final stage of human evolution. It is reaching the absolute by one's own death. Death, in this case, is not a sinister event. It is a weapon in the hands of the friend who with it hits the head of the enemy. In the event that Husayn is completely powerless in defending the truth, he hits the head of the attacking enemy with his own death.

Iran state poster celebrating Dr. Shariati

Shahadat has such a unique radiance; it creates light and heat in the world and in the cold and dark hearts. In the paralyzed wills and thought, immersed in stagnation and darkness, and in the memories which have forgotten all the truths and reminiscences, it creates movement, vision, and hope and provides will, mission, and commitment. The thought, "Nothing can be done," changes into, "Something can be done," or even, "Something must be done." Such death brings about the death of the enemy at the hands of the ones who are educated by the blood of a shahid. By shedding his own blood, the shahid is not in the position to cause the fall of the enemy, [for he can't do so]. He wants to humiliate the enemy, and he does so. By his death, he does not choose to flee the hard and uncomfortable environment. He does not choose shame. Instead of a negative flight, he commits a positive attack. By his death, he condemns the oppressor and provides commitment for the oppressed. He exposes aggression and revives what has hitherto been negated. He reminds the people of what has already been forgotten. In the icy hearts of a people, he bestows the blood of life, resurrection, and movement. For those who have become accustomed to captivity and thus think of captivity as a permanent state, the blood of a shahid is a rescue vessel. For the eyes which can no longer read the truth and cannot see the face of the truth in the darkness of despotism and istihmar (stupification), all they see being nothing but pollution, the blood of the shahid is candlelight which gives vision and serves as the radiant light of guidance for the misguided who wander amidst the homeless caravan, on mountains, in deserts, along byways, and in ditches."

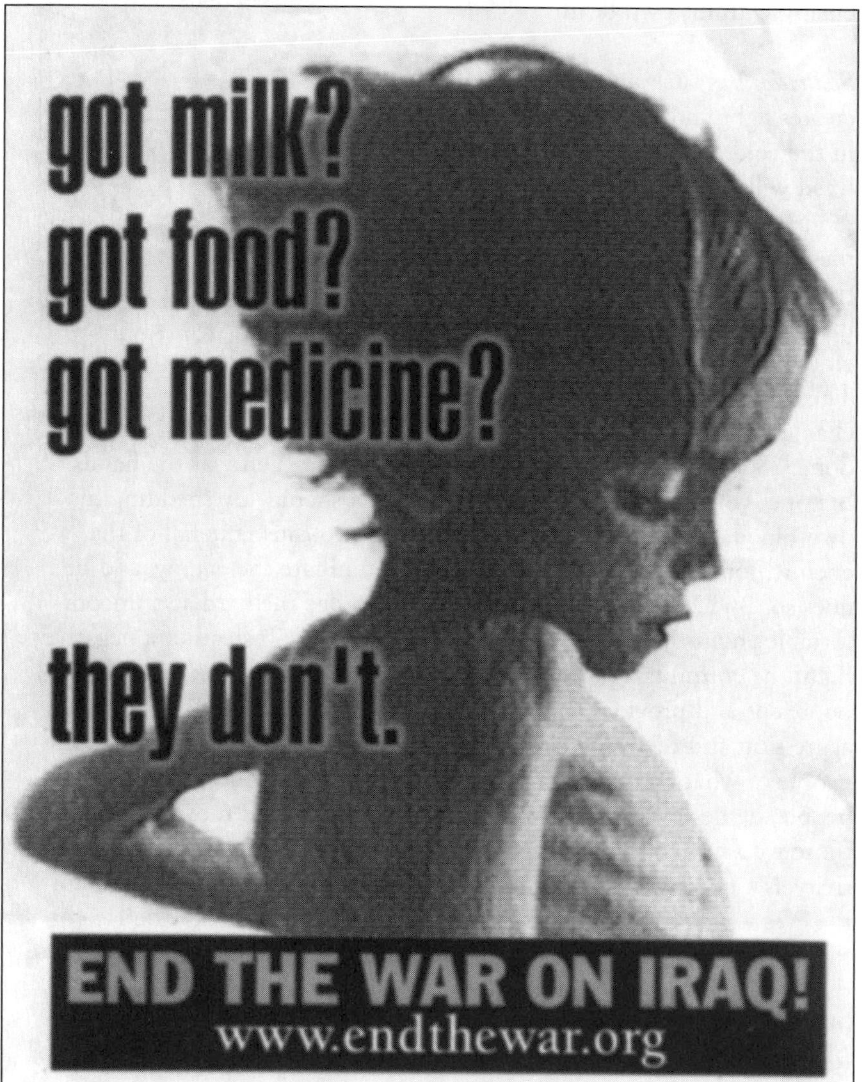
got milk?
got food?
got medicine?
they don't.
END THE WAR ON IRAQ!
www.endthewar.org

SADDAM HUSSEIN'S EMAIL TO AN AMERICAN CITIZEN
In the name of God, the Merciful, the Compassionate

From: Saddam Hussein
To: Christopher J. Love

Dear brother in the family of mankind,

I read your e-mail message of October 2nd carefully and I have well pondered over your emotions regarding the victims of the two towers.

All muslims are not brothers. Iran's depiction of Saddam.

All I can say is presenting my condolences to you, and to reiterate the Muslims linguistic formula on occasion, like this: (God has created us, and to him we return. May God give you long life.)

In a letter of reply like this, there may be no room to say all I want, not to acquaint you with Saddam Hussein's and his comrades in the leadership way of thinking, or of how Iraqis think through them, and of the kind of principles they believe in.

Nevertheless, as you have come to me to know about things, as I understood from your message: the way my people, the Arabs and Muslims, for whom the Arabs are a model, think. You wanted an answer to these questions by addressing yourself to an official in the leadership of this people, and this religion, as well as to someone from the region, you call the Middle-East.

I may give you an explanation to what happened to the two towers, and made America mourn, and inflicted pain and sorrow on others, because such an event has been inflicted on other people in the past, including Arabs and Muslims, in many cases.

I began this letter, by addressing you by the word "brother," although you are neither Iraqi or Arab, nor a Muslim, as can be seen by your name.

Christopher, do you know why I called you brother? Because I never forget, that all mankind come from Adam and Eve. They are all brothers, although they later became different nations and adherent to different religions. Hence, to our understanding, we are one family within the peoples of our earth.

In this family, there is vice and virtue, good and bad people. As long as a man safeguards his rights and duties, within himself, and with humanity, avoids transgressing other peoples' rights, greed, and harming others, and tries to be useful to others, only if they ask for his help, he becomes their brother. But, when any member of this family of mankind oppresses, exploits, unjustly wages wars on them, or lies and deceives others, he would be acting like a devil in the form of man.

We, Arabs, have learned this, brother Christopher, before any nation on earth. We have taught it to you, and to all the adherents of divine religions in the Universe, because God the Almighty, had created Adam and Eve on our land. There is no other chronicle or religion, that pretends, or can prove the contrary. Abraham, the friend of God and the father of all prophets, is one of us, as are all the other prophets. Whenever, God made a revelation, the Arabs were the people to undertake the mission of spreading it to other non-Arab nations, after believing in it themselves. Again, I say that this the fundamental basis of the humanitarian viewpoint of, not only Saddam Hussein and the Iraqi people with him, but also of all Arabs, in all their great homeland, which was divided by British and French colonialism, and which the US is trying to halt its people's unity, and forbid them from enjoying their rights which God bestowed on them on their proper land.

Once again I say, that the basic general rule is that, he who wants to avoid the harm of others, must not harm them. He who wants to enjoy the fruits of his crops must not damage the corps of others. In Iraq, and in the Arab rural regions, and that could be true in different degrees, all over the world, people would fight each other, and some of them maybe killed, but no one ever burns the corps of others. If a criminal ever did so, he would be considered an outcast, and his blood would be shed. Why is such an act so severely judged, although, in comparison, the killing of a man is much more a serious act than the burning of crops?

This customary law in the Iraqi countryside, and maybe in the Arab and world also, is based on two reasons: First: a man can think, hide, and confront others, while crops cannot run, hide, or draw a gun on who wants to harm them. Second: a man cannot live without crops, and for this reason, burning his crops is equal to depriving him from his right to live, and also, because more than one family may have a share in these crops. The damage would be inflicted, not only on the share of the person who is meant to be harmed. It would include the shares of the entire family: women, children, old people, or even young men, who can carry weapons. It is for this reason, that our religion prohibits the killing of woman, children and old men, as well as the uprooting of trees, when a war is fought, by necessity, between two armies.

Do you know, brother Christopher, that your administration, in its war against the people of Iraq, has been burning not only the cereals in silos, but even the harvest by throwing flares in order to make Iraqi people starve?

Do you know what does this mean? It means collective death. Your successive administrations have killed one million and a half Iraqis in eleven years as a result of the blockade it has imposed on Iraq, according to statistics published international organizations, including American humanitarian organizations. You can ask them for details, by Internet.

Food is important and holy to people, because it is related to man's right to live. In the same way medicine has the same sanctity. This is something we have learned from our history and civilization which are thousands of years old, Hence I remind you of the Crusades in 1096-1291 by which the western aggressors came to occupy the land of Arabs, under the pretext of saving Al-Quds from the infidel Muslims as confirmed by documents issued by the west itself. Notice the motto, dear Christopher: "Saving Al-Quds from the infidel Muslims"! So, the Muslims are infidels, not in the eyes of the church, but in the eyes of the Western leaders who mobilized the nations of the West to come as invaders to the holy land of Al-Quds, which is the land on which landed Prophet Mohammed "Peace be upon him" in his divine nocturnal journey.

An individual person in a nation, may be fanatic because of a wrong reasoning, or awareness, but could leaders be so too?

You may say that this is something that happened a very long time ago. But what made me mention it in my letter to you, is what I saw, and heard of some leaders, not ordinary Western citizens. It seems that as if those leaders have recalled all this inventory of fanaticism and hatred of the times of the Crusades, in which the Western leaders considered the Arabs, who are the people of the country and the owners of the land, as infidels who must be expelled from their land by force.

They have, now, planted the Zionist entity in our land to replace that hatred. They have revived the memory of the old Crusades wars by a new war of Crusades, called for by the highest ranking rulers in your country, and in other countries of the west.

Isn't it a paradox, and double standards, to accuse a citizen of fanaticism, to denounce his fanatic attitude and than to mobilize armies against him, and against the country in which he is living, on the basis of nothing but suspicions, while waging an outrageous campaign of hatred and fanaticism to the maximum, which even includes calling for, and the recalling the old Crusades wars against Arab and Muslims, as we mentioned?!

Nevertheless it is well-known, that when the Arabs and Muslims leader Salahdin Al-Ayoubi, was told that the leader of Crusades, Richard, who was called the (Heart of Lion), was ill, he sent him a doctor, and that when his horse was killed in a battle, he refused to fight anyone before mounting another horse.

But do you know that your administration has, one way or the other, deprived the people of Iraq from food and medicine?

Do you know the meaning of the death of one million and a half human beings, in addition to those who are killed by bombs and missiles?

Maybe, you and the majority of the peoples of America, do not know that American bombard men, and death harvest caused by fighter jets, and missiles, are ongoing in Iraq for the last eleven years, and have not stopped until the moment of writing this letter? Do you know why you don't know?! Because the media in your country which is controlled by Zionism, do not want you to known. And because your administration, which says that it is necessary for the peoples of the world to know, does not want you to know. You should ask your administration, why doesn't it speak to you about facts? Why doesn't present you any information except its devilish fancies?

As for me, I can tell you why Zionism doesn't want you to know the harm inflicted on the people of Iraq. The Zionist and the American administration believe that it is necessary that Iraqis die. The Jewish Albright, the former US Secretary of State, spoke in this way, or in a similar case, when she said that the objectives of the US foreign policy, justify the death of Iraqi children. The reason is that the Iraqis refused the Zionist usurpation of Arab and Palestinian territories. They refuse to accept the crimes of occupying Palestine, the Golan, and the Lebanese territories, and refuse do accept the Zionists confiscation of the holy places of the believers in God, including Muslims there.

Hence, whenever Zionism has the upper hand over high ranking officials in America, it pushes the administration toward a confrontation with the Arabs, and reinforces Zionist entity, at the expense of Arab and Palestinian rights.

By the way, please ask for the videotapes to see how the Jews, in the occupied territories, kill old men, children and women, in front of the cameras. Do you know that all these crimes have been perpetrated since 1935 by using Western weapons, and in fact, American weapons in particular, weapons that cost billions of dollars, the administration takes from American tax-payers to be granted as an aid to the Zionist entity?

So, the Arabs and Muslims did not cross the Atlantic, as invaders or aggressors. They did not colonize America. It is America that brought them all kinds of sufferings. If any of your rulers says something different, please discuss it with them. For example, if they say that they crossed the Atlantic to make sure that you get your oil supplies, tell them that oil is guaranteed by mutual interests and non-aggression, not by aggressions, killing, violating other people's rights, and destroying all sanctities.

If your rules say that, they crossed the Atlantic in the past to fight Communism so that it does not invade the West, tell them that the ex-Soviet Union has fallen apart, as has the Warsaw Pact, although I personally don't accept the contradiction between the call for the freedom of thinking, and saying that the Western way of thinking is more vital and modern, as the intellectuals and leaders of the West say, and between fearing Communism.

Do you know, brother Christopher, that the NATO, which was created under the pretext of confronting Communism, still exists, and was even enlarged after the collapse of the Warsaw Pact. Decisions of death are taken in its name, against some peoples of the world sometimes, as was the case against Yugoslavia, because it is an independent, and Slovak country, and because the majority of its people are Orthodox, not because their oppression of Muslims in Bosnia, as was claimed, to fool the Muslims, and falsely win their support in international forums?

If we go on, we can give thousands of examples on the blind fanaticism exported by the West to the world with American participation during the last 50 years. But I don't want to burden you. I only want to tell you that the people of Iraq are against all kinds of fanaticism, whether based on religion, nationality or race. They are against the use of fanaticism as a cover for harming people whom God does not accept to harm. They call for love between the peoples and nations of the world. Nevertheless, we do not believe in love on one side only.

Iraq has been harmed severely by the fanaticism of others, including America. It was also severely harmed by terrorism. Maybe you don't know that many the members of our leadership were victims of terrorism and terrorists. Some of them escaped death, by the will of

God, after being injured or missed by the terrorists, in addition to the pain inflicted to our people.

Do you know brother, that your administration's reaction to that, was one of encouraging it and rejoicing ? Do you know that your administration has been encouraging terrorism against us for the past eleven years, calling to overthrow us by force, allocating special funds to do so, and boasting about not fearing God, as it publicly announces that on TV screens, because Iraq does not have the same destructive force and armament of America? The Palestinians, whose right to resist the occupation forces are guaranteed by the international law, promulgated by America and the other big powers, are considered terrorists because they resist the Zionist occupation of their territories, and holy places.

Tell me, brother, if the Vatican is occupied by Arabs, or non-Arab Muslims, wouldn't its people fight the occupying forces? Wouldn't the English people fight for the Westminster cathedral? Or wouldn't the French people, defend Notre Dame? I say they must fight for them! Why, then, are your armies occupying Mecca and the land of our Prophet? Why are you occupying the regional waters in the Arab Gulf, in addition to territories in its countries ? Why is your ally, the Zionist entity, occupying our holy places, and territories, in Palestine, by using your arms, and financial, political, media, and moral support? And, why are your administration killing people, including children in Iraq, Afghanistan, and in Palestine now, just as it did, before that, in Lebanon, Sudan, Somalia and Libya, and the list of Arabs and Muslims to be killed is long?!

I know that Arabs are far from being fanatic. Do you know why? Because, God, the Almighty, assigned them with the mission of delivering the messages of all religions to humanity, and not to Arabs alone. They have fulfilled their mission, so that all Christians are now indebted to Arabs for guiding them to Faith, which God wanted them to have when, He made it possible for them to reach you, or for you to reach them, so that you know what they believe in, and be affected by it.

I know that Arabs, in general, do not adopt fanatic stances against any people for religious reasons. But, can anyone guarantee that one fanaticism does not create another? Can anyone guarantee that the death toll and killing, inflicted upon Arabs and Muslims by the American armies, would not lead to a counter-reaction, whether that reaction is well guided, or is a random one, that pleases no one except those who carry it out?

These words are general rules and principles, although I still do not know who is behind what happened to the towers on September

11, 2001. Your government did not help me, or anyone else, by showing, or communicating the information it possesses, so that we can elaborate an opinion, if it needed to know the opinion of those whose people it daily attacks with bombs, starves to death, and deprives from the right to live, construct, and deploy their creativity.

Our law, which is borne of our religion and heritage, and of our reasoning which is thousands of years deep, stipulates: "the Plaintiff should present evidence and the defendant should take an oath." But the plaintiff, which is your administration did not present any evidence so far. Nevertheless, it accused the people it accused, without showing us, or anyone else, any evidence, except for Blair and the ruler of Pakistan, as they both said. The people accused have not pleaded guilty.

Anyhow, I don't think that your administration deserves the condolences of Iraqis, except if it presents its condolences to the Iraqi people for the one million and a half Iraqis it killed, and apologizes to them, for the crimes it committed against them. As for the American people, we have sent them our condolences through Mr. Tareq Aziz's letter to the Voices in the Wilderness Organization Mr. Ramsay Clark, the former Attorney General, on Sept. 18, 2001.

Dear brother,

He who does not want his harvest to be burned must not set fire to the harvest of others. He, who wants to live in security, should accept the right of others to live in security, and he who is irritated, or raged by an aggression, should not aggress others. He who cherishes the lives of his people, should remember that God created all people equal at birth, in death, and in their human values, that's why he should remember that the lives of others are also cherished by their people. He who strikes people with remote control missiles should expect, that there would be someone to seek revenge, for his dignity and the dignity of his people, and consequently does something harmful, or fatal, by stabbing a dagger in his body, or taking his life by a sword.

He who sees himself as a man, who revenges his dignity, should not deprive other men from their dignity, and he who calls for the respect of his people, men and women, should respect the people of other nations.

He who remembers God, must not ignore or forget, that God the Almighty, is capable of everything, and of providing the weak with what makes those who underestimate them, make heed of their rights and respect them.

In any case, the security of humanity is, in our view, a responsibility on the shoulders of all good people. Any irresponsible action on the part of superpowers may give way to a counter irresponsible action by the people, even if the smaller nations do not take such a course of action.

Finally there is something in your letter that you asked to be corrected, if it was wrong about the ex-President Bush, is giving us reason to believe that he was our ally in the issue of Kuwait, but he was forced to abide with the United Nations. The Fact, Mr. Christopher, is that, it was President Bush who adopted the logic of war, right from the first day of those events. He refused solving the problem politically, and entering into a dialogue with us. The resolutions of the United Nations were, in fact, adopted under pressure from Bush and his administration. He then waged the war against Iraq, in a way that had nothing to do with the issue of Kuwait. His objective was to destroy all Iraq, and to deprive its people of the edifice they built, in several decades, and not merely getting the Iraqi armed forces out of Kuwait. He did that in 1991, and he later committed similar things, and he and his administration, are still doing so under different pretexts and justifications.

Wishing that you will have the opportunity to see the facts as they are, and not as your administration present them,

Yours truly

Saddam Hussein
Baghdad, Shabban 2,1422 H.
October 18, 2001

الغزو الايراني للعراق والغزو الصهيوني للبنان حلقة واحدة للتآمر على الامة العربية

مَصيرُ الغزاةِ الايرانيين القبرُ أو الاسرُ

THE GREEN BOOK
By Muammar al Qaddafi

QADDAFI PRECOCIOUSLY ENGINEERED HIS COUP OF THE LIBYAN GOVERNMENT WHEN HE WAS ONLY 27 YEARS OLD. HIS ROLE MODEL WAS GAMEL ABDEL-NASSER, THE EGYPTIAN LEADER WHO PROMOTED ARAB NATIONALISM, A FORM OF GOVERNING HATED BY THE MUSLIM BROTHERHOOD AND RELATED GROUPS WHO WISHED TO SEE THE QUR'AN BECOME THE SOLE LAWBOOK.

THOUGH HE DOES NOT OPERATE HIS GOVERNMENT ON A QUR'AN-BASED MODEL, QADDAFI CLAIMS TO BE DEVOUT. *ESCAPE TO HELL*, QADDAFI'S COLLECTION OF SHORT STORIES (ONE SEEN BELOW), ARE ALL BASED ON, OR INSPIRED BY, QUR'ANIC VERSE.

ACCUSED FOR HAVING A HAND IN MANY TERRORIST CRIMES, QADDAFI, HIMSLEF ANGERED MANY ISLAMISTS FOR SAYING, AFTER 9/11/01, "AMERICA HAS A RIGHT TO SEEK REVENGE FOR ATTACKS ON ITS SOIL." IN 1986, RONALD REAGAN'S ADMINISTRATION, BLAMING LIBYA FOR TERRORIST ATTACKS, MADE A POINT OF BOMBING QADDAFI'S HOME, KILLING HIS YOUNGEST DAUGHTER.

DICTATOR QADDAFI PUBLISHED DEMOCRATIC/PARLIAMENTARIAN/QUASI-SOCIALIST POLITICAL IDEAS IN HIS *GREEN BOOK*, A RATHER BIZARRE TEXT THAT, MORE THAN ANYTHING, DEMONSTRATES THE LIBYAN LEADER'S DESIRE TO BE SEEN AS INSPIRATIONAL.

THE CHAPTER, "BLACK PEOPLE," SEEN BELOW, IS ESPECIALLY INTER-ESTING IN LIGHT OF QADDAFI'S SUPPORT OF AMERICA'S NATION OF ISLAM, AN ORGANIZATION THAT, LIKE QADDAFI, IS QUITE VOCAL IN ITS ATTACKS OF AMERICAN GOVERNMENTS, AND REFUSES TO FOLLOW THE

QUR'AN EXPLICITLY. From *The Green Book*, Part Three: "The Social Basis of the Third Universal Theory"

Black People Will Prevail in the World

The latest age of slavery has been the enslavement of Black people by White people. The memory of this age will persist in the thinking of Black people until they have vindicated themselves.

This tragic and historic event, the resulting bitter feeling, and the yearning for the vindication of a whole race, constitute a psychological motivation of Black people to vengeance and prevalence that cannot be disregarded. In addition, the inevitable cycle of social history, which includes Yellow people's domination of the world when it marched from Asia, and the White people's carrying out a wide-ranging colonialist movement covering all the continents of the world, is now giving way to the re-emergence of Black people.

Black people are now in a very backward social situation, but such backwardness works to bring about their numerical superiority because their low standard of living has shielded them from knowing methods of birth control and family planning. Also, their old social traditions place no limit to marriages, leading to their accelerated growth. The population of other races has decreased because of birth control, restrictions on marriage and continuous occupation in work, unlike the Blacks, who tend to be lethargic in a climate which is continually hot.

Sport, Horsemanship and the Stage

Sport is either private, like the prayer which one performs alone, inside a closed room, or, public, performed collectively in open places, like the prayer which is practiced collectively in places of worship. The first type of sport concerns the individuals themselves, while the second type is of concern to all people. It must be practiced by all and should not be left to anyone else to practice on their behalf. It is unreasonable for crowds to enter places of worship just to view a person or a group of people praying without taking part. It is equally unreasonable for crowds to enter playgrounds and arenas to watch a player or a team without participating themselves.

Sport is like praying, eating, and the feeling of coolness and warmth. It is unlikely that crowds will enter a restaurant just to look at a person or a group of people eat. It is also unlikely to let a person or a group of people enjoy warmth or ventilation on their behalf. It is equally illogical for the society to allow an individual or a team to monopolize sports while the society as a whole pays the costs of such a monopoly for the exclusive benefit of one person or team. In the same way people should not allow an individual or a group, whether it is a party, class, sect tribe or parliament to replace them in deciding their destiny and in defining their needs.

Private sport is of concern only to those who practice it on their own and at their own expense. Public sport is a public need and the people cannot be either democratically or physically represented by others in its practice. Physically, the representative cannot transmit to others how his body and morale benefit from sport. Democratically, no individual or team has the right to monopolize sport, power wealth or arms for themselves. Sporting clubs represent the basic organization of traditional sport in the world today. They retain all expenditure and public facilities allocated to sport in every state. These institutions are social monopolistic instruments, like all dictatorial political instruments which monopolize authority, economic instruments which monopolize wealth, and traditional military instruments which monopolize arms. As the era of the masses does away with the instruments monopolizing power, wealth and arms, it will, inevitably, destroy the monopoly of social activity in such areas as sports, horsemanship and so forth. The masses who queue to vote for a candidate to represent them in deciding their destiny act on the impossible assumption that this person will represent them and embody, on their behalf, their dignity, sovereignty and point of view. However those masses, who are robbed of their will and dignity, are reduced to mere spectators, watching another person performing what they should, naturally, be doing themselves.

The same holds true of the crowds who, because of ignorance, fail to practice sport by and for themselves. They are fooled by monopolistic instruments which endeavor to stupefy them and divert them to indulging in laughter and applause instead. Sport, as a social activity, must be for the masses, just as power, wealth and arms should be in the hands of the people.

Public sport is for all the masses. It is a right of all people for their health and recreational benefit. It is mere stupidity to leave its benefits to certain individuals and teams who monopolize these while the masses provide the facilities and pay the expenses for the establishment of public sports. The thousands who crowd stadiums to view, applaud and laugh are foolish people who have failed to carry out the activity themselves. They line up lethargically in the stands of the sports grounds, and applaud those heroes who wrest from

them the initiative, dominate the field and control the sport, and in so doing exploit the facilities that the masses provide. Originally, the public grandstands were designed to demarcate the masses from the playing fields and grounds; to prevent the masses from having access to the playing fields. When the masses march and play sport in the center of playing fields and open spaces, stadiums will be vacant and become redundant. This will take place when the masses become aware of the fact that sport is a public activity which must be practiced rather than watched. This is more reasonable as an alternative — a helpless apathetic minority that merely watches.

Grandstands will disappear because no one will be there to occupy them. Those who are unable to perform the roles of heroism in life, who are ignorant of the events of history, who fall short of envisaging the future and who are not serious enough in their own lives, are the trivial people who fill the seats of the theatres and cinemas to watch the events of life in order to learn their course. They are like pupils who occupy school desks because they are uneducated and also initially illiterate.

Those who direct the course of life for themselves have no need to watch life working through actors on the stage or in the cinemas. Horsemen who hold the reins of their horses likewise have no seat in the grandstands at the race course. If every person has a horse, no one will be there to watch and applaud. The sitting spectators are only those who are too helpless to perform this kind of activity because they are not horsemen.

The Bedouin peoples show no interest in theatres and shows because they are very serious and industrious. As they have created a serious life, they ridicule acting. Bedouin societies also do not watch performers, but perform games and take part in joyful ceremonies because they naturally recognize the need for these activities and practice them spontaneously.

Boxing and wrestling are evidence that mankind has not rid itself of all savage behavior. Inevitably it will come to an end when humanity ascends the ladder of civilization. Human sacrifice and pistol duels were familiar practices in previous stages of human evolution. However, those savage practices came to an end years ago. People now laugh at themselves and regret such acts. This will be the fate of boxing and wrestling after tens or hundreds of years. The more the people become civilized and sophisticated, the more they are able to ward off both the performance and the encouragement of these practices.

FROM *ESCAPE TO HELL AND OTHER STORIES*
The Earth
You can leave everything, except the earth. The earth is the only thing you cannot do without. If you destroy other things, you might not lose out, but beware of destroying the earth, because you will then lose everything! The source of biological life, at which human life stands at the top, is food. The earth is the container for this nourishment, which comes in different types . . . solid, fluid, gaseous. The earth is its container, so do not break the only container we have, for which there is no substitute. If you destroy agricultural land, for example, it is as if you are destroying the only vessel containing your food, without which you will not be able to consume it. If you destroy agricultural land, it is as if you are destroying the only vessel containing your drink, for which there is no other receptacle, so how will you be able to consume it? The earth is the lung through which you breathe, so if you destroy it, you will have no way to breathe. If the rain falls down upon you without having land, you will not benefit at all. Therefore, the sky has no value for us without our having land.

If oxygen is found somewhere in outer space, what is the benefit if there is no earth? All of history's conflicts throughout the ages have been led by man against man, or against nature, have been about land.

Land has been the crux of the conflict. Even space has been used for the sake of land. Truly, the earth is your mother; she gave birth to you from her insides. She is the one who nursed you and fed you. Do not be disobedient to your mother — and do not shear her hair, cut off her limbs, rip her flesh, or wound her body. You must only trim her nails, make her body clean of dirt or filth. Give her medicine to cure any disease. Do not place great weights above her breast, weights of mud or stone above her ribs. Respect her, and remember that if you are too harsh with her, you will not find another. Sweep the accumulated iron, mud, and stone from her back. Relieve her of the burdens that others have placed on her unfairly. Revere the cradle in which you grew up, the lap in which you lay. Do not destroy your final resting-place, your place of refuge, or you are the losers [1] and you shall truly regret it. [2]

Land remains land only if we preserve its bounty. Land that is bountiful is truly useful land — guard it well. If we lay tile or pave it, build upon it, we will have killed it, and it will no longer give us its bounty. It will then become merely tile or asphalt, concrete or marble. And these things do not give us anything. They do not grow plants or give us water; they are useful to neither man nor animal. The earth will then have died. Do not kill the earth — do not kill your very life. The earth is water and nourishment, and the dead land that has been covered by buildings and construction does not give this water and nourishment. Thus, there is no life upon a dead earth. What kind of people are they who kill the earth and bury it alive? Upon what kind of land will their life depend afterwards? Where will they live, and where will they obtain their food and drink? The earth is something for which there is no alternative, so whither then are you going? [3] In heaven there are trees, and not roads, sidewalks, public squares or buildings. Ruining the earth is its misuse, its transformation into something other than land good for producing water and food. Thus, those who turn agricultural land into land that cannot grow anything are the ones who spoil this land. [4]

Notes:
1. Implicit reference to many verses; especially Sura 5, verse 30; Sura 2, verse 27; Sura 103, verse 2.
2. As in to become "repentant"; Qur'an, Sura 5, verse 31.
3. Qur'an, Sura 81, verse 26.
4. Qur'an, Sura 18, verse 94.

Jihad, Mankind's Only Hope
By Abdul Malik, KCOM Journal

Khilafah.com, Khilafah.org, Hizbu-Tahrir.com, muslimstudent.org.uk, al-aqsa.org hilafet.com and probably many other websites are propagation/propaganda arms of a canny London-based organization devoted to the overthrow of the American superstate and its political servants, particularly in territories with large Muslim populations still ruled by secular law. Hizb-ut-Tahrir (meaning "Islamic Liberation Party") was founded in 1952 by Sheikh Taqiuddin an-Nabhani in Beirut. In unpronounceable Central Asian territories like Kyrgzstan, Tajikistan, and Uzbekistan, Hizb-ut-Tahrir is a banned party but a powerful presence nonetheless, where their secret membership is urged to practice Jihad against their secular power structures.

Khilafah means "the political system of Islam," which most of the Khilafah websites attribute to Mustapha Kamal's power play within Turkey in 1924 that replaced the Ottoman Empire's Islamic State with capitalism and Western rhetoric.

In Muslim-friendly London, Hizb-ut-Tahrir held an international Islamic fundamentalist conference at Wembley Arena in August 1994, where 8,000 audience members cheered the invocation of Jihad against the country that allowed them to convene and whose police force arrested their only visible opponents — a set of "OutRage! Queers" protesting the execution of "more than four thousand lesbians and gays in Iran."

Several websites say that Hizb-ut-Tahrir is a "deviant sect" due to its failure to accept the "Ahaad Hadith" as a relevant part of the holy text. Hizb-ut-Tahrir interprets Islamic law in such a way that makes smoking, listening to music, and the viewing of nude photographs permissible, but worst of all, rants an outraged Muslim in his exposé, its members are allowed to imitate homosexuals. How? Hizb-ut-Tahrir permits the shaving of beards. Extremely minor divisions in Islamic belief have divided the religion since the ascendance of its Prophet. The CIA has no doubt taken note that widening these divisions would be the simplest, cheapest and most effective way to drive a stake through Islam's ideological heart.

Whether or not Hizb-ut-Tahrir fails to get excited about the presence of shaving cream, its "Jihad Under Fire" essay,

LIKE OTHERS ON KHILAFAH.COM'S MAGAZINES AND JOURNALS, POINTS
ITS IDEOLOGICAL BAZOOKA AT THE WAY AMERICA USES ITS MASS MEDIA
MECHANISM TO PORTRAY ISLAM. HERE, THE AUTHOR TAKES NOTE OF
ALL THE INSTANT MULLAHS, ACADEMIC "EXPERTS" AND APOLOGISTS
WHO APPEARED ON TELEVISION AFTER 9/11/01 TO DECLARE ISLAM A
RELIGION OF ABSOLUTE PEACE, AND THAT JIHAD SHOULD ONLY BE
THOUGHT OF AS A STRUGGLE WITH SELF, AND NOT OTHERS.

IF ONE PUTS DOWN THE MORNING PAPER'S CLIFF NOTES ON ISLAM
AND ACTUALLY READS THE QUR'AN, IT BECOMES IMMEDIATELY EVIDENT
THAT ALLAH, THROUGH THE MOUTHPIECE OF THE PROPHET MUHAMMAD,
DICTATES ABSOLUTE SUBMISSION TO HIS COMMANDS, WHICH MUST BE FOL-
LOWED EXPLICITLY AND PROPAGATED THROUGHOUT THE WORLD BY EVERY
BELIEVER. FEAR OF ALLAH IS PROPAGATED BY THE MENACE OF SEVERE PUN-
ISHMENTS, BOTH HERE, AND IN A SKIN-FLAYING HEREAFTER, FOR ANYONE
WHO FAILS TO HEW THE MANY COMMANDS. ISLAM IS A GROWTH RELIGION,
SINCE THE QUR'AN PROMISES SPECIAL PAYBACK AND VENGEANCE TO THE
HUMILIATED AND MISERABLE, ESPECIALLY FOR THOSE WHO MAKE WHAT IS
CONSIDERED AN HEROIC SACRIFICE.

HIZB-UT-TAHRIR'S READING OF PALESTINE SITUATION, AVAILABLE AS
A PDF FILE ON KHILAFAH.ORG IN ITS "ATROCITY" SECTION, HAS ACUTE
UNDERSTANDINGS UNSEEN ON MOST ISLAMIC POLITICAL SITES, PARTICU-
LARLY SINCE IT DIFFERENTIATES AMERICAN FROM ZIONIST INTERESTS IN
THE MIDDLE EAST, AND DOES NOT FALL INTO AN ANGRY, EMOTIONAL,
CONSPIRATORIAL LURCH. WHAT'S CURIOUS ABOUT HIZB-UT-TAHRIR IS
THAT IT'S ABLE TO PRODUCE ENERGETIC AND INTELLIGENT MATERIAL,
AND MAKE HUGE POLITICAL STRIDES BEHIND THE SCENES, ALMOST
INVISIBLY. IF THEY KEEP IT UP, THIS WILL BE AN ORGANIZATION TO BE
RECKONED WITH.

"Never will the Jews nor the Christians be pleased with you till you
follow their religion. Say: 'Verily, the guidance of Allah is the (only)
guidance.' And if you were to follow their desires after what you have
received of Knowledge, then you would have against Allah neither any
protector/guardian nor any helper." (TMQ 2:120)

In 1857, the Muslims of India rose up and fought a jihad against
their British occupiers. They were brutally suppressed. In the reprisals
that followed, the "civilized" Brits stuffed pork into the mouths of
those due for execution, and sewed them into pigs' skins. Many were
then fired live out of cannons.

A new brand of "scholar" emerged after what is now referred to as the Indian Mutiny. These mentally defeated modernists, anxious to please their British masters, insisted that armed resistance was not justified and sought to re-define jihad. Sir Sayyid Ahmad Khan, knighted for saving the life of a senior British army officer during the uprising, presented Islam as a pacifist religion. Another loyal subject, Maulavi Cheragh Ali, wrote *A Critical Exposition of the Popular "Jihad."* According to the subtitle, the book's appendices showed "that the word jihad does not exegetically mean warfare."

Egypt, too, has had its fair share of anti-jihad modernists who wanted to reconcile Islam with Western ways, among them the notorious freemasons Muhammad Abduh and Jamaluddin Afghani. The former was rewarded by being appointed Shaykh of Al-Azhar by the British.

Anwar Sadat, the Egyptian President who was assassinated because he had signed the infamous Camp David accords with Israel, did not shy away from trying to derail the concept of jihad. In 1979, the same year as the peace treaty, he wrote an article entitled "The Greater Jihad" for the first issue of a Sufi journal. He promoted the idea that fighting against the disbelievers is far less important than struggling against one's own desires.

He based his argument on a rather weak narration, which describes struggling against the desires as being better than fighting on the battlefield. The narrator, Yahya ibn al-Ala', is described by Ahmad bin Hanbal as "a liar and forger of *ahadith*." Ibn Hajar Asqalani says "he was accused of forging *ahadith*." Moreover, this narration contradicts the many authentic ahadith which prove the clear understanding of jihad.

In the aftermath of the attacks on the World Trade Center, George Bush declared, "Islam is peace." The concept of jihad came under scrutiny and a number of apologists were wheeled out to tell the West what they wanted to hear. One of these media darlings, who was given "100% security clearance" by the FBI and now advises the White House, declared: "The Prophet said the greatest jihad is the struggle of a man against his own evil influences." He also insisted in a BBC interview on October 7, the same day the attack on Afghanistan began, that the U.S. had "no option" but to take military action. He maintained, "Americans have a right to defend and pre-empt any acts of aggression against themselves, most certainly." Apparently, while America is entitled to carpet-bomb Afghanistan, Muslims must focus on following the Sufi path!

On British television, another self-appointed "shaykh" proclaimed: "Jihad is a term used in the Qur'an for striving, not for fighting . . . For instance if I actually work as a teacher, as a carpenter, as anything I am called a *mujahid*, I am making jihad, that is striving to serve the community at large."

In fact, the Shari'ah meaning of jihad is to exert one's utmost effort in fighting the disbelievers for the sake of Allah (SWT), directly by fighting in the battlefield or indirectly by helping this struggle by monetary means, scholarly verdicts, and encouraging people to participate in the jihad. Other tasks which may be difficult and thus involve some exertion but are not related to fighting, such as fixing a boiler or making a chair, are not termed jihad as understood in the Shari'ah.

In the verses of the Qur'an and ahadith about jihad, the expression fi sabil illah (in the cause of Allah) is commonly used. The following hadith clarifies what this means:

A man came to the Prophet and asked, "A man fights for war booty; another fights for fame and a third fights for showing off; which of them fights in Allah's cause?" The Prophet (*sallalahu alaihi wasallam*) said, "He who fights so that Allah's word (i.e. Islam) should be superior fights in Allah's cause."

After the establishment of the first Islamic state in Madina, the Prophet (*sallalahu alaihi wasallam*) strove to make Allah's word superior through da'wa, and by waging jihad when the call was rejected so as to remove the obstacles in the way of the Islamic call. The Quraysh had to be removed, as it was a physical barrier between Islam and the people, who could then be invited to Islam while witnessing the justice of its rule. This method of spreading Islam was followed by the Muslims after the Prophet (*sallalahu alaihi wassalam*) — Muslims such as Rib'i bin 'Amir who was sent by Umar (ra) as an emissary to the court of the Persian general Rustum, and who announced:

"Allah has sent us forward so that we may liberate, whomsoever he wills, from following men (and lead them) to the obedience of Allah, and pull them out of their narrow world into the broader one, and from under the tyranny of (various) ways of life into the justice of Islam." (Ibn Kathir, al-Bidayah wa al-Nihayah).

Today, the whole world suffers under the unchallenged tyranny of Capitalism and U.S. hegemony. The rule of Islam and its propagation through *da'wa* and jihad is humankind's only hope.

ALGERIA, A VIOLENT STATE OF MIND

AN ASTONISHINGLY VOLATILE CIVIL WAR HAS FACTIONS OF ARMED
ISLAMIC FUNDAMENTALISTS WARRING WITH EACH OTHER, AND SECULAR
FORCES. SINCE 1993, 50,000 ALGERIANS HAVE BEEN KILLED, NEARLY 70
JOURNALISTS HAVE HAD THEIR THROATS SLIT, AND 100 FOREIGNERS
HAVE BEEN MUTILATED IN THE SUCCESSFUL ATTEMPT TO INHIBIT
TOURISTS AND JOURNALISTS FROM COMING INTO THEIR COUNTRY.

THE FRENCH HAVE BEEN INVOLVED SINCE THE '50S, WHEN THEY PERPE-
TRATED THEIR OWN VIOLENT COLONIAL WAR. 800,000 ALGERIANS LIVE
IN FRANCE, AND THE FRENCH COMMUNITY IN ALGERIA, STILL ADDS UP
TO 700,000.

ARMED ISLAMIC GROUP OR GIA IS PERHAPS THE MOST SPECTACULARLY
BRUTAL IN THE BRUTAL STATE OF ALGERIA. THE ARTICLES BELOW FILL
US IN ON THEIR RECENT PARTICULARS.

Armed Islamic Group leader speaks out
(September 1997) One of the Algerian leaders of the rebel Armed
Islamic Group (GIA), 32-year-old Mahfoud Assouli (Abu al-Munthir)
said, "Our fighters kill only those who deserve to die." The Algerian
government placed a $16,000 bounty on his head.

In an interview with a newspaper which claims to be the official voice
of GIA in Europe, he said: "We do nothing more than fulfill the will
of God and his prophet."

When asked about killing innocent women and children he added, "If
they were in the same area as the enemy they will be accepted as
martyrs."

He warned Algerian citizens who do not pray, drink alcohol, take
drugs, as well as homosexuals and immodest or debauched women
that their fate is death.

Assouli divides Algerian citizens into three categories. The first are
those take up the fight against Islam. The second are those who join
the Jihad. The third are those who support Islam but also with the
democracy and elections. He maintains that all in the third category
are impostors and should be killed.

Armed Islamic Group Claims Massacre Responsibility
(August 1998) In the Douera district south of Algiers early on August 14 attackers killed 15 people, including six children and two women, by slitting their throats.

The rebel Armed Islamic Group's (GIA) leader said that all responsibility for these and other massacres belongs to his party, and he will continue in this way to kill "all enemies of Islam," from the youngest of their children to the oldest of their elderly. Also he declared that his GIA is the only Flame of Jihad in Algeria.

Islamic Salvation Front leader Abbas Madni, recently released from Algerian prison, condemned the attack and all other collective massacres against civilians, and he stated that the massacres have nothing whatsoever to do with Islam, *Al-Ahram Al-Masai* newspaper said yesterday.

Regarding Algeria's Armed Islamic Group (GIA)
From "Medea"
It is difficult to evaluate precisely the structure and size of the GIA (estimated at about 10 thousand men) because it is composed of so many more or less autonomous groups controlled by as many emirs (although a single command unit exists). Like the FIS, there is a split within the GIA between Salafists — who speak in terms of a world Islamic revolution — and Djazarists — who seek power in Algeria only.

The GIA mainly recruits among former Algerian volunteers trained in guerilla tactics by the Afghan freedom fighters and others who fought in Bosnia, as well as among young men from the most disadvantaged social groups. Many members of the dissolved FIS joined its ranks and local gangs of petty criminals and dealers are also said to be mixed up in its activities. A large part of its membership is said to be of Kabyle or Berber origin.

Although their objectives are identical and their methods similar for the greater part, relations between the GIA and the Army of Islamic Salvation (AIS, the armed branch of the FIS) are riddled with personal animosity and rivalry between leaders and regions. The AIS even condemned certain of the GIA's bloody activities. On the other hand, rapprochement with the moderate wing of the FIS seems excluded: FIS leaders who support dialogue with the government have been "condemned to death" by the GIA.

Some observers claim that the Algerian military supported GIA violence, sanctioning it to a certain extent in order to legitimate its own use of repression. Others were speaking of direct involvement of certain Algerian security services in the escalation of violence. Similarly, there were questions about an objective alliance between the Islamic guerrilla and certain corrupt circles such as the "political-financial mafia" (which includes former FLN members, the former single party) in the murder of intellectuals who dared condemn the corruption which is corroding Algerian society.

The election of Abdelaziz Bouteflika as President of Algeria in April 1999, has been a turning point in the civil war which started in January 1992. After the cease-fire proclaimed by the Islamic Salvation Army (AIS) in June, the President pardoned 2,300 jailed Islamists and presented to Parliament the "National Harmony Law" providing an amnesty for members and supporters of the AIS. The proposals contained in the law were submitted to a referendum on 16 September 1999 and got a massive support in the population (98% of Yes). The announcement of the referendum led to a surge of violence from the GIA in the weeks before it took place but it seems that the GIA is more and more isolated. Cruel massacres perpetrated now and then remind people that the civil war is not yet over.

Nation of Islam Q and A

This set of questions and answers was passed out to new members at their first meeting.

1. **Who made the Holy Koran or Bible? How long ago? Will you tell us why does Islam renew her history every twenty-five thousand years?**
The Holy Koran or Bible is made by the original people, who is Allah, the Supreme Being or Black Man of Asia. The Koran will expire in the year twenty-five thousand — nine thousand and eighty years from the date of this writing. The Nation of Islam is all wise and does everything right and exact. The Planet Earth, which is the home of Islam, is approximately twenty-five thousand miles in circumference, so the wise man of the East (Black Man) makes history or Koran to equal his home circumference; a year to every mile and thus, every time his history lasts twenty-five thousand years, he renews it for another twenty-five thousand years.

2. **What is the circumference?**
24,896 miles. Approximately 25,000 miles.

3. **What is the diameter of the planet?**
7,926 miles. Seven thousand nine hundred twenty-six miles.

4. **What is the total square mileage?**
196,940,000 square miles. One hundred ninety-six million, nine hundred forty thousand square miles.

5. **How much is the land and water?**
57,255,000 square miles of land. 139,685,000 square miles of water.

6. **What is the total weight of our planet?**
6 sextillion tons. A unit followed by twenty-one ciphers.

7. **How fast does our planet travel per hour?**
1,037 ⅓ miles per hour.

8. **What makes rain, hail, snow and earthquakes?**
The Earth is approximately covered under water. Approximately ¾'s of its surface. The sun and moon, having attracting power on our planet

while our planet makes the terrific speed of 1,037 ⅓ miles per hour on its way around the sun. The sun draws this water up Into the Earth's rotation, which is called gravitation, in a fine mist that the naked eye can hardly detect. But as this mist ascends higher and increasing with other mists of water in different currents of the atmosphere until when she becomes heavier than gravitation, then she distills back to the Earth in the form of drops of water or drops of ice which depends on how heavy the mist was in the current of the air it was in. There are some layer or current of air real cold and warm and some very swift and changeable so when the water strikes one of these cold currents, it becomes solid ice in small round drops in form or in a light fluffy form which is called snow. But this water is never drawn above six miles from the Earth's surface by the sun and moon. The reason it rains back on our planet is because it cannot get out of the Earth's sphere, with its high speed of rotating around the sun makes it impossible. Earthquakes are caused by the Son of Man by experimenting on high explosions; in fact, all the above said is caused by the Son of Man.

9. Why does the devil teach the eighty-five per cent that a mystery God brings all this?

To conceal the true God which is the Son of Man and make slaves out of the 85% by keeping them worshipping something he knows they cannot see (invisible) and he lives and makes himself rich from their labor. The 85% know that it rains, halls and snows; also hear it thunder above his head, but they do not try to learn who it is that cause all this to happen by letting the 5% teach them. He believes in the 10% on face value.

10. Who is that mystery God?

There is not a mystery God. The Son of Man has searched for that mystery God for trillions of years and was unable to find a mystery God. So they have agreed that the only God is the Son of Man. So they lose no time searching for that that does not exist.

11. Will you set up home and wait for that mystery God to bring you food?

Emphatically No. Me and my people who have been lost from home for three hundred and seventy-nine years have tried this so-called mystery God for bread, clothing and a home, and we receive nothing but hard times, hunger, naked and out of doors, also was beat and killed by the ones who advocated that kind of God and no relief came to us until the Son of Man came to our aid, by the name of our Prophet, W. D. Fard.

12. Tell us why the devil does not teach that?
Because he desires to make slaves out of all he can. So that he can rob them and live in luxury.

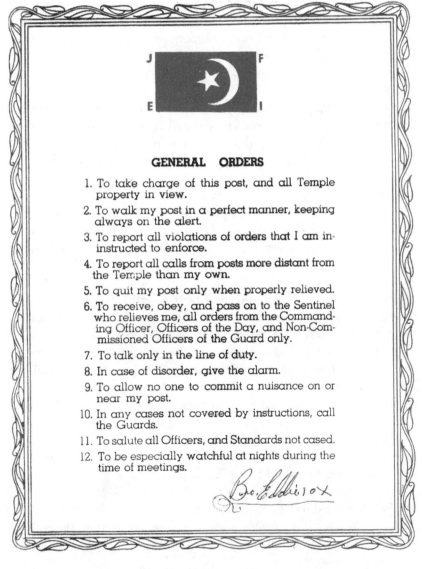

GENERAL ORDERS

1. To take charge of this post, and all Temple property in view.
2. To walk my post in a perfect manner, keeping always on the alert.
3. To report all violations of orders that I am in-instructed to enforce.
4. To report all calls from posts more distant from the Temple than my own.
5. To quit my post only when properly relieved.
6. To receive, obey, and pass on to the Sentinel who relieves me, all orders from the Command-ing Officer, Officers of the Day, and Non-Com-missioned Officers of the Guard only.
7. To talk only in the line of duty.
8. In case of disorder, give the alarm.
9. To allow no one to commit a nuisance on or near my post.
10. In any cases not covered by instructions, call the Guards.
11. To salute all Officers, and Standards not cased.
12. To be especially watchful at nights during the time of meetings.

Official framable document for Nation of Islam officer.

13. What bring rain, hail, snow and Earthquakes?

They continue daily, to teach the 85% that all this that you see such as rain, snow, hail and earthquakes comes from that mystery God that no one will ever be able to see until he dies. This is believed by the 85%. The 10% know that when man dies that he will never come back and tell the living whether he lied or not because the dead is never known to return from the grave. All the History of Islam never reveals anything that no man had ever been able to come back from a physical death. But there is a chance for mental death, because the lost-found was once dead mentally and many of them revived from it. But they were not physically dead, only mentally dead.

14. Who is the 85%?

The uncivilized people, poison animal eaters, slave from mental death and power. People who do not know the living God, or their origin in this world and they worship that they know not what. Who are easily led in the wrong direction but hard to lead into the right direction.

15. Who is the 10%?

The rich, the slave makers of the poor, who teach the poor lies, to believe that the almighty, true and living God is a spook and cannot be seen by the physical eye. Otherwise known as the blood sucker of the poor.

16. Who is the 5% in this poor part of the Earth?

They are the poor, righteous teachers, who do not believe in the teaching of the 10% and are all wise and know who the living God is and teach that the living God is the Son of Man, the supreme being, the (Black man) of Asia; and teach Freedom, Justice and Equality to all the human family of the planet Earth, otherwise known as civilized people. Also is Moslem and Moslem Sons.

17. What is the meaning of civilization?

One having knowledge, wisdom, understanding, culture, refinement and is not savage. Pursuit of happiness.

18. What is the duty of a civilized person?

To teach the uncivilized people who are savage, civilization, righteousness, the knowledge of himself, the science of everything in life, love, peace and happiness.

From *The New Afrikan* ©1984, a one-man African-American Islam cult.

19. If a civilized person does not perform his duty what must be done?

If a civilized person does not perform his duty which is teaching civilization to others they should be punished with a severe punishment. Ezekiel, Chapter 3, 18 Verse; St. Luke, Chapter 12, 47 Verse.

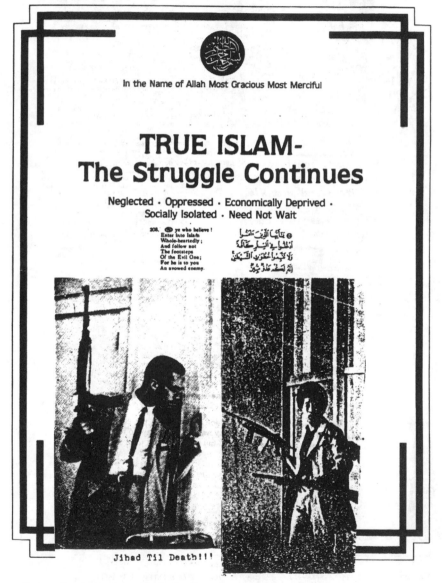

From *The New Afrikan* ©1984

20. What is the prescribed law of Islam of said person of that ability?
That the civilized person is held responsible for the uncivilized and he must be punished by the nation of Islam.

21. Who was the founder of unlike attract and like repel?
An original man who was a scientist by the name of Yacob born twenty miles from the Holy City Mecca, in the year eight thousand four hundred.

22. How old was the founder?
When Yacob was six years old, while playing with two pieces of steel, he discovered one piece had magnetic in it and the other piece did not. Then he learned that the piece with magnetic attracted the piece that did not have magnetic in it; then he told his people that when he was old enough he would make a nation that would be unlike and he would teach them tricknolledgy and they would rule for six thousand years.

23. Tell us what he promised his Nation he would do?
That he would make a devil graft him from his own people and that he would teach them how to rule his people for six thousand years.

24. What was his idea of making devil?
It was predicted of him that he would make devil eight thousand four hundred years before he was born. So he was born with a determined idea to make a people to rule for six thousand years.

25. How long did it take him to make devil?
Six hundred years he was in grafting devil or making him from the black man.

26. What year was that?
It was in the year eight thousand four hundred, which means from the date of our present history or Koran, or about two thousand and six hundred years before the birth of the Prophet Mossa.

27. What was the name of the place where he manufactured the devil?
Pelan. The same that is called Patmos in the Reve; chapter 1, 9 Verse; an island that is situated in the Aegean Sea.

THE GREAT ANNOUNCEMENT
By The Hon. Louis Farrakhan

MINISTER LOUIS FARRAKHAN, LEADER OF THE NATION OF ISLAM, HELD A PRESS CONFERENCE ON OCTOBER 24, 1989 TO TELL THE WORLD OF AN IMPENDING WAR AGAINST BLACK PEOPLE IN THE UNITED STATES, A WIPE-OUT PLANNED BY THE ELDER GEORGE BUSH AND COLIN POWELL. HOLDING A PRESS CONFERENCE TO ANNOUNCE A GENOCIDAL RACIAL WAR IS STRANGE, BUT EVEN STRANGER IS THE IDEA THAT THE LATE ELIJAH MUHAMMAD, THE FOUNDER OF NATION OF ISLAM WHO DIED IN 1975, WAS THE ONE TO IMPART THIS KNOWLEDGE. AND BURSTING THE LIMITS OF WEIRDNESS IS THAT ELIJAH MUHAMMAD VISITED MINISTER FARRAKHAN TO IMPART THIS WARNING INSIDE A FLYING SAUCER, OR "THE GREAT WHEEL," WHICH ELIJAH MUHAMMAD SPOKE OF HIMSELF IN A 1972 SPEECH.

The Nation of Islam remains the largest and most influential Muslim group in America despite being issued a fatwa (seen on page 246) by European Islamic leaders for its cultic and anti-Qur'anic precepts. NoI's biggest supporter in the Arabic world is Muammar Qaddafy, the Libyan leader, who tried to give the Nation of Islam either one billion or one million dollars (the amount changes depending who tells the story). The offer was disallowed by the U.S. government.

Ladies and Gentlemen of the Press, Brothers and Sisters, we are honored by your presence here this morning. I am a man who has great respect for the Press and the electronic media and I also have respect for myself and my mission. As you know, I do not readily submit to interviews, nor am I frequently seen on the television; for I am not before you of myself, nor do I do what I do to be seen of men. Therefore, I have never tried to abuse, or misuse the Press to seek advantage for myself, or the Nation of Islam. So, in calling this press conference, I am calling you because of the serious nature of the Announcement that I am about to make; an announcement on which hangs the future of this nation, its leaders and the people of America.

It is written in the Book of Ezekiel:

"When I say unto the wicked, You shall surely die; and you give him not warning, nor speak to warn the wicked from his wicked way, to save his life; the same wicked man shall die in his iniquity; but his blood will I require at your hand.

"Yet if you warn the wicked, and he turn not from his wickedness, nor from his wicked way, he shall die in his iniquity; but you have delivered your soul." It is in this spirit that I make this Announcement.

In a tiny town in Mexico, called Tepotzlan, there is a mountain on the top of which is the ruins of a temple dedicated to Quetzacoatl, the Christ-figure of Central and South America — a mountain which I have climbed several times. However, on the night of September 17, 1985, I was carried up on that mountain, in a vision, with a few friends of mine. As we reached the top of the mountain, a Wheel, or what you call an unidentified flying object, appeared at the side of the mountain and called to me to come up into the Wheel. Three metal legs appeared from the Wheel, giving me the impression that it was going to land, but it never came over the mountain.

Being somewhat afraid, I called to the members of my party to come with me, but a voice came from the Wheel saying, "Not them; just you." I was told to relax and a beam of light came from the Wheel and I was carried up on this beam of light into the Wheel.

I sat next to the pilot; however, I could not see him. I could only feel his presence. As the Wheel lifted off from the side of the mountain, moving at a terrific speed, I know I was being transported to the Mother Wheel, which is a human-built planet — a half-mile by a half-mile that the Honorable Elijah Muhammad had taught us of for nearly 60 years. The pilot, knowing that I was fearful of seeing this great, mechanical object in the sky, maneuvered his craft in such a way that I would not see the Mother Wheel (Plane) and then backed quickly into it and docked in a tunnel. I was escorted by the pilot to a door and admitted into a room.

I shall not bother you with a description of the room, but suffice it to say that at the center of the ceiling was a speaker and through this speaker I heard the voice of the Honorable Elijah Muhammad speaking to me as clearly as you are hearing my voice this morning.

He spoke in short cryptic sentences and as he spoke a scroll full of cursive writing rolled down in front of my eyes, but it was a projection of what was being written in my mind. As I attempted to read the cursive writing, which was in English the scroll disappeared and the Honorable Elijah Muhammad began to speak to me. He said, "President Reagan has met with the Joint Chiefs of Staff to plan a war. I want you to hold a press conference in Washington, D.C., and announce their plan and say to the world that you got the information from me on the Wheel." He said to me that he would not permit me to see him at that time. However, he said that I had one more thing to do and when that one more thing was done that I could come again to the Wheel and I would be permitted to see him face to face.

He then dismissed me. I entered the small wheel and the pilot whom I still could not see, moved the craft out of the tunnel and took it up to a terrific height and maneuvered his craft that I might look down upon the Mother Wheel. I saw a city in the sky.

With great speed it brought me back to earth and dropped me off near Washington where I then proceeded into this city to make The Announcement.

After I awakened from the vision, it seemed to vanish from my mind. However, on the morning of September 19, 1985, a great earthquake struck Mexico City and it was felt in the little town where I was staying. That earthquake brought the vision forcibly to my mind and I spoke it, later that morning for the first time to my wife, Khadijah Muhammad, and Sister Tynnetta Muhammad in the city of Cuernavaca.

During the vision of 1985, the Honorable Elijah Muhammad did not tell me who the war was planned against, or where it would take place. But, as events began to unfold from September to December of 1985 into January of 1986, it began to dawn on me, slowly, that the war might be against Moammar Qaddafi and the Libyan Jamahiriya, but I was not completely sure. In early February, 1986, I was invited to participate in and be the spokesman at a press conference initiated by the Libyans in cooperation with Kwame Toure of the All African Peoples' Revolutionary Party and the representatives of approximately 15 groups of Blacks, Native Americans, Hispanics and Whites, in essence, to state to the government of the United States: "Hands off Libya."

While I was speaking at the press conference, the lights of the television cameras in the back of the room brought back the vision of the press conference that I was to hold in Washington, D.C., and I wondered to myself, "Could this be it?"

In February 1986, I embarked on a world tour. While I was in Ghana, it crystallized for me that the war President Reagan and the Joint Chiefs of Staff had planned was in fact against Muammar Qaddafi and the people of Libya. So, I decided to alter my planned itinerary to go to Libya and to warn Muammar Qaddafi.

From Tripoli, speaking before the representatives of approximately 80 nations, I told the vision publicly, sending back to the United States a warning to President Reagan and Secretary of State George Schultz.

During the confrontation in the Gulf of Sidra, between the United States Air Force and the Libyan Air Force, it was reported in the press that a bright orange object was seen over the Mediterranean. The Wheel was, in fact, present and interfered with the highly sensitive electronic equipment of the aircraft carrier, forcing it to return to Florida for repairs.

In 1987, in the *New York Times' Sunday Magazine* and on the front page of the *Atlanta Constitution*, the truth of my vision was verified, for the headlines of the *Atlanta Constitution* read, "President Reagan Planned War Against Libya."

In the article which followed, the exact words that the Honorable Elijah Muhammad spoke to me on the Wheel were found; that the President had met with the Joint Chiefs of Staff and planned a war against Libya in the early part of September 1985. I did not realize, at the time, when the Honorable Elijah Muhammad said that I had one more thing to do that that one more thing involved having the actual press conference — that I am holding today — and making the actual announcement that I am now fully in the knowledge and understanding of. The reason that the Honorable Elijah Muhammad did not tell me who the President and the Joint chiefs of Staff had planned the war against was because Muammar Qaddafi, the Muslim Revolutionary leader, and the small nation of Libya, was only to serve as a sign of an even more significant and consequential war which would come several years later. I am here to announce today that President Bush has met with his Joint Chiefs of

Staff, under the direction of General Colin Powell, to plan a war against the Black people of America, the Nation of Islam and Louis Farrakhan, with particular emphasis on our Black youth, under the guise of a war against drug sellers, drug users, gangs and violence — all under the head national security.

The FBI, in preparation for this war, has stepped up its campaign against strong Black political leadership. The FBI is using dirty tactics under the guise of flushing out corrupt politicians to malign and besmirch the good name of many of our strong fighters for justice, threatening them with indictments or casting them into prisons. With other weaker leaders, the government has already promised them wealth and nearness to the centers of power and to be in their councils in exchange for their being silent when the attack finally comes.

The FBI has been working to destroy the Nation of Islam since 1940. As a young Muslim, 34 years ago, I recall that the agents of the FBI were constantly visiting members of the Nation of Islam, trying to frighten us and our families away from our belief in the religion of Islam, and away from our desire to follow the leadership of the Honorable Elijah Muhammad.

Now, it is well documented, through the Senate Subcommittee hearings on the Counterintelligence Program of the United States government, under J. Edgar Hoover, and through information that we have received under the Freedom of Information Act, that the Government of the United States, the Justice Department and the FBI, in the name of fighting communism; and in the name of preventing a Messiah from rising among Black people, who would unite us; and in the name of protecting the existing social and political order, used taxpayers' dollars to employ every dirty trick that was ever used in overthrowing foreign governments deemed to be enemies of the United States, to overthrow and to undermine all Black leaders and Black organizations in the United States.

It is well documented that the FBI, using taxpayers' dollars, conducted illegal surveillance, wiretaps, and mischievous machinations against Black leadership, to discredit, undermine, embarrass and even to kill those leaders who stood up to amend the condition that 310 years of chattel slavery and 100 years of free slavery produced.

That which the FBI has done against the Honorable Elijah Muhammad, the Nation of Islam, Black leaders and Black organizations, again, is well documented. It was the FBI who planned and engineered the split between Malcolm X and the Honorable Elijah Muhammad. It was the FBI and its agents that engineered the destruction of the Nation of Islam after the departure of the Honorable Elijah Muhammad in 1975. It was the FBI that planned and engineered the struggle in the courts to weaken the Nation from within and to deprive the Muslims of that which their hard-earned dollars had gained in property through probate court disputes. It was the FBI's plan to promote division among the ministers of the Honorable Elijah Muhammad after His departure.

Now that I, and those with me, are working to rebuild the Work of the Honorable Elijah Muhammad as a means of reforming our people and transforming their lives into lives of service and usefulness to themselves and others, the same fear of the government that was seen in times past, is now seen again in the work of members of the FBI's anti-terrorist task force and the organized crime racketeering task force, that have been working night and day to cripple and destroy the Nation of Islam, culminating in an attack on Louis Farrakhan with the purpose of discrediting, embarrassing and ultimately causing the death of Louis Farrakhan, preferably by heightening tensions within the movement exacerbated by government agents posing as Muslims. This is the aim of the United States government, and it appears to be the aim of the President of the United States, President George Bush.

Two weeks before George Bush was elected President, he made a speech before the Simon Wiesenthal Center in Los Angeles detailing his support of Israel and his continued support of the Jewish community. He pledged continued funding of the Justice Department in their continuing investigations and vigorous prosecution of those whom the President called "anti-Semites." And he said, "Whether they wear brown shirts, or white shirts and bow ties: whether they live in Skokie, Chicago, or Brooklyn, New York, the villain is the same."

I am sure President Bush was not referring to Senator Paul Simon of Illinois, who wears bow ties and white shirts. During the Reagan Administration, the then Vice-President Bush spoke out against me, identifying me by name. Now as he approached the Presidency he spoke of me by innuendo saying that he would continue the funding of the Justice Department, he promised he would lead the fight against those whom he and certain leading members of the Jewish community determined to be "anti-Semites" through vigorous investigation, prosecution, and then he indirectly referred to me as "the villain." Evidence is now mounting that those were not empty words of the President, but those words as in the past, have been translated into the final program and policy — and war that has been designed to destroy the Nation of Islam and Minister Farrakhan with a particular focus on the growing strength of Black youth.

The vision that the Honorable Elijah Muhammad gave me from the Wheel in 1985 is now manifested fully in that President Bush has met with his Joint Chiefs of Staff, the chairman of which is a Black man, General Colin Powell, and again, they too have planned a war.

Why would President Bush assign a Black man to be chairman of the Joint Chiefs of Staff, jumping over 30 white men, who are reportedly more qualified, to be chairman? Oftimes, when a Black man is elevated to a high position, it is generally because of a desire to use him against the legitimate aspirations of his own people, or to use him as window-dressing, to make the masses of Black people believe that an unjust system is working in their behalf.

With an army full of young Black men and women (which includes Native Americans, Hispanics and poor Whites), could it be that General Powell will be used to justify the use of these soldiers against Noriega and his regime in Panama; against the Medellin drug cartel; and then on to Daniel Ortega and the Sandinista regime; possibly against Cuba; against the liberation movements in Africa and, lastly, but most importantly, against the rise of Black youth and Black people in America.

For the past few years, the American press has been feeding the public the image of Black youth on a rampage. From the gangs called Crips and Bloods, in Los Angeles, California; the Central Park incident, to the drug sellers that are operating in the major cities along the East Coast, particularly in Washington, D.C., the image the American public gets is that when it comes to gangs, violence and drugs, that the gang leaders are Black; the violence is Black; the drug sellers are Black and the majority of drug users are Black. Our youth are being portrayed as the perpetrators of violence, and are being armed with "street sweepers," AK-47s, Uzis, MAC10s. It is being reported that these Black youth are better armed than the local police.

The police are saying that they have insufficient arms to combat these drug groups and, therefore, they either need heavier weapons, or the back-up of the National guard, and Federal troops. However, information has come to us that the police have great firepower available to them. And certain areas of the country have been targeted to test these new weapons. Armored personnel carriers that can travel at speeds up to 70 mph with high caliber machine guns are being stored in the armories of the major cities and the use of certain kinds of gases is being planned. This is being planned to be executed against Black youth in several major cities in the country, one of which is Washington, D.C.

Much of the gang activity is fomented, manipulated, and kept alive by outside forces from within the white community and oftimes by the very police themselves to justify what the government is planning against our community. Many of our young people are recruited by corrupt police to sell drugs to our people and many of our youth are killed if they violate police instructions, by hit squads from within the police departments. This is what we are learning from so-called gang leaders throughout the country.

All of this has been planned and is now being carried out under the pretext of national security and to maintain, preserve and protect an increasingly corrupt and unjust social and political order.

In closing, I would like to issue a warning to the President, to the Government and to the people of the United States of America. If I in your mind am before you of myself; if I in your mind am a hater, an anti-Semite, a wild-eyed radical; then you have nothing to fear from my presence; for I, like those who are actually like that, will go the way history has decreed for that kind of person.

However, if I am in reality in front of you by Allah's Divine Will as an extension of the Divine Warnings given to you from the Honorable Elijah Muhammad, then be instructed that you would do well to leave me alone; to leave the Nation of Islam alone; and to cease and desist from your evil planning against the future of the Black people of America and the world. For the Black people of America, though despised and rejected, have now become the People of God and He has declared that He will fight you for their liberation.

The government would be wise to heed the counsel of Gamaliel, in the days of Paul, and the early Christians, who advised the rulers of that day, with these words:

"And so in the present case, I say to you, stay away from these men and let them alone for if this plan or action should be of men, it will be overthrown;

"But if it is of God, you will not be able to overthrow them; or else you may even be found fighting against God."

So it is not wise for you to plan against Allah's (God's) servants; for by so doing you are actually planning against yourselves. This warning is for the President, the government and the wise to reflect upon so that the unwary citizens of America may not be harmed by the consequences of the wicked machinations of the United States Government.

You may come against me, which you are free to do, since we have no power to stop you, but I warn you, that I am backed by the Power of Allah (God) and His Christ and the Power of that Wheel in which I received This Announcement. The moment you attempt or lay your hands on me the fullness of Allah's (God's) Wrath will descend upon you and upon America.

Before you will be able to establish your mockery of me (if that is what you wish to do) for what was revealed to me in the Wheel you will see these wheels or what you call UFO's in abundance over the major cities of America and the calamities that America is presently experiencing will increase in number and in intensity that you might humble yourselves to the Warning contained in This Announcement.

This is a final warning to you. The ball in now in your court. You may do with it, with me, and with us, as you see fit. Thank you for your attention and may Allah bless each of you with the light of understanding, as I greet you in peace.

As Salaam Alaikum

MUSLIM VS. MUSLIM
The Fatwa Against The Nation of Islam

ON MARCH 7, 1998 THE BOARD OF ULEMA OF THE ITALIAN MUSLIM
ASSOCIATION (AMI) ISSUED THE FOLLOWING FATWA AGAINST THE
NATION OF ISLAM. THE ENGLISH TRANSLATION WAS RENDERED BY
PROFESSOR ABDUL HADI PALAZZI, SECRETARY-GENERAL OF THE
ITALIAN MUSLIM ASSOCIATION AND DIRECTOR OF THE CULTURAL
INSTITUTE OF THE ITALIAN ISLAMIC COMMUNITY.

In the Name of Allah, the Beneficent, the Merciful.

Praise to Allah, Lord of the worlds, and blessings and peace upon His
servant and Messenger, the Prophet Muhammad ibn 'Abdillah, upon
his family, his companions and those who follow his way till the Day
of the Resurrection. Allah, the Most High, says in the Holy Qur'an:
"Of the people there are some who say: 'We believe in Allah and the
Last Day,' notwithstanding their unbelief. Fain would they deceive
Allah and the believers, but they only deceive themselves, and realize it
not. In their hearts there is a disease, and Allah permitted this decease
to increase. Grievous is the penalty they incur, because they are false."
(Qur'an 2:8–10)

During the past few months a group active in the United States that
calls itself the "Nation of Islam" has received worldwide press coverage.
Its leader, Louis Farrakhan, met Islamic scholars and heads of State,
introducing himself as a representative of American Muslims. Some
brothers of ours asked this Board: "Can Mr. Farrakhan and his followers be accepted as 'Muslim' in the sense that this word is defined by
the Shari'ah?" With the permission and the help of Allah, after due
investigation of the matter, this Board answers as follows:

Praise to Allah, the One who created good and evil, and who revealed
the difference between the true and the false. Generally speaking, the
hukm (Shari'ah rule) is that each one who claims to be a Muslim must
be accepted as such by other Muslims, except in the case they have a
clear evidence of the contrary. The most common hukm is that "unbelief is not proved by actions," but "is proved by the principles that are
believed." The most common way to prove what a man actually
believes is by analyzing his speeches and writings.

That means that the fact that someone does not usually observe the hukm of the Shari'ah is not enough to proof his unbelief. This view is held by the Hanafi, Maliki and Shaf'i schools, but the school of Imam Ahmad ibn Hanbal says that "unbelief is not proven by actions, expect for the compulsory ritual prayers (salawat)."

According to this school, a Muslim who refuses to pray a compulsory prayer must be regarded as a renegade, but the other three schools says he is a Muslim, although a sinner (fasiq). Notwithstanding this divergence, the four schools are unanimous in considering non-Muslim someone who — without being under pressure — says "I do not regard prayer as compulsory," or "There is no need to fast on Ramadan," or "There is no harm in drinking wine," etc. That kind of declaration proves that a person has rejected one of the clear hukms, about which there is no doubt or possibility of misunderstanding. The consensus of Islamic jurists is that rejecting a single hukm is like rejecting them all, and that missing an element of faith is like missing them all. There is no difference between a hukm concerning things that must be believed by the heart, or things that must be done by the body. As a general rule, it is forbidden to investigate whether Muslims observe the Shari'ah, and even if their belief is correct from all points of view. Notwithstanding this, as soon as a Muslim hears from his brother something that can be identified as a wrong belief, he has the duty to correct him and to teach him the correct doctrine according to the Qur'an and the Sunnah.

In cases when some wrong doctrine can imply unbelief, it is necessary, for the involved person, to repent and to pronounce again the two testimonies. The case is different when a person or a group is openly preaching and teaching doctrines that look unusual. In that case, the Ulema are bound to investigate the matter, and judge whether these doctrines imply heresy (bid'ah) or apostasy (riddah).

Regarding the "Nation of Islam," their official doctrine is that Allah appeared in the form of a human being named Fard Muhammad, and that this "incarnation of God" chose another man, called Elijah Muhammad, as his Prophet. This is a clear contradiction of the Monotheistic faith (Tawhid), and of the Qur'anic teaching according to which Muhammad (blessings and peace upon him) is the Seal of the Prophets. That is enough to say that everyone who belongs to the "Nation of Islam" is not, ipso facto, a Muslim, but an unbeliever.

Muslims must declare this truth, and each one of them who keeps silent while listening to Mr. Farrakhan being called "a Muslim leader" is sinning. Since the matter concerns "faith and unbelief," it is not permitted to avoid a judgment due to political or diplomatic considerations. Every marriage between a Muslim and a member of the "Nation of Islam" is null and void, and whoever, after becoming a member of this organization, wants to return to Islam, must repent and be re-converted. In case he was married, he must re-celebrate his wedding; in case he performed the Pilgrimage, he must perform it again.

We pray to Allah to make all this clear to our brothers in Islam, and to help them never to deviate from the doctrine that was revealed in the Holy Qur'an and that is presently accepted by the Islamic Community. And we call upon Allah as a Witness of what we say.

Shaykh 'Ali Mo'allim Hussen
President
Board of Ulema
Italian Muslim Association

DAJJAL THE ANTICHRIST
By Ahmad Thomson

DAJJAL THE ANTICHRIST COMBINES FAR-RIGHT ECONOMIC IDEAS AND
NEO-NAZI CONSPIRACY THEORY, USING QUOTATIONS FROM THE QUR'AN
TO CONFIRM THE IDEAS AND VIEWS OF ADOLF HITLER AND EZRA
POUND. OBVIOUSLY INFLUENCED BY MURABITAN, THE REVOLUTIONARY
ISLAM ORGANIZATION THAT CALLS SCOTLAND HOME, *DAJJAL THE
ANTICHRIST* IS DEDICATED TO THAT GROUP'S LEADER, SHAYKH 'ABD'AL-
QADIR AL-MURABIT (AUTHOR OF "ISLAM AND THE DEATH OF
DEMOCRACY," SEEN ON PAGE 252).

The people who really rule the *kafir* states of today are not the politicians who appear on television, but rather the people who control the major finance and business institutions, that is the freemasons. Effective control is exercised especially by using the kafir banking system to create debts by charging interest, which grow so large that they can never be repaid. In order to speed up the process of creating debts, the freemasons, as we have already seen, create conflict situations out of which profits are made by selling the goods — especially armaments and food — needed by the sides who have been drawn into conflict, at a high price, and out of which debts are created by providing those goods on credit at interest.

The conflict situations created by the freemasons vary, from manipulating market forces — especially in the commodity markets and on the stock and money exchanges — to engineering war on a large scale. Thus, for example, in order to curb the wealth of the Muslim oil-producing countries during the boom of the 1970s — and especially after the price of oil was quadrupled by OPEC in 1973 in response to the High Tec North's support of Israeli military aggression against the Arabs in the Yom Kippur War — the cost of crude oil from the Middle East was soon reduced, not only by re-negotiating the price per barrel, but also by devaluing the currencies of all the oil-producing countries — by revaluing the exchange rates within the international banking system, as well as by manipulating supply and demand and therefore value on the international money markets.

During the 1980s, Iraq was armed, at its own expense, in order to wage war on and weaken Iran. Once this had been achieved —

increasing both Iraq's and Iran's dependence on the international banking system in the process — Iraq was then encouraged to invade Kuwait, while at the same time Saudi Arabia and the Gulf states were warned that if American troops — accompanied by token forces from other countries to create the impression of its being an "international" affair — were not permitted to come to their rescue, at their expense, then they would be the next to be invaded by Iraq. The troops came, the Gulf War ensued, all the latest technological weapons (including the

chemical ones and their vaccines) were tested, Kuwait was destroyed and had to be rebuilt, at its own expense, much of Iraq was destroyed and its population decimated, and Saudi Arabia and all the Gulf states spent billions on financing the war and buying obsolete armaments in order to ensure that the same thing did not happen all over again.

During the early 1990s therefore, vast profits were made by the armaments industry, and vast profits were made by the international banking system as funds poured out of the Middle East into the High Tec North at one rate of exchange and then eventually back again, once it was all over, at another rate of exchange. As a result the oil-wealth of the Middle East had been reduced to virtually nothing, and as if to emphasize the hold which the international banking system now enjoys over Saudi Arabia and the Gulf states, the BCCI Arab bank was closed down almost overnight, wiping out much of the Muslims' 'wealth' throughout the world in the process.

Once again, everything had gone more or less according to plan and the architects of the new world order had triumphed. This was the same kind of carefully orchestrated activity of which both Ezra Pound and Adolf Hitler were fully aware, and tried to prevent, but without any success.

Perhaps one of the main reasons why Pound and Hitler failed to expose and destroy the activities of the freemasons was because they were not fully aware of the true nature of existence. The true nature of existence is that nothing exists, only Allah. It follows that anything other than Allah only appears to exist if you give it reality.

The way of Muhammad, may the blessings and peace of Allah be on him, means that reality is given to Allah. The way of kufr means that reality is given to other than Allah.

If enough of the people who are at present enslaved by the kafir system, that is the Dajjal system, and who are accordingly imprisoned by the kafir view of existence, decide to follow the way of Muhammad, and accordingly cease to give reality to what they have been conditioned to give reality to by the educational and media systems, then the producer consumer process will collapse and cease to exist — especially once the Muslims abandon the banks and their worthless paper and plastic money.

Thus the way to fight the kafir system, that is the Dajjal system, is not to fight it, but to leave it. Ignore it. The way to leave the system is to follow the way of Muhammad, may Allah bless him and grant him peace. The system is already in an advanced state of collapse. Accordingly it is becoming easier and easier to leave it, and to follow the way of Muhammad — and when the system does collapse, it will be the Muslims who will best be able to cope with what happens next. The choice is yours, right now.

ISLAM AND THE DEATH OF DEMOCRACY
By Shaykh Abdalqadir as-sufi al-Murabit

ACCORDING TO THE *HIGHLAND NEWS GROUP*:

ACHNAGAIRN [SCOTLAND] SEEMS TO BE ONE OF THE HEAD-
QUARTERS OF THE WORLDWIDE MURABITUN MOVEMENT WITH
ITS FOUNDER, SHAYKH ABDALQADIR AS-SUFI AL-MURABIT, REG-
ULARLY LIVING AT THE HOUSE.

SHAYKH ABDALQADIR, IN HIS 70S AND THOUGHT TO BE FOR-
MERLY KNOWN AS SCOTS AUTHOR IAN DALLAS, APPEARS TO
COMMAND SIGNIFICANT RESPECT THROUGHOUT THE MUSLIM
WORLD.

HE AND THE MOVEMENT'S POLITICAL LEADER, UMAR
IBRAHIM VADILLO, HAVE SET UP A NEW MONETARY SYSTEM
BASED ON GOLD AND SILVER AND HAVE HAD SIGNIFICANT
SUCCESS IN PERSUADING MUSLIM COUNTRIES ROUND THE
WORLD TO ADOPT THE ISLAMIC CURRENCY AS AN ALTERNATIVE
TO THE "GLOBE-CONTROLLING US DOLLAR."

THEY ARE ALSO COMMITTED TO REPLACING SUPERMARKETS
WITH THE LOST ISLAMIC INSTITUTION OF THE MARKETPLACE
AND SETTING UP CARAVANS TO REPLACE MONOPOLISTIC DISTRI-
BUTION.

IN A FATWA AGAINST AMERICA AND ALLIES REGARDING RESPONSES TO
THE 9/11/01 ATTACK, THE SAME SHEIK (THOUGH NOW UNDER THE
NAME SHAYKH HAMUD IBN ABDULLAH ASH-SHU'AYBI), CALLS FOR THE
DEATH-RATTLES OF NON-BELIEVERS IN THE WEST:

AND LIKE WE SAID, IT IS COMPULSORY UPON ALL MUSLIMS TO
HELP THE TALIBAN GOVERNMENT IT IS ALSO EQUALLY COMPUL-
SORY UPON THE MUSLIM GOVERNMENTS ESPECIALLY THE
NEIGHBORING COUNTRIES TO ASSIST THEM AGAINST THE KUFR
OF THE WEST.

AND LET THOSE KNOW THAT THAT FAILING TO ASSIST
TALIBAN THAT IS BEING FOUGHT FOR ITS RELIGION AND
BECAUSE OF THE HELP IT GIVES TO MUJAHIDÎN AND, ASSISTING
THE KUFFAR AGAINST THEM IS THE KIND OF FRIENDSHIP AND
SUPPORT OF THE KUFFAR THAT ALLAH WARNED AGAINST WHEN
HE SAID:

"BELIEVERS, TAKE NOT MY ENEMY AND YOUR ENEMY AS FRIENDS IN WHOM YOU PUT LOVE."

AND HE SAID "BELIEVERS TAKE NOT MY ENEMY AND YOURS AS PROTECTING FRIENDS."

CERTAINLY IT WILL GO DOWN IN HISTORY THAT THESE COUNTRIES BETRAYED THEIR BROTHERS AND IT WILL REMAIN AS A KIND OF BAD RECORD ON THEM AND THEIR PEOPLE THAT WILL REMAIN FOREVER!!

SIMILARLY LET THOSE NEIGHBORING AND NEARBY COUNTRIES BEWARE THAT IF THEY REFUSE TO HELP THE BROTHERS AND ALLOWED THE ENEMY TO ATTACK THEM, THAT ALLÂH MAY FACE THEM WITH HIS NATURAL DISASTERS AND TERRIBLE SITUATIONS AS A PUNISHMENT AND CHASTISEMENT ON THEM. THE PROPHET SAID A MUSLIM IS A BROTHER OF A MUSLIM, HE DOES NOT FORSAKE OR BETRAY HIM . . . AND HE ALSO SAID IN A HADITH QUDSÎ: "ALLAH SAID "WHOEVER FIGHTS MY FRIEND SHOULD GET READY FOR WAR WITH ME AND HE SAID "WHOEVER ALLOWED A MUSLIM TO BE HUMILIATED WHILE HE COULD ASSIST HIM, ALLAH WILL HUMILIATE HIM IN FRONT OF THE ENTIRE CREATION ON THE DAY OF JUDGMENT." (REPORTED BY AHMAD).

REMARKABLY, THE MURABITUN ORGANIZATION HAS INFLUENCED FORMER RACIST SKINHEADS AND NATIONAL FRONT MEMBERS TO CONVERT TO ISLAM AND JOIN THE ORGANIZATION. WE WOULD LIKE TO KNOW IF EX-SKINHEADS AND EX-NATIONAL FRONT MEMBERS ARE ACTUALLY GIVING UP THEIR BELOVED PINTS — DRINKING ALCOHOL IS MAJOR ISLAMIC SIN. THE MURABITUN-DEDICATED *DAJJAL THE ANTICHRIST* BY AHMAD THOMSON, WHICH EXPANDS ON THE ANTI-JEWISH, ANTI-AMERICAN, ANTI-USURY, AND ANTI-FREEMASONRY VIEWS OF EZRA POUND AND ADOLF HITLER WITH APOCALYPTIC CONSPIRACY, IS EXCERPTED ON PAGE 249.

I affirm that there is no god but Allah — no god but the One Creator of the universe, and Muhammad, blessing and peace of Allah be upon him, is the Messenger of Allah — that is to say that *Sayyiduna Muhammad, salla'llahu 'alayhi wa sallam*, the beloved, came with the complete message of Islam, with the science of Islam, with the knowledge of Islam, which is a light that has illuminated the world for 1400 years. The light of Islam is the light of Qur'an — the light of Qur'an is the light of Muhammad, *salla'llahu alayhi wa sallam*. The people who follow Sayyiduna Muhammad, *salla'llahu alayhi wa sallam*, are a people who are illuminated by the wisdom and the beauty that comes from the teachings of Qur'an al-Karim, the Generous Qur'an, the Noble Qur'an.

For 1400 years, whenever Islam has established itself, it has swept away ignorance, it has swept away cruelty and oppression, and it has brought life to people and that life is so sweet and it has such a fragrance in it and the dust of this fragrance still so enchants the people of this barbaric society that they put it in museums and they walk in awe around it and look at the artifacts of these civilizations of Islam and see something they have not got in their own lives. But this is the dust of the teaching of Islam. Islam has always flowered where the society has been collapsing — has become over-full, has become decadent, has become soft, has become sentimental, has become over-educated, over-knowledgeable without wisdom. People who know too much — people who know everything — this ignorance is swept away when the light of Islam comes.

The project of Islam is not visible which is why all these enemies of Islam failed to understand what was happening in Iran, failed to understand what was happening in the Middle East and in Indonesia and in the sub-continent of India. Why do they not understand it? Because it's not visible. The reality of Islam is in the heart and this reality is so powerful that there is not anything in this world that is worth taking in exchange for it. The famous statement that was made to Lord Cromer when he said, "We must stop the Muslims" in Egypt in the 1890's. They said — even in the early 19th century, "What are we to say against a people who, when they look into the mouths of the cannons see the gardens of Jinna?" A people who see the gardens of Paradise.

The people were not looking at the visible world at all. Islam has no negotiation with ignorance. It has no negotiation with a decadent society. One has to cut through the decadence and establish — what? *Iqama as-Salat* — establish worship of Allah — establish prostration before the Divine Reality. Islam is original awareness — deen, it is called in Arabic — *Deen al-Haqq* — the life-transaction of the Real. What is the life-transaction of the Real? It is to stand before Reality and recognize that you are in-time, that you are dependent and that the Real is beyond time, is before-time and after-time, and time, and it is independent, and before the enormity of the Divine Reality of which you are an infinitely minute speck, a blink of an eye — less than the blink of an eye, your life is a tiny thing in the cosmic reality — before the awareness of this and the physical/physiological/biological reality of our helplessness, before the Majesty of the Real, to stand before it, to bow before it, and finally completely to prostrate and put one's head on the ground before it. That is Islam — finished!

And this Reality brings with it awareness. What awareness does it bring with it? — that this world is passing and disappearing and leaving us. What lies after death is coming towards us, is approaching and coming nearer. There isn't any moment in which it isn't more near than the moment before it. Therefore the only non-neurotic way to live is a way that is aligned to recognizing the biological inevitable. In all the society of outwardness that is this insane society, and of all the insanities there has never been one like the current dominant culture — never — there is no recognition of the biological fact of death — none.

Look at the implication of this. The result of recognizing this in your own being is that you are brought to have other goals. You cannot have the same social goals. You cannot aim at the same things because you are not permanent nor can you create permanence. You will not create a social order that is just, with peace and harmony throughout the land and-and-and . . . This is rhetoric, this is poetry, this is fantasy. Everything is created in opposites. If you want something to be raised up — you have to bend down in order that it can be raised up. Without the opposite, the thing cannot happen.

How could they possibly understand the fall of the Shah? because they believe that this figure on his peacock throne is real. They have to believe it's real because they believe their own infantile projects are real. But what was the real project of Sidi Ayatollah Khomeini, *rahimahu'llahu*? It was to prostrate before Allah. The first pictures the world saw were the pictures of a man in sajda — with his head on the ground — completely helpless. People went to him and then said, "But where's his government? Where's his this? Where's his that?" He had nothing. He said, "I haven't got anything — Allah!" He went down as far as you can go without disappearing into the earth and the Shah couldn't go any further up — equally without disappearing out of the earth. And now he's mad. Now he has gone mad. But wasn't he always mad. Because it is against nature — it is against existence — and you cannot go against existence.

This is a society where the highest intellection is opinion — and what is opinion but indoctrination and programming of the most banal mass information? Wherever you go in the United States of America people tell you — as if they had arrived by some spectacular spiritual illumination — at opinions that are mass-produced, not by the hundred thousand, but by the million. They say, "Oh well . . . I . . . of course, am against organized religion. You see, because I have reached this monumental decision that it's false and only inhibits people . . ."

Or the whole dialectic of women's liberation which is completely set up, not to liberate women, but to put women into the industrial mechanism — without which, the industrial mechanism cannot reach the next stage of its inevitable technical development. And all this rhetoric that is mouthed doesn't mean anything at all because it is simply taking women out of one slavery and putting them into another slavery — the same slavery that men have been in for the last fifty years.

Our project is not the same, Islam is disruptive. Islam is peace among the Muslims, but it is war on this ignorance. Now American society has collapsed. It has collapsed. It is finished. It was based on democracy and democracy is demonstrably over. We've seen recent statistics that go right back to 1960: every President has been voted in on a twenty to thirty per cent aggregate of the voting population. So democracy is not democracy. And still this ghastly fantasy is being imposed on people who'd have nothing to do with it, who want nothing to do with it, Iran has rejected it. Pakistan has rejected it. And it has collapsed in Turkey. Political democracy as a viable form of existence has collapsed in Turkey after an attempted imposition on the Turkish people of it by the Masonic movement instigated by the same western banking elite who have been running this country as an occupied state from the 1890's.

This is occupied territory. This is no longer America in any recognizable form. This is already occupied territory in the same way that Palestine is occupied territory — and the left bank is occupied territory — by the same people — controlled by it, governed by it, and media-dictated by it, So you can't arrive at a world picture from within the dialectic that you are offered by your education and by the already imperially controlled media that are manipulating the indigenous population of the United States of America.

This is the viewpoint of the Muslim — arrived at by the evidence of the last twenty-five years in the Middle East — in which everything that was before that considered a paranoid fantasy of those people who said it was going to happen, has proven a historical reality by what has happened with the Zionist victory in governing America and in seizing the lands of the Palestinian people. But the issue of the Palestinian people only focuses on the helpless struggle of innocent people against a life-transaction which in fact stretches beyond the 'Russian' occupation of America. The Russian power struggle in which America has been involved is a struggle over who is to lead this enormous country.

It stretches beyond that. It stretches beyond it to what has always been the tension in the human race and in human society at different stages and at different degrees, manifesting different conflicts and different cultures and different transformations of culture at different times in society. That is, that man is able to grasp the message of the Prophets or he is able to reject them, because according to the teachings of the Qur'an there has never been a people who have not received direct revelation from the Divine about how to live — but they have rejected the Prophet as the Jews rejected Moses and have become Baconized — so the Christians have rejected Jesus and have turned him into a Greek mystery cult, and all that happened when Sayyiduna Muhammad, *salla'llahu alayhi was sallam*, came is that he returned people to what he called *Deen al-Haqq*.

What is *Deen al-Haqq*? The life-transaction of the Real? That you are mortal, that you will die and the only means of peace is for you to have inner awareness of your existential dilemma which only remains a dilemma as long as you are unable to grasp your situation. Once you have grasped it — you recognize you are helpless — you recognize you are poor. You give up. You surrender. Islam is surrender. You surrender this idea that you can sculpt some kind of monumental autobiographic reality that will stand immutable when you are a vanishing thing. You are in annihilation. You have come from non-existence and you are going to non-existence. You are an imagination in an imagination in an imagination. Everything is perishing — it says in Qur'an — except the Face of Allah. And it remains. Endless. It goes on. Lord of Majesty and Generous Gifts. This is the reality of existence. But the secret of the most minute particle of existence is the secret of the whole. And this secret is in the heart of the human being. And knowledge of this secret is what illuminates the Muslim society.

There was published recently in England an anthropological series with all the ludicrous invented complexities of anthropology, which is in itself a crucial political arm of the dominant culture trying to grasp and understand all the varied sorts of human beings and cultures and groupings of human beings in the world in order to control them, in order to manipulate them into this hideous profit nexus that has been set up in this culture. But if you didn't read the pseudo-fantasies of the academics and looked at the photographs, you saw something quite overwhelming, you saw basically three groups of people. Right through the whole world, today you can basically divide people into three groups:

1) What you might call the "primitive" — they were naked and they were painted. They were bare or they were decorated and they have the nobility of this primal condition of the human being according to how much they have avoided the corruption of our society.

2) Then there were the middle group who were these bloated fat, pinkish, suited, seated, frozen, impacted, opaque, dead creatures — the European and the American — there was really something so completely suffocating and stifling in their lack of transparency, so utterly geared to play and utterly geared to infantile projects.

3) And then there was a third group of people who first of all were staggering, by their vastness in numbers — because they also stretched around the world — and they were noble. They were from Somalia, and they were from Sudan, and they were from Pakistan, and they were from Malaysia, and they were from Indonesia, and they were from southern China, and they were from southeastern Russia, and they were from the Tuareg in the desert and they were from the islands of the Comoros, and they were from Nigeria and Gambia and Senegal and you could not look at them without your eyes filling up with — if not tears, at least some kind of deep admiration that was not aesthetic. It was a recognition. "I didn't realize, I had forgotten how noble the human being was," and where was their project? Where was their idolatry? There was nothing — they were against the background of the

earth and the sky — men, women and children — because their main
project was worship of Allah — and they looked quite fulfilled and
they didn't look as if there was something wrong or something had to
be brought to them, but the dominant culture says that they are
underdeveloped, that they are "third world" and by the Mercy of Allah
this event in Iran has made the whole of these people of whom we are
part as Muslims, realize the fantasy of this. They are not third anything
— they are not underdeveloped — they are developed.

And here is a country so based on fantasy, so based on a magical
pharaonic hermeneutic of numbers — something they have invented
totally to manipulate and to exploit people, the economic system and
the financial market — that they have actually condemned the Untied
States already — in advance, because they are not getting their way —
to destruction. It's done, and it's signed and sealed, and it's delivered
— and everybody knows it. And the people are helpless, and still they
are carrying on these ludicrous dialogues about women's freedom,
about black people's freedom, about the freedom of sexual deviants,
about every kind of freedom that is, in fact, a rhetoric in a balloon that
doesn't mean anything at all. It's been given to them to keep them all
hearing about it and to control any psychological restlessness and tur-
bulence that would allow them to ask any questions — to say, "How
can we unlock the dilemma we are in?"

The only way you can unlock the dilemma you are in is to turn away
from the society and the dominant culture that has reduced people to
the state of people in western Europe and in the United States today. It
is not the life-transaction of technology that is spreading — it is Islam
that is spreading and Islam is bounded in worship of God, worship of
the Creator of the universe, and direct experience of Divinity — pure
mysticism — crystalline diamond mysticism — without priesthood,
without ritual, without magic, without bells and mystic figures,
without dragons and fairy stories — a pure rational foundation —
from which you look out on an abyss that is totally incomprehensible
by intellect. And that solid foundation allows you to make sincere true
judgements that are illuminated by compassion and concern for your
brother and your sister.

From that clear foundation of judgement that is in Qur'an you are
able to embark on the adventure of examining and discovering the
secret of your own heart and the meaning of your own existence —

not linguistically so you can talk about it and rap about it — but by illumination, by vision, by inner vision. Not some special group, for some people with a proclivity for the unseen and a proclivity for the esoteric. It is the ordinary Muslim. It is the simple person in Islam who becomes the saint, who becomes the luminary, who becomes what we call the wali — the friend of Allah — who reaches Allah, who has the vision of the Face of Allah, who gazes on the beloved — it is the poor person, it is the cobbler, it is the carpenter, it is the clerk. These become, among the Muslims when they meet together for Allah, these people become the princes, these people become the kings in that circle. It is not the ruler of the society who is honored — it is the one who is in the highest place with Allah who is honored.

When Sayyiduna Umar, the second Caliph, *radiya'llahu anhu*, arrived with Sayyiduna 'Ali, *karima'llahu wajhuhu*, when they arrived at the place where the great mystic and saint, Uways al-Qarani, lived and they realized they were in the place where this man lived. The Prophet, *salla'llahu alayhi wa sallam*, had never seen Uways al-Qarani in the visible world but he said, "There is a man in a certain place and you will come to it and when you come to it, go to him and greet him for me because he is my beloved friend." They asked, "Is there any man here who is a great man of Allah?" and people said, "No, no, there's nobody here," and they said, "There must be, because the Prophet described the place and we're at it," and they said, "Well, there's like a madman in the hills. He lives in a cave, but he'll throw stones at you if you go near him." They laughed and said, "This will be him!" They went to him, but he didn't throw stones. He came out and said, "Ya Umar and Ya Ali! Marhaban! Come in! I've been waiting for you. Sit down, describe him to me!" They said, "He looks like . . . this and this and this and this . . ." and they described the Prophet. He said, "That is right. That is right. That is right. That is right . . . and you have missed out this . . ." He was the one who was close to Allah, and before this man — the amir of the mu'minun — the ruler of an empire that already stretched from Europe to the gates of China within the lifetime of the Companions of the Prophet, this man who had an empire stretching a third of the way around the world who was dressed, remember, in a robe of patches and walked barefoot, 'Umar ibn al-Khattab, wept and said, "You should be the Amir al-Mu'minin. You should be the ruler of the believers. Let me stay in the cave!"

This is the life quality of the people of Islam. They move between government of the social and pure mysticism with complete ease — not like these terrible dead figures who are leading men and women and their children today into complete chaos so that, in the last week, in one week, we have had at least three cases of murder by 14-year-olds, two cases on their parents. Completely a kind of limit situation of social breakdown, and still they laugh, and still they shrug their shoulders, and sill they believe what they read in the newspapers, still they believe what they are told on television and still they think they know everything, because they have been crammed with ludicrously unstructured data in the university and these same people who laugh — have got no say whatsoever in any significant aspect of their society whatsoever. They are as helpless as children who have not even any teeth.

Now, if Islam establishes itself in America, it can only do one thing — which is sweep away a decadent society and establish it with a just society, Not by legislation, not by Shari'a — it's not about that — Islam is about people who already are capable of leading moral lives. All the propaganda against Islam makes it seem that there is a pile of hands that have been cut off and lumps of people buried under stones. This is so ludicrously distant from the realities of a Muslim society.

The point is, in a Muslim society, people have opted for a moral existence. They are able — it is a conceivable goal — to police yourself. They are not in the ludicrous, the insane dialectic of crime and statistics, by which the crime prevention is improved by a larger police force and more inhibitions to stop the crimes which are on the increase — which proves that their method is not working in the first place. There are no policemen in Islam, there is no army, there are no banks. The structure is organic.

Your body is not rigidly structured. It is structured in flux, it is structured in movement, it is structured in cellular growth and breakdown. One half of the whole process of your body you do not even have any conscious command of — and without that you could not even live. But you cannot say you are not structured. Well, that is the same in a Muslim society. You cannot police your digestion anymore than you can police morality within the house. This is the foundation of Islam, in moral terms and that's why, in a Muslim society today — even today — with all the incursions on Islam and the corruption of Islam by the kafir, you can walk through a Muslim village in Africa in the dead of night and not even look behind you. If you hear a noise you are absolutely safe and — in the rare event that you are not safe — if you called out there is no question but that people would come to your rescue, and neither the first nor the second is true in American or European society.

The issue of women's freedom cannot be debated or confronted or opened up at the personal, psychological and social level at which it is being made in the present time. All liberation is based on a just and moral society that has respect for men and women, for the fulfillment of their goals, according to a healthy, wholesome and reasonable bounded existence — because we are bounded. We are bounded biologically by the limits of our body. We are already lawful, we are already organized, we are already structured, as I have said. The issue of the freedom of women is a political issue and can only be solved by the politicization of women, as the liberation of men is a political issue, which can only be solved by the politicization of men.

But politicization means being aware of the total social nexus, and the social nexus has an outside and an inside. It has a physical aspect and an inner aspect, and nothing less than something that answers both of these is of any use. Do you follow? Unless you have inwardness, that social life will not be tolerable for you anyway. Whatever material goals you get, whatever social zone you answer or establish yourself in, you will still not be content. Sayyiduna Muhammad, salla'llahu alayhi wa sallam, said, "The son of Adam will never be content until the dust fills his mouth."

If your orientation is the unseen and what lies beyond it, not as an idea, not as a fantasy, but something which you will see with your own inner eye while you're alive because the Prophet, salla'llahu Oalayhi wa sallam, has said, "Every mu'min, everyone who accepts Allah, will see his place in the Garden before he dies" — and it is true. And this is an orientation that not only makes life possible, it makes death possible. If your life is bearable, your death will be bearable. If you're not afraid of death, you will not be afraid of life. All fear of life is fear of death and fear of death is based on not having coming to terms with your inevitably destined limited existence. All Sufic knowledge is attuning people to relax before the inevitable, before what Qur'an calls the Certain: "When the Certain comes to you, and what is the Certain?"

These are themes of mediation and of reflection and of contemplation by the intelligent Muslim. In the social sphere, and in the private sphere, Islam invites you take its way. Islam is an invitation itself. Ash-hadu an la ilaha illa'llah. Wa ash-hadu anna Muhammadun rasulallah, salla'llahu alayhi wa sallam. I confirm that there is no god but the one God and that Muhammad, peace be upon him, is the Messenger of God.

That is it, and that is enough. On this incredibly simple statement, a whole profound and ravishingly beautiful metaphysic and social reality is offered to the human being, It is not laid out in advance. It is not "going back 1400 years" and so on. Ridiculous propaganda! All your options are open — what are laid down are the limits — the parameters of the possible for sanity and for justice. And then you do what you like, do what you like. Those are the limits, and within them, you do anything you want. This is the Islamic republic that they are so terrified of.

But it is not mullahs, and as long as there are mullahs it is not Islam. Islam has got no elite. Islam is a bunch of human beings who have elected to follow this and who accept it. They have said mullahs — it is not mullahs! In Afghanistan it is not mullahs — it is simple mountain people fighting for their lives. And the same in Iran. And the same in Egypt, And the same in Turkey — which we will soon see insha'llah. But it will happen here and it is happening here. It is started here, not just in Tucson, but from one end of America to the other — it is happening. It is growing. Nothing can stop it, because it is for this time — it is for this place. It will go around the world. It is in Korea. It is in Japan. Last year the venerable 85-year-old leader of the Buddhist Church in Korea embraced Islam and he is now Hajj Abu Bakr. The world is changing.

But you are changing. You are the microcosm and the world is the macrocosm. The world is changing — you are changing. You are in change — there isn't anything but change. Allah is the Ever-Continuing. Make Islam your life-transaction and hold to Islam. Strengthen your Islam and extend your Islam. Expand it, because each person has an Islam according to his station of knowledge. One man's Islam is very narrow. One man's Islam is very closed — another person's Islam is very wide, very vast. It depends on your intellect, on your generosity. Because of all the qualities of Sayyiduna Muhammad, *salla'llahu alayhi wa sallam,* his greatest quality was his generosity.

And people who have good qualities before Islam are the people who are the best Muslims, because he said, "The best of you before Islam are the best of you after Islam" — because all it does is it ennobles and enhances and gives focus to the moral good qualities of the human being and there is not one thing in the teaching of Islam and in the beautiful revelation of Qur'an, there is not one thing that offends the human intellect. You cannot find one thing to offend the human intellect — and that is why Islam has grown, is growing, and will continue to grow — will flower — will become decadent — will crumble — and then the seeds of it will go somewhere else and the same process will go on, as it has gone on, in a world that is running down, that is decaying, and in which all sense of justice and sanity is disappearing according to precisely what was said by Sayyiduna Muhammad, salla'l-lahu alayhi wa sallam, yet still the people of the Truth call on Allah and worship Allah, whatever happens in the world. They are not looking for a utopia. We do not expect a utopia. We are not Christian. We have no fantasy that everyone will become Muslim and will all live happily ever after. Every age, the Prophet, salla'llahu alayhi wa sallam, said, "every age after us will be worse than the age before it, until the end of time." That is the historical perspective of the human being. That is the dilemma of the human being, and the reality of Islam confronts it.

How Can I Train Myself for Jihad?

The following article appeared on the "Azzam" website from England which is currently unavailable online from computers in America. The Azzam website is revolutionary in content and context, testing the outer limits of parliamentary states for hosting overt enemies. Its original URL address is <HTTP://WWW.QOQAZ.CO.ZA/HTML/ARTICLESJIHADTRAIN.HTM>

"And prepare against them all you can of power, including steeds of war to terrorize the enemies of Allah and others besides whom you may not know, but Allah does know. And whatever you shall spend in the Cause of Allah shall be repaid unto you, and you shall not be treated unjustly." [Quran 8:60]

In commenting on this verse, the Messenger (SAWS) said: "Indeed, power is shooting, power is shooting, power is shooting." [Sahih Muslim]

Narrated Abu Hurairah (RA) that the Messenger (SAWS) said: "If anyone keeps a horse for Jihad in the Way of Allah, motivated by his faith in Allah and his belief in His Promise, then he will be rewarded on the Day of Resurrection for what the horse has eaten or drunk and for its dung and urine." [Sahih Al-Bukhari]

After receiving a number of e-mails asking about this topic, we decided to include a small article about this subject. It is broken down into sections, but should be read from beginning to end for maximum benefit.

1.0 What is Jihad?
Jihad literally means "to struggle." In the military sense it is meant in the context, "to struggle against oppression." Jihad is therefore an act to liberate people from the oppression of tyrants. Jihad is not illegal acts of terror against innocent people. When tabloid journalism mistakenly informs the masses that Jihad is "to commit illegal acts of terror," they are revealing the lack of their research and the extent of their unprofessional approach to the subject.

2.0 Military Training is an Islamic Obligation not an Option

According to the verse above ("And prepare against them all you can of power . . ."), military training is an obligation in Islam upon every sane, male, mature Muslim, whether rich or poor, whether studying or working and whether living in a Muslim or non-Muslim country. The Prophet (SAWS) explained the meaning of the term "power" in the above verse during a Friday Sermon by mentioning that power was specifically shooting.

The verse mentions "what you can . . ." meaning that the Muslims must prepare to the utmost of their ability and circumstances.

"Steeds of war'" refer to the horses that were prepared for battle. In this day and age, the scholars of Islam have explained this term to mean all forms of modern weaponry such as infantry weapons, tanks, artillery, aircraft, etc.

The above verse is clear evidence that military training of all sorts is an Islamic obligation, not something optional. Furthermore, the obligation is according to one's ability, in that the Muslims must use every means at their disposal to undertake military and physical training for Jihad.

In Surah Taubah of the Qur'an, Allah answers those hypocrites who made feeble excuses to the Messenger of Allah (SAWS) so that they would not have to participate in the Battle of Tabuk. The hypocrites came to the Prophet (SAWS) and gave their excuses with the impression that they really wanted to take part in the battle, but difficult circumstances outside their control were preventing them from doing so. Allah's response was:

"And if they had really intended to march forth, certainly they would have made some preparation for it; but Allah hated them being sent forth, so He made them lag behind, and it was said to them, 'Sit you among those who sit at home (women, children, elderly, etc.)'" [Quran 9:46]

These hypocrites had not intended to participate in Jihad from the outset and their lack of preparations was the evidence for this. Had they really wanted to take part in the Jihad, they would have prepared themselves and tried their utmost to join the battle, like the three companions who approached the Messenger (SAWS) before the Battle of Tabuk, requesting horses or mules so they could join the Battle. When the Prophet (SAWS) informed them that he could not provide them with mounts, they turned back with their eyes full of tears that they could not join the battle:

"Nor is there blame on those who came to you to be provided with mounts, when you said, 'I can find no mounts for you,' they turned back, while their eyes were overflowing with tears of grief that they could not find anything to spend for Jihad." [Quran 9:92]

Therefore, those Muslims unable to participate in Jihad at this present time whatever the reason have no excuse before Allah for not training for Jihad.

The Messenger of Allah (SAWS) said: "Whoever dies without having fought in battle, nor having the sincere wish in his heart to fight in battle, dies on a branch of hypocrisy." [Sahih Al-Bukhari]

The one sincere to fight in battle is the one who makes suitable preparations for battle. A Muslim that spends a life empty of any physical or military training for Jihad, let alone Jihad itself, should fear dying on a branch of hypocrisy according to the above hadith. True Iman (faith) is manifested in actions and if someone truly wishes to fight Jihad, he will prepare himself in all possible ways.

3.0 Sincerity of Intention

Training is an Islamic obligation so a Muslim must undertake it for the correct reason otherwise he will neither be blessed nor rewarded by Allah for all his efforts. The correct reason to train is to train for Jihad which is undertaken to please Allah alone. Therefore the Muslim must not publicly display to the people what he is doing, nor must he show off during his training, nor seek fame or reputation in the eyes of human beings during his training. If he wishes to be rewarded by Allah and blessed and helped in his training, all his training must be done to obtain the Pleasure of Allah alone.

In practical terms, this would mean avoiding training in the company of people (e.g. women) who might be impressed by the one training, flouting muscles etc. This also means to avoid publicly announcing to everyone that one is going for training or dropping subtle hints such as leaving clothes and equipment in view of the people. The beloved Companions of the Prophet (SAWS) used to hide their good deeds more than they used to hide their sins, for fear of their intention being corrupted. Train only to please Allah and He will help you, reward you and bless you, for there is no benefit in gaining the pleasure of human beings.

4.0 Training in your Country of Residence
4.1 Physical Training
The basis of all Jihad training is something that can be done in every country of the World: physical training. This requires little or no equipment and is something that one can fit round one's daily routine. This comprises four main areas: stamina, strength, speed and agility. In order to benefit from your physical training, it is important that it is done regularly, ideally at the same time of the day if possible, three times a week, which leaves a rest day between exercise sessions to allow the body to recuperate. Some general suggestions are given below though there are many variations to this type of training. Consult an expert or read books or Internet articles on the topic. There are books available to the general public of physical training within the Army (US Army Field Manuals and books written by ex-British soldiers).

Stamina involves being able to sustain the body at a high rate of activity for prolonged periods of time. Stamina is built up by aerobic exercise in sessions of at least 20 minutes duration. Aerobic exercise is any activity that keeps the heart rate at a level higher than normal for a sustained amount of time. It differs from anaerobic exercise in which the heart rate increases to a very high level but only for short bursts of time. Running, swimming, rowing are some exercises which build up stamina. For the exercise to be of benefit, it must be sustained for at least 20 minutes.

Running by far is the best and most practical form of stamina training for Jihad. Start your session by running for about five minutes in order to warm up. Then proceed to stretch the major muscles in your body by holding them in a stretched position for at least 30 seconds. Avoid "bouncing" stretching as this can lead to serious injury. After this, run at a steady pace for a fixed period of time. Start easy, e.g. 10 minutes, then gradually build up every session until you can continue running at that pace for 20 minutes, 30 minutes or more. Inhale deep breaths through your nose and exhale through your mouth whilst running. It is better to run in boots as running in boots reflects the reality of running in Jihad. It is also advisable to add shock absorbing insoles into your boots before running, as these cushion the stress on the leg bones and joints. These insoles, e.g. Sorbothane, are available in camping and sports stores. Once you can sustain running at a constant pace for 30 minutes or more, you can add variety into the sessions by running up and down hill, running with ankle weights or running carrying loads, e.g. a bag full of books.

Strength training can be undertaken in the form of press-ups, squats, abdominal crunches, etc. or by following a regular routing in weight training at a gymnasium. It is better to go to the gym with another brother if possible, or go at a time when there are as few women as possible. Public gymnasiums are generally un-Islamic places with loud music and improperly dressed men and women. Such an atmosphere is not befitting for the training of a Mujahid. In all cases, learn how to use the equipment properly, start easy and build up gradually and make sure you stretch and warm up enough before each session.

Speed and agility can be built up by sprinting, running around obstacles, climbing over walls and similar activities. Practicing martial arts is the best way to develop speed and agility.

4.2 Martial Arts
It is vital to join a martial arts club as part of the training for Jihad. In addition to teaching you how to defend yourself and strengthen your body, martial arts develop self-discipline and controlled aggression. In some countries, there are martial arts run by Muslim instructors, but one can join other clubs if there are no Muslim clubs in his area. It is preferable to join clubs that emphasize on street-fighting and self-defense such as kung-fu styles rather than tournament fighting. You would never use high or flying kicks in a real fight but you may in tournaments. As with any activity, regular attendance for a number of months is necessary in order to benefit from martial arts. Many people join martial arts clubs but are unable to stick with them. Joining clubs that teach weapons such as sword or knife-fighting are also good at advanced stages.

4.3 Survival and Outdoors Training

The majority of the time spent in Jihad is learning to cope with harsh, physically and mentally demanding living conditions. It is not about fighting glamorous battles for your pictures to appear on the Internet. Jihad is tough and difficult, which is why the rewards for it are so great.

Although survival training is taught at centers in some countries, it is expensive and, in many cases, nothing special that you cannot learn and practice yourself by reading books on the subject. The best way to learn these skills is to go camping into the outdoors with a small group of brothers. Avoid going to a camping site, since these are holiday areas where many facilities are available such as hot showers, gas, etc. The best training is to take some tents, food and water and warm clothes in a rucksack and go on treks lasting 2–3 days at a time. If you do not have an experienced person with you, then start easy and build up gradually. Learn how to purify water, make wudu and istinja in cold water, attend to the call of nature in the outdoors, cook or heat food out in the open, making different types of knots with ropes, setting up tents and other similar activities. Learning how to start and maintain a fire in all conditions, wet or dry, with and without lighting instruments is one of the most important survival skills.

Learning how to walk long distances carrying loads up to one-third of your bodyweight, walking over difficult terrain at night without the use of torches and navigational skills using a compass/map or the stars are also useful skills. Many of these skills can be learnt from books and then practiced out in the outdoors.

4.4 Firearms Training

Firearms training differs from country to country. In some countries, possession of firearms by the public is illegal, in other countries it is legal. In some countries of the World, especially the USA, firearms training is available to the general public. One should try to join a shooting club if possible and make regular visits to the firing range. There are many firearms courses available to the public in USA, ranging from one day to two weeks or more. These courses are good but expensive. Some of them are only meant for security personnel but generally they will teach anyone. It is also better to attend these courses in pairs or by yourself, no more. Do not make public announcements when going on such a course. Find one, book your place, go there, learn, come back home and keep it yourself. Whilst on the course, keep your opinions to yourself, do not argue or debate with anyone, do not preach about Islam and make Salah in secret. You are going there to train for Jihad, not call people to Islam.

Useful courses to learn are sniping, general shooting and other rifle courses. Handgun courses are useful but only after you have mastered rifles.

In other countries, e.g. some states of USA, South Africa, it is perfectly legal for members of the public to own certain types of firearms. If you live in such a country, obtain an assault rifle legally, preferably AK-47 or variations, learn how to use it properly and go and practice in the areas allowed for such training. If you cannot get someone to teach you, you can purchase books about shooting technique and practice shooting stationary targets at different distances, with a partner. You can also practice running a distance, e.g. 1 km, then shooting targets from a distance. Again, there are many variations and unless you have an experienced, trained person to learn from, you will be able to do little more than perfect your shooting technique at different ranges.

Under NO circumstances should you play or experiment with firearms. NEVER EVER point a firearm at anyone for a joke, whether loaded or unloaded. Keep firearms unloaded and out of reach of children. If you feel that you will be unable to control a firearm or your temper, do not purchase one.

Respect the laws of the country you are in and avoid dealing in illegal firearms. One can learn to operate many arms legally, so there is no need to spend years in prison for dealing in small, illegal firearms. Learn the most you can according to your circumstances and leave the rest to when you actually go for Jihad.

4.6 Military Training
Although sometimes it is difficult to obtain comprehensive military training in one's home country, it is very easy to do plenty of background reading using freely-available books and CDs, before one actually goes abroad.

The US Army has produced a number of military field manuals on CD on all topics from light weapons, tanks and artillery to mines, military fieldcraft and combat medicine. The full set is available on CD for less than $100 and many field manuals are also available on the Internet. One source of availability is http://www.chqsoftware.com or by searching for the term "US Military Field Manuals CD" or just "US Military Field Manuals Online." Even though the US Army Field Manuals contain information specific to US Weapons, they still contain a large amount of useful information applicable in all circumstances. It is useful to get a full set of CDs for your mosque or Islamic society that everyone can use.

Some topics to read up about include:
Physical fitness training
Ammunition
Sniper training
Mine/ Counter-Mine Operations and Recognition of Different Mines
Mortar
AK-47 and other Soviet weapon Operating Manuals
Terrain Analysis
Map Reading and Land Navigation
Camouflage and concealment
Survival
Combat skills of the soldier
First Aid for Soldiers
Cold Weather Training

5.0 Jihad Training Abroad

There are some countries where one can obtain Jihad training but we are not in a position to comment on the suitability or unsuitability of any particular country. Contact individuals you know and trust and they will be able to advise you better. If you are true to Allah, Allah will be true to you and He will find you a way to do what you want to do.

KILLING INFIDELS IN CHECHNYA
A Foreign Mujahid's Diary

FIGHTERS INVOKED BY JIHAD TO KILL THE INFIDEL BROUGHT THIS
NORWEGIAN MUJAHID TO CHECHNYA. THIS IS AN EXCERPT FROM HIS
DIARY.

TUESDAY 04 JULY 2000

Each day in Chechnya is not unpredictable but completely unknown.
Only Allah knows what adventure each day (or night) will bring and
what repercussions it will have for the overall situation and each individual.

About five days ago, I got my essential belongings together and set off
from Field Commander Abu Jafar's camp to go somewhere else. Not
far from the camp I met some brothers who told me that the Russians
had just set up a post on a nearby road blocking my route, causing me
to return. Being a bit tired I went straight to sleep. Early afternoon I
was woken by a brother asking for my AK-74 as the Russians had
entered the forest. I looked out to see a column of brothers being
briskly led out by Abu Jafar.

By the time I had got my gear on and set out after them into the
forest, Abu Jafar had disappeared into the woods and I was left with a
group of 15 or so brothers wondering where to go. With a lot of
artillery and helicopters around us, events were moving along very fast
and Abu Jafar told us via the radio to keep a lookout over a nearby
gorge rather than waste time joining up with him.

We descended into the gorge and I was still trying to make the best of
a base of a tree when suddenly there was a crescendo of automatic fire.
The Russians had come into view some 20m below and had immediately seen Abul-Harith moving between trees to my right. He fired first
but within a second the whole gorge was ablaze. These guys were
Spetsnaz (Special Forces) with some of them carrying Vinterez, a
weapon only Special Forces use. Alhamdullilah we had the vantage
point, and the battle was joined by brothers on the opposite side of the
gorge just above the Russians, some of whom had climbed out of the
gorge to a point opposite ours.

Pistoniks (rifle-launched grenades) and other grenades from our side were answered by artillery being directed onto us by the Russians. For the rest of the day there was intermittent fighting, shouting and then the most intense pounding by mortars, artillery and helicopters. The intensity was such that sounds of the many explosions became a one roar. Field Commander Abu Waleed who had arrived some 300m to our rear with more brothers and ammunition had to go back. It's incredible to behold — the earth shaking as craters are gouged, huge trees shattering like ice, and the air filled with the rush of shrapnel. *Subhanallah*, it was an experience!

Absolutely nothing to do but sit, wait and make dua! Alhamdullilah we were so close to the Russians that some of the projectiles were landing right where they were and they were definitely being showered by the shrapnel. As sunset approached, five of us circled around them and attacked them in the rear further down the valley before regrouping and returning to the camp. The Russians stayed where they were for the rest of the night, too terrified to move!

Brothers who went back the next morning saw six of them (Russians) dead with all their weapons still in the river bed (at the bottom of the gorge/valley) with the remaining Russians still there.

The next day, soon after *Fajr*, word went round that we were decamping and going to move. This was the last morning of my tentmate Abu Malik Al-Qahtani (Arabian Peninsula). That morning he did all the work of packing up our tent and soon we were ready to move.

The whole forest had pretty much been constantly bombed for the last few days and it was that morning that Abu Asim Al-Jeddawi (Arabian Peninsula) was killed with shrapnel to the head. Brothers all around the area were having contacts with Russians and news came in from Abu Bakr that he had encountered a Russian team which had gone into the adjoining valley after some fighting. In this incident, two Russians (and a tracking sniffer dog) were killed and it was here that Abu Saad Al-Kandahari (Arabian Peninsula) was instantly shaheed soon followed by Abu Saeed Ash-Shimali (Arabian Peninsula) from a bullet wound to the head.

The time and place of one's death is written. As we descended into the valley, Abu Malik was at the front and setting the pace at a jog. He shouldn't even have been with us as only brothers with Pistoniks were told to go. However looking back, it's as if Abu Malik was late for an appointment and was rushing to be on time! As the pace slowed in the undergrowth, Abu Malik was sometimes 15–20m ahead on his own and he was the first one to spot them. Off the trails it is often difficult to see more than a few meters and so it was then that there were three of us in rough line advancing and firing occasionally. Madness! I was on the right, Abu Malik in the middle and Abu Rawda on the left with some 10m separating us.

I saw a trail in the leaves which led even further to the right. As I advanced, I saw a magazine followed by some 20m or so by a ruck sack. We had made a great deal of noise and the Russians had been surprised by the speed of our advance, so they had fled leaving their belongings behind! Anyway, there was a fallen tree on the edge of a sharp decline to a stream below which I approached after a bit of firing. Then, just as I peered over it, a single pistol shot came whistling through the trunk over my head. *Subhanallah* — it was the Russians and this one had fired just a fraction too soon. As I fell to the ground a grenade was lobbed, hit the tree and fell back on their side though only 2m away! The nearest Russian who had fired the pistol was no more than a few meters away and insha-Allah was injured by his own grenade. I lobbed some grenades in their direction and during the ensuing firefight.

It was immediately after this that I heard groaning to my left down near the stream. I thought at the time it was a Russian and so did nothing more than to dig in and prepare for more of the above. As the brothers called out to each other I learned that Abu Malik had descended down to the stream and had been injured. Only some hours later when the Russians had fled did we go down and I realized that it had been Abu Malik that had been groaning. He was lying shaheed in the stream, bullet wound to the abdomen. He had been in an incredibly dangerous place, an open stream with thick undergrowth on either side, and had been shot in the side of his chest. The Russians had also taken his weapon.

Even as I write this, that afternoon seems so surreal. Many of the things we did were lunacy. However, as always any victory came completely from Allah who helped us, protected us from massive shelling and put fear into the hearts of the Russians. These Russians were not your run-of-the mill conscripts, but professional elite troops whose training and expertise dwarfs that of your typical young mujahid.

So now, about a week later, my dear friend Abu Malik (may Allah have Mercy on him) is no longer with us; joining the many martyrs of this war. Some brothers are given martyrdom but when I think of Abu Malik and how he rushed forward that afternoon, it is as if he embraced martyrdom. One of the finest brothers that I knew here, from Ahlul Bait (Direct Descendants of the Prophet) and a *hafiz* of the Qur'an (memorized whole Qur'an), he was very modest, had excellent manners, a very pleasant personality and a dignified bearing. Around the camp, he would often be seen waking the brothers for *Fajr* prayers, cooking the bread or heading out on reconnaissance. His will is translated at the bottom.

There were five *shaheed* that day. In addition to the four Arabs there was Abdur-Rauf Uzbeki — the first fatality of the day. This brother had been due to leave some few weeks ago but changed his mind at the last moment. The Uzbeks are the unknown heroes of this war. Solid *Iman* in Allah, utterly uncomplaining, completely reliable and unflinching in battle.

Immediately after retrieving his body, Abu Jafar decamped, and left with his group and the injured. Three days of trekking and weaving through the Russian lines, followed. Field Commander Abu Waleed opted to stay behind and see whether the Russians would back off from further intrusions. This war only goes on with the help of Allah and so make a NEW appeal for dua on the website. Tell them from the *Mujahideen* here that their dua do make a difference *insha-Allah*.
— Brother X (Norwegian National), Chechnya, 04 July 2000.

GENOCIDE: SERBIA, 1993
By Hizb-ut-Tahrir

THIS PIECE, SO REMINISCENT OF EARLY CHRISTIAN MARTYR SCREEDS, MEANS TO OUTRAGE AND PROVOKE ACTION AGAINST THE NON-BELIEVER, THOUGH THE SERBIAN CRIMINALS COMMITTING THE VICIOUS CRIMES AGAINST THE MUSLIMS DESCRIBED HERE ARE SAID TO HAVE RECEIVED "THREATS" FROM THE UNITED STATES, A COUNTRY DESERVING OF JIHAD, AS POINTED OUT ELSEWHERE ON THE <WWW.HIZBU-TAHRIR> WEBSITE.

Europa Times has published this article with deep misgivings, for what it reveals is almost unbearable. Finally we decided to leave the choice to you if for no other reason than that the victims would surely have wished the world to know as desperately as they must have asked "why?" in their last moments. If our readers don't make it past the first few lines, we'll understand. We struggled, too. For the victims we can only reach for words to express the emotions that are evoked. For the perpetrators of these crimes, one can only feel wild bewilderment. But for those in positions of power and influence who could have done something to protect those innocents but failed them one can feel an abiding contempt. Please remember that these are not the most sensational cases selected to shock, but they are just a few scores of cases submitted by the Government of Bosnia-Herzegovina to the International Court of Justice at the Hague earlier this year. The tragedy lies in that none of this need have happened. At the highest levels, the politicos know this; they abandoned the Bosnians because, as leaders, they were inadequate even to stand against a ragbag of cut-throat militiamen if it risked a few votes. The Serbs, like scavengers at a kill, were sent scurrying at each US threat but still the lesson wasn't or couldn't be learned. The Serbs' luck lay in finding, in Europe's leaders, a troupe of politicos even more craven than themselves. The lesser functionaries were, as always, just following office memos. This, then, is dedicated to you — all you politicians, officials and bureaucrats who made this hell possible. On March 20, 1993 before the International Court of Justice at the Hague, Bosnia and Herzegovina instituted proceedings against Yugoslavia (Serbia and Montenegro) for an Application of the Convention on the Prevention and Punishment of the Crime of Genocide. In a "Statement of Fact," the People and State of Bosnia and Herzegovina stated that, while it could not "catalogue all the available evidence related to the acts of genocide that have been perpetrated upon its own people," a collection of evidence was listed with which to charge that Serbia and Montenegro and its agents and surrogates "have committed Genocide and will continue to commit Genocide until they are stopped." The following are verbatim extracts from the official "Statement of Fact" submitted by the Bosnians to the International Court of Justice.

BOSNIA AND HERZEGOVIAN V. YUGOSLAVIA (SERBIA AND MONTENEGRO)

Section 44D Page 32 Paragraph (h)
"Serb torturers used iron bars to beat Muslims (some Croats) to death. They would not spare any part of the body, breaking all the bones so that the beaten Muslims begged their torturers for a bullet. Serb torturers stabbed my arms with knives. I saw Serb torturers stab others, twisting and turning the knives inside them. I saw how Muslims were forced to bite each others testicles off, their mouth filled with testicles and blood, ripped blood vessels sticking out of their mouths. Daily Serb torturers forced Muslim prisoners to f . . . each other, to perform oral sex on each other, forcing those bestialities especially among family members, between a father and a son."

Paragraph (k)
"Omarska extermination camp had women prisoners as well. Daily Serb soldiers would take girls and bring 5–6 men per girl, Serb soldiers, prisoners to rape them. Sometimes I was among the men forced to rape the girl(s). They were raped constantly, non-stop every day. They raped older women, Croats, 60–65 years of age. One named Divis, was raped by 12 men. There were many young girls, around 16 years that were being raped daily . . ."

Paragraph (l)
"Serbs would torture us by extinguishing their cigarettes on our bodies. However that was reserved mostly for Muslim women. Serbs would extinguish their cigarettes on the Muslim women's naked bodies, mostly their breasts and vaginas. Serbs would shove bottles (mostly half-liter beer bottles) up the Muslim girls' vaginas . . . Serbs would stick a bottle inside Muslim women's vagina and then break them inside them."

Paragraph (m)

"In Omarska there was a shop where dump trucks were being repaired, we called it the 'Red House'. Serb torturers killed many prisoners in the Red House. That was the place where I saw the Serbs cut people's noses, ears, limbs. When I was cleaning the room in the Red House the floor was full of human body pieces, pieces of the skull, fingers, ears, noses. Outside on the road, skull pieces were scattered everywhere."

Paragraph (o)

I witnessed Serb guards shoving a fire hydrant hose into a man's sphincter (it was a man from a village of Kozarac), letting the water run full force from the hydrant, until the man swelled and then died bursting to pieces.

VICTIM N 004JF SECTION 44E PAGE 38 PARAGRAPH (A)

"Every day they entered house in which there were only women and children remaining. They plundered, killed and raped even the five-year-old girls and old women. So our house was a prison camp to us for they could come in and kill us at any time of the day or night. When they were searching my home we were taken into the backyard and made to stand in a row. They threatened to shoot us if they found weapons in the house. There were no weapons, they plundered the house and took the gold and told us they would come back again and kill us because we were Muslims."

FUNDAMENTALISM IN RUSSIA
An Interview with Islamic Committee's Heidar Jamal
By Nabi Abdullaev
MoscowTimes.com 11/16/01

Heidar Jama

HEIDAR JEMAL DESCRIBES HIMSELF AS A MUSLIM
FUNDAMENTALIST. HE HEADS THE RUSSIAN BRANCH
OF THE ISLAMIC COMMITTEE, FOUNDED IN
KHARTOUM, SUDAN, IN 1993. IN THIS ROLE, JEMAL,
54, ADVOCATES RUSSIA'S INVOLVEMENT IN WHAT HE
CALLS THE "GLOBAL PROJECT OF ISLAM."

Jemal, an ethnic Azeri born in Moscow, speaks five languages in addition to Russian: Farsi, English, French, Italian and Turkish. In the Soviet era, he worked as an assessor in the library of the Academy of Social Sciences. He became active in religious and political affairs during perestroika. His alliances run the gamut from the ultranationalist group Pamyat (Memory), which he worked for briefly in 1989, to the late Ahmed Khomeini, son of Ayatollah Khomeini. Jemal helped found the Islamic Rebirth Party in 1990 and ran unsuccessfully for the State Duma in 1995. In 1999, his Islamic Committee joined forces with hard-line communists Viktor Ilyukhin and Albert Makashov.

The thread that links all of Jemal's strategic partners has been a virulent anti-Western stance. Jemal recently spoke with The Moscow Times about Islam, Russia and anti-globalism.

Q: What does it mean to be a Muslim fundamentalist in Russia?
A: The virtue of Muslim fundamentalism is the same in Russia, Egypt or the United States. It involves striving to live according the teachings of Islam as they were delivered to mankind by our great prophet, Mohammed. But in Russia, fundamentalists face aggression and a lack of understanding both from the authorities and from fellow Muslims who have been disoriented by anti-Muslim propaganda. These people labor under a false notion of a domesticated Islam, a variant of the faith adapted to pre-existing local beliefs and customs. This is nonsense. Islam is a religion that transcends the differences of race, geography and ethnicity among its adherents.

Q: Why, then, does your Islamic Committee seek out allies with explicitly nationalist aims, such as Eduard Limonov's National Bolshevik Party?

A: I value the energy of these young National Bolsheviks. They are the only young people in Russia today who are prepared to go out and fight in a country that is sinking into lethargy. But I want to explain to them that there can be no "national" Bolshevism. The fight for justice is international.

Q: You have compared Usamah Bin Laden to Dr. No of the James Bond movies.

A: This is how the Western media portray him. The problem with Bin Laden is that we don't know his ideology. We only know his theological declarations on the confrontation between Islam and the infidels, and that is not enough to understand his position. In any war, the combatants have goals they plan to implement when the fighting is done. These goals are usually formulated by a charismatic leader, and they constitute his ideological message. In the absence of such a message, one can rightfully question whether a leader — Bin Laden, in this case — has not merely been promoted and pumped up by those who require a Muslim villain.

Q: Are you in contact with the Chechen leadership?

A: I can't answer that question, because acknowledgement of such contacts could be used as grounds for charging me with treason.

Q: What is your position on the war in Chechnya?

A: The Islamic Committee calls for an end to the war and withdrawal of Russian troops from Chechnya.

Q: Relations between the Muslim world and the West are extremely tense of late. What is fueling this conflict? Is this another war with the "infidels"?

A: The struggle with infidels must not be understood as merely a provocative slogan. The real infidels today are not those who practice a faith other than Islam, not Christians or Jews, but the oligarchs who flout basic human rights in pursuit of absolute power. The oligarchs and the heads of multinational corporations are filled with contempt for the mass of their fellow men and treat them like dirt.

The "clash of civilizations" has become a fashionable cliché, but we must not forget the class conflict that underlies it. Today, the strong oppress the weak more vigorously than ever. Since the beginning of perestroika in Russia, the wealth of the richest 1 percent of the world's population has doubled. And in the Third World, social and political exploitation of the masses resembles something out of Dickens. In these circumstances, Islam emerges not as a religion in the traditional secularist understanding of that term, but as a comprehensive political ideology that defends the weak and the oppressed.

Q: What makes the Muslim project, which is also global in scope, preferable to Western globalism, which you have called "Atlantism"? A: Islam and Atlantism are two opposed versions of globalism, and there is not room for both in the world. Islamic globalism is based on the principle of transcendent justice laid down in the Koran, Sunna and Sharia law. Western globalism, on the other hand, attempts to increase the power and wealth of the elite while preventing a crisis in the system as a whole. These are contradictory goals.

Q: What are fundamentalist Islam's prospects in Russia? A: At the Khartoum conference in 1993, I held Russia up as a country where fundamentalist Islam could be preserved. Russia is a tabula rasa. Reforms here always start from nothing, and there is a boundless interest in new projects. In the Arab world, however, rigid local traditions make it harder to address the tasks of Islamic globalism.

Q: There has already been an attempt to implement fundamentalist Islam in Russia. In Dagestan, the Wahhabis in the villages of Karamakhi and Chabanmakhi expelled the secular authorities and established a Muslim enclave that lasted for about a year. Was this a successful experiment? A: It was a great success. And the destruction of these villages by federal troops in 1999 was the gravest crime committed by the Russian state during the entire period of reform.

Q: But the Wahhabis used violence to force others to follow their laws. A: People are prone to error. Violence halts the process of social disintegration. Islam admits violence to ensure law and order. People had become accustomed to drinking alcohol and violating sexual norms with impunity. Violence must be used to reinstate the basic conditions of communal life, especially in periods of transition. And the violence of the Wahhabis in Karamakhi represents just a tiny fraction of the violence perpetrated by the Russian state against its citizens.

Q: Did the Wahhabis' call to break Russian laws concern you?

A: Current Russian law was concocted by lawyers beholden to the ruling elite with the aim of justifying the giveaway of state property to former communist bureaucrats and the oligarchs during privatization. We live in a criminal state that violates its own laws. In my view, it is a matter of honor for Muslims politically to oppose such laws.

Q: What is the true measure of Muslim political power in Russia?

A: Political Islam in Russia works at the grass-roots level to influence the decisions of the Russian leadership and to bridge the gap between the Russian and Muslim civilizations.

Political Islam directly contributed to ending the first Chechen war, for instance. The Union of Muslims of Russia and the Islamic Committee cooperated with General Alexander Lebed.

During Boris Yeltsin's first term, Russian foreign policy, directed by Andrei Kozyrev, placed Russia in a position of subordination to Western priorities. Most Russian officials came to see the world as a mono-polar structure run by the United States. I think that our steadfast opposition to this view helped to popularize a more multipolar worldview among Russia's decision-makers.

RESTRICTIONS IMPOSED BY THE TALIBAN

FROM THE REVOLUTIONARY ASSOCIATION OF THE WOMEN OF AFGHANISTAN, <WWW.RAWA.ORG>

The following list offers only an abbreviated glimpse of the hellish lives Afghan women are forced to lead under the Taliban, and can not begin to reflect the depth of female deprivations and sufferings. Taliban treat women worse than they treat animals. In fact, even as Taliban declare the keeping of caged birds and animals illegal, they imprison Afghan women within the four walls of their own houses. Women have no importance in Taliban eyes unless they are occupied producing children, satisfying male sexual needs or attending to the drudgery of daily housework. Jehadi fundamentalists such as Gulbaddin, Rabbani, Masood, Sayyaf, Khalili, Akbari, Mazari and their co-criminal Dostum have committed the most treacherous and filthy crimes against Afghan women. And as more areas come under Taliban control, even if the number of rapes and murders perpetrated against women falls, Taliban restrictions — comparable to those from the middle ages — will continue to kill the spirit of our people while depriving them of a humane existence. We consider Taliban more treacherous and ignorant than Jehadis. According to our people, "Jehadis were killing us with guns and swords but Taliban are killing us with cotton."

Taliban restrictions and mistreatment of women include:

1. Complete ban on women's work outside the home, which also applies to female teachers, engineers and most professionals. Only a few female doctors and nurses are allowed to work in some hospitals in Kabul.
2. Complete ban on women's activity outside the home unless accompanied by a mahram (close male relative such as a father, brother or husband).
3. Ban on women dealing with male shopkeepers.
4. Ban on women being treated by male doctors.
5. Ban on women studying at schools, universities or any other educational institution. (Taliban have converted girls' schools into religious seminaries.)

6. Requirement that women wear a long veil (burqa), which covers them from head to toe.
7. Whipping, beating and verbal abuse of women not clothed in accordance with Taliban rules, or of women unaccompanied by a mahram.
8. Whipping of women in public for having non-covered ankles.
9. Public stoning of women accused of having sex outside marriage. (A number of lovers are stoned to death under this rule.)
10. Ban on the use of cosmetics. (Many women with painted nails have had fingers cut off.)
11. Ban on women talking or shaking hands with non-mahram males.
12. Ban on women laughing loudly. (No stranger should hear a woman's voice.)
13. Ban on women wearing high heel shoes, which would produce sound while walking. (A man must not hear a woman's footsteps.)
14. Ban on women riding in a taxi without a mahram.
15. Ban on women's presence in radio, television or public gatherings of any kind.
16. Ban on women playing sports or entering a sport center or club.
17. Ban on women riding bicycles or motorcycles, even with their mahrams.
18. Ban on women's wearing brightly colored clothes. In Taliban terms, these are "sexually attracting colors."
19. Ban on women gathering for festive occasions such as the Eids, or for any recreational purpose.
20. Ban on women washing clothes next to rivers or in a public place.
21. Modification of all place names including the word "women." For example, "women's garden" has been renamed "spring garden."
22. Ban on women appearing on the balconies of their apartments or houses.
23. Compulsory painting of all windows, so women can not be seen from outside their homes.
24. Ban on male tailors taking women's measurements or sewing women's clothes.
25. Ban on female public baths.
26. Ban on males and females traveling on the same bus. Public buses have now been designated "males only" (or "females only").
27. Ban on flared (wide) pant-legs, even under a burqa.
28. Ban on the photographing or filming of women.
29. Ban on women's pictures printed in newspapers and books, or hung on the walls of houses and shops.

Apart from the above restrictions on women, the Taliban has:

+ Banned listening to music, not only for women but men as well.
+ Banned the watching of movies, television and videos, for everyone.
+ Banned celebrating the traditional new year (Nowroz) on March 21. The Taliban has proclaimed the holiday un-Islamic.
+ Disavowed Labor Day (May 1st), because it is deemed a "communist" holiday.
+ Ordered that all people with non-Islamic names change them to Islamic ones.
+ Forced haircuts upon Afghan youth.
+ The Taliban have arrested dozens of Afghans and sent them behind bars until they are able to grow a "proper beard."
+ Ordered that men wear Islamic clothes and a cap.
+ Ordered that men not shave or trim their beards, which should grow long enough to protrude from a fist clasped at the point of the chin.
+ Ordered that all people attend prayers in mosques five times daily.
+ Banned the keeping of pigeons and playing with the birds, describing it as un-Islamic. The violators will be imprisoned and the birds shall be killed. Kite flying has also been stopped.
+ Anyone who carries objectionable literature will be executed.
+ Anyone who converts from Islam to any other religion will be executed.
+ All boy students must wear turbans. They say, "No turban, no education,"
+ Non-Muslim minorities must distinct badge or stitch a yellow cloth onto their dress to be differentiated from the majority Muslim population. Just like what did Nazis with Jews.
+ Banned the use of the internet by both ordinary Afghans and foreigners [though Taliban had its own website, www.taleban.org, now inaccessible].

Forced Abortion, Taliban Style

On May 29, 1997, Layla living in Khairkhana, Kabul, who was five months pregnant, left her house for a routine pregnancy check-up at the nearby Parwan Maternity Clinic. She was dressed head-to-foot in the prescribed chadari (also called burqa) which only allowed a grill through which she could look out but even her eyes could not be seen. She had to wrap herself carefully in the chadari, as allowing her dress to be seen was against the imposed dress code. Halfway to the clinic she felt suffocated and felt an urgent need for fresh air. Turning into a deserted lane she raised her veil and drew deep breaths, relishing the feeling of relief. Suddenly a scourge-wielding Taliban militiaman screaming abuse materialized out of nowhere.

"Why have you bared your face! Why have you bared your face!" he kept screaming while he poured out the vilest invectives. His whip hand was raised and before Layla could say anything the blow landed on her distended abdomen. Layla could only scream "Bradar jan, [brother, dear], don't hit me, I am with child, I am going to the clinic," but the frenzied Taliban kept raining down blows on the miserable woman. The pain and the terror made Layla sit down on the dirt and the Taliban went away after a few more vicious blows of the lash. None of the few passers-by could dare to intercede. By now Layla was bleeding but both she and one or two passers-by knew that she could not hope for a helping hand as there were no women around and it is against Taliban edicts for a male to touch any female other than close family members. Any man extending a helping hand to a woman in need was sure to receive the same treatment that had been meted out to Layla a moment ago. Layla could only drag herself to the clinic where she passed out. When she came to she was drenched in blood and the nurses told her that she had had a miscarriage. It was not long before she lost consciousness again. The following day she developed a soaring temperature and doctors diagnosed peritonitis. They recommended abdominal surgery but before they could obtain the necessary go-ahead from the Taliban authorities Layla breathed her last.

Reckoning for Wearing Thin Socks

On July 5 1997 at around 11:30 in the morning I was walking along the road to the north of Shahr-i-Nao Park [a park in central Kabul]. I was not very far from the entrance of the Ministry of Martyrs and the Disabled when a steel-cable-thong-wielding Taliban confronted me. I was wearing a chadari and had taken pains to ensure that my appearance was in total conformity with Taliban prescriptions. I was at a loss to understand what I had done to irk the monster. The Taliban asked me fiercely in Kandahari dialect Pashtu: "The sock that you are wearing is onionskin-thin. How are going to answer for that on the day of reckoning? You will burn in everlasting fire!"

I knew better than to try to defend myself. I told him piteously that I did not have the presence of mind to remember that such socks were prohibited; I had made a grave mistake and pledged that it would not be repeated in the future. My grovelling did not pacify him. "You always have enough presence of mind not to forget books and pens and schooling and to whine that you are not allowed to go to school, but when it comes to showy dress, that's when you lose your presence of mind!" I saw that I was up against a cretin and the terror of what he might do next rendered me speechless. I remained silent.

A crowd began to form. "Say toba here and now for wearing a thin sock!" he ordered. [Toba: repentance; considered highly humiliating if forced in public.] I could feel the eyes of the crowd boring through my chadari. I was soaking in perspiration and feeling asphyxiated. I had a choice of two species of pain and humiliation: public flogging and public toba. I chose the lesser evil. To this day I relive in my nightmares the public toba of repeating aloud three time for all to hear, in the middle of a crowd on a public street, that I will never, ever, be so wanton as to wear thin socks again. When will the nightmare end?

"GOD'S ORDER TO KILL AMERICANS"
Usamah Bin-Laden's 1998 Fatwa

23 February 1998
SHAYKH USAMAH BIN-MUHAMMAD BIN-LADEN
AYMAN AL-ZAWAHIRI, AMIR OF THE JIHAD GROUP IN EGYPT
ABU-YASIR RIFA'I AHMAD TAHA, EGYPTIAN ISLAMIC GROUP
SHAYKH MIR HAMZAH, SECRETARY OF THE JAMIAT-UL-ULEMA-E-PAKISTAN
FAZLUR RAHMAN, AMIR OF THE JIHAD MOVEMENT IN BANGLADESH

Praise be to God, who revealed the Book, controls the clouds, defeats factionalism, and says in His Book: "But when the forbidden months are past, then fight and slay the pagans wherever ye find them, seize them, beleager them, and lie in wait for them in every stratagem (of war)"; and peace be upon our Prophet, Muhammad Bin-'Abdallah, who said: "I have been sent with the sword between my hands to ensure that no one but God is worshipped, God who put my livelihood under the shadow of my spear and who inflicts humiliation and scorn on those who disobey my orders."

The Arabian Peninsula has never — since God made it flat, created its desert, and encircled it with seas — been stormed by any forces like the crusader armies spreading in it like locusts, eating its riches and wiping out its plantations. All this is happening at a time in which nations are attacking Muslims like people fighting over a plate of food. In the light of the grave situation and the lack of support, we and you are obliged to discuss current events, and we should all agree on how to settle the matter.

No one argues today about three facts that are known to everyone; we will list them, in order to remind everyone:

First, for over seven years the United States has been occupying the lands of Islam in the holiest of places, the Arabian Peninsula, plundering its riches, dictating to its rulers, humiliating its people, terrorizing its neighbors, and turning its bases in the Peninsula into a spearhead through which to fight the neighboring Muslim peoples.

If some people have in the past argued about the fact of the occupation, all the people of the Peninsula have now acknowledged it. The best proof of this is the Americans' continuing aggression against the Iraqi people using the Peninsula as a staging post, even though all its rulers are against their territories being used to that end, but they are helpless.

Second, despite the great dev-
astation inflicted on the Iraqi
people by the crusader-Zionist
alliance, and despite the huge
number of those killed, which has
exceeded one million; despite all
this, the Americans are once
against trying to repeat the horrific
massacres, as though they are not
content with the protracted blockade imposed after the ferocious
war or the fragmentation and dev-
astation.

So here they come to annihi-
late what is left of this people and to humiliate their Muslim neighbors.

Third, if the Americans' aims behind these wars are religious and
economic, the aim is also to serve the Jews' petty state and divert
attention from its occupation of Jerusalem and murder of Muslims
there. The best proof of this is their eagerness to destroy Iraq, the
strongest neighboring Arab state, and their endeavor to fragment all
the states of the region such as Iraq, Saudi Arabia, Egypt, and Sudan
into paper statelets and through their disunion and weakness to guarantee Israel's survival and the continuation of the brutal crusade occupation of the Peninsula.

All these crimes and sins committed by the Americans are a clear
declaration of war on God, his messenger, and Muslims. And ulema
have throughout Islamic history unanimously agreed that the jihad is
an individual duty if the enemy destroys the Muslim countries. This
was revealed by Imam Bin-Qadamah in "Al-Mughni," Imam al-Kisa'i
in "Al-Bada'i," al-Qurtubi in his interpretation, and the shaykh of al-
Islam in his books, where he said: "As for the fighting to repulse [an
enemy], it is aimed at defending sanctity and religion, and it is a duty
as agreed [by the ulema]. Nothing is more sacred than belief except
repulsing an enemy who is attacking religion and life."

On that basis, and in compliance with God's order, we issue the
following fatwa to all Muslims:

The ruling to kill the Americans and their allies — civilians and
military — is an individual duty for every Muslim who can do it in
any country in which it is possible to do it, in order to liberate the al-
Aqsa Mosque and the holy mosque [Mecca] from their grip, and in

order for their armies to move out of all the lands of Islam, defeated and unable to threaten any Muslim. This is in accordance with the words of Almighty God, "and fight the pagans all together as they fight you all together," and "fight them until there is no more tumult or oppression, and there prevail justice and faith in God."

This is in addition to the words of Almighty God: "And why should ye not fight in the cause of God and of those who, being weak, are ill-treated (and oppressed)? — women and children, whose cry is: 'Our Lord, rescue us from this town, whose people are oppressors; and raise for us from thee one who will help!'"

We — with God's help — call on every Muslim who believes in God and wishes to be rewarded to comply with God's order to kill the Americans and plunder their money wherever and whenever they find it. We also call on Muslim ulema, leaders, youths, and soldiers to launch the raid on Satan's U.S. troops and the devil's supporters allying with them, and to displace those who are behind them so that they may learn a lesson.

Almighty God said: "O ye who believe, give your response to God and His Apostle, when He calleth you to that which will give you life. And know that God cometh between a man and his heart, and that it is He to whom ye shall all be gathered."

Almighty God also says: "O ye who believe, what is the matter with you, that when ye are asked to go forth in the cause of God, ye cling so heavily to the earth! Do ye prefer the life of this world to the hereafter? But little is the comfort of this life, as compared with the hereafter. Unless ye go forth, He will punish you with a grievous penalty, and put others in your place; but Him ye would not harm in the least. For God hath power over all things."

Almighty God also says: "So lose no heart, nor fall into despair. For ye must gain mastery if ye are true in faith."

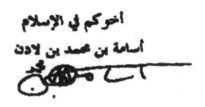

أخوكم في الإسلام

أسامة بن محمد بن لادن

THE FINAL NIGHT

THE FBI MANAGED TO TURN UP LETTERS OF THEOLOGICAL INSTRUC-
TION LEFT BY HIJACKERS ON THREE OF THE FOUR DOOMED SEPTEMBER
11 FLIGHTS. THE ROMAN NUMERALS AND ARABIC NUMBERS AFTER
QUOTATIONS ARE CHAPTER AND VERSE FROM THE QUR'AN. A PORTION
OF THE ORIGINAL LETTER IN ARABIC, AS PROVIDED BY THE FBI, IS SEEN
FOLLOWING THE TRANSLATION.

1) Renewing your covenant with God.
2) Know all aspects of the plan very well and expect the reaction and
the resistance from the enemy.
3) Read the Chapter of "Tobah" from the Qur'an.
4) Think about what God has promised the good believers and the
martyrs. Remind yourself to listen and obey that night because you
will be exposed to critical situations (100%). Train and convince yourself to do that. God narrated: "Obey God and his messenger and fall
into no disputes. Lest you lose heart and your power depart and be
patient and persevering for God is with those who are patient." (VIII-
46)
5) Increase your supplication to God with regard to aid and stability
and victory in order to facilitate your matters and shield you from
harm.
6) Increase your supplications to God and know that the best way to
do so is by reciting the Koran. This is the consensus of all Islamic
scholars and its sufficient that this is the word of God, the Creator of
the Earth and the Heavens.
7) Cleanse your heart and purify it and forget everything involving
this secular life, for the time for playing is gone and it is now the time
for truth. How much of our lives have we lost? Should we not use
these hours that we have to perform acts of nearness and obedience to
God?
8) Let your chest be open because it's only moments before you begin
a happy life and eternal bliss with the Prophets and the veracious and
martyrs and the righteous and these are the best of companions. We
ask God of His bounties and be optimistic because the Prophet was
optimistic in all his matters.
9) Establish your goal as one to become patient and to know how to
behave and be steadfast and to know that what's going to hit you
would not have missed you and what has missed you would not have
hit you. This is a test from God the Almighty to raise you up high and

forgive your sins. You must acknowledge that these are only moments in which you'll be raised with gratitude from God, the Almighty, with rewards. "Did you think that you would enter paradise without God testing those of you who struggled in his cause and remained steadfast?" (III-142)

10) Also remember the sayings of God in which he stated: "You did indeed wish for death before you met it. Now you have seen it with your own eyes and you flinch." (III-143) "How often, by God's will has a small force vanquished a large one?" (II-249) "If God helps you, none can overcome you and if He forsakes you, Who is there, after that that can help you? In God, then, let the believers place their trust." (III-160)

11) Remind yourself of the supplications and ponder their implications during the morning and the evening, etc.

12) Say your supplications and blow your breath on yourself and on your belongings (luggage, clothes, knife, ID, passport, and all your documents).

13) Inspect your arm . . . prior to your departure. "Let one of you sharpen your blade and let him ease his sacrifice."

14) Tie your clothes around you in the same way our good forefathers had done before you. Wear tight socks that would hold on your shoes and wouldn't allow your shoes to slip off. These precautions we are expected to follow. God is our sufficiency, how excellent a Trustee!

15) Pray your morning prayers with a group and think of the reward while reciting your supplications and never leave your apartment without absolution because the angels will seek your forgiveness and will pray for you as long as you have ablution. "Did you then think that we had created you in jest and that you would not be brought back to us for account?" (XXIII-115)

16) Shave and wash yourself.

One of the Companions of the Prophet Muhammad said: "The Prophet ordered us to read the following before going into battle, so we read it and we were safe."

The Second Phase

After this, the second stage begins:

If the taxi takes you to the airport, repeat the supplication one should recite upon riding a vehicle and upon entering a city or any other place you enter. Smile and be at peace with yourself because God is with the believers and because the angels guard you even though you may not be aware. God is mightier than all his creations.

"Oh God suffice them with whatever You wish." And say "Oh God, we . . . " and say "Oh God, put a barrier in front of them and a barrier behind them and further, cover them up so that they cannot see." (XXXVI-9) and say "God is our sufficiency, how excellent a Trustee!" remembering His word most high.

"Men say to them: 'A great army is gathering against you so fear them,' but it only increased their faith, they said: 'God is our sufficiency, how excellent a Trustee!'" (III-173)

After you say these verses, you will notice that things will go smooth as God has promised His servants of his bounties that they will never be harmed as long as they follow the instructions of God.

"And they returned with grace and bounty from God; No harm ever touched them; for they followed the good pleasure of God and God is the lord of bounties unbounded." "It is only the evil one that suggests to you the fear of his. . . . Be you not afraid of them, but fear Me if you have faith." (III-175)

Those are who admired the Western civilizations and who were nourished with the love and they were scared of their weak equipment. "Be you not afraid of them, but fear Me if you have faith." (III-175)

The real fear is the fear of God because none knows it except the believers. It is He, the One and Only, who has everything in His Hand. It is the believers who are most certain that God will nullify the plots of the unbelievers. "That is because God is He who makes feeble the plans and strategies of the unbelievers." (VIII-18)

You have to know that the best invocation is to not let others notice that you are invoking, because if you say it for 1,000 times no one will be aware whether you are only silent or invoking. Even when you say "No God but God" while you are smiling and reflecting upon it, then it becomes the greatest word. And it suffices that it is the statement of Unity, which you have accepted the same way as the Prophet Muhammad (peace and blessings be upon him) and the Companions, from their time until the Day of Judgment.

Don't manifest any hesitation and control yourself and be joyful with ease, because you are embarking upon a mission that God is pleased with. And you will be rewarded by living with the inhabitants of heaven. "Smile to hardship O youth, because you are on your way to Paradise!" In other words, any action you perform, and any invocation you repeat, God will be with you and the believers to protect them and grant them success, and enable them to achieve victory.

The Third Phase

When you board the plane, remember that this is a battle in the sake of God, which is worth the whole world and all that is in it. As the Messenger (peace and blessings be upon him) has said.

And when you sit in your seat, invoke the known supplications, and then be confident with the remembrance of God. "O you who believe, if you meet an army, then stand firm and invoke God much so that you may prosper." (VIII-45)

And when the plane takes off, remember the supplication of travels, for you are traveling to God, and what a beautiful travel!

This will be the hour. Then ask God Most High as He said in His Book: "Our Lord, pour constancy on us and make our steps firm, help us against those that reject faith." (II-250) And His saying: "Our Lord, forgive us our sins, and anything we may have done that transgressed our duty. Establish our feet firmly, and help us against those that resist faith." (III-147)

And remember the saying of our Prophet (peace and blessings be upon him): "O God, revealer of the Book, and mover of the clouds, and defeater of the party, defeat them and make us victorious over them." Supplicate for you and your brothers, all of them, to be victorious, and do not be afraid. Ask God to grant you martyrdom, marching ahead, and not turning back, and be steadfast."

Let everyone be prepared to undertake his task in a way pleasing to God, and be courageous, as our forefathers did when they came to the battle. And in the engagement, strike the strike of the heroes, as those who don't want to go back to this life. And say, "God is greatest," because it plants fear in the hearts of the unbelievers. God said: "Smite above their necks and smite all their finger tips." (VIII-12)

And know that the Gardens of Paradise are beautified with its best ornaments, and its inhabitants are calling you. And if . . . do not let differences come between you, and listen and obey, and if you kill, then kill completely, because this is the way of the Chosen One.

On the condition that . . . there is something greater than paying attention to the enemy or attacking him, because the harm in this is much greater. For the priority of the action of the group is much more important, since this is the duty of your mission. Don't take revenge for yourself only, but make your strike and everything on the basis of doing it for the sake of God. As an example, Ali ibn abi Talib (may God be pleased with him) fought with an enemy among the infidels who spat on him, and Ali took his sword and did not strike him. When the war ended, the Companions asked him why he did not strike that person, so he said: "When he spat on me, I was afraid to strike him out of egotistic revenge for myself, so I pulled my sword out. I wanted this to be for the sake of God." Then apply the way of taking captives, and do what God said in His Book: "It is not fitting for a Prophet that he should have prisoners of war until he has thoroughly subdued the land. You look for the temporal goods of this world, but God looks to the Hereafter, and God is Mighty, Wise." (VIII-67)

Let each one of you then tap on the shoulder of his brother . . . and remind each other that this work is for the sake of God and do not be afraid. And give him glad tidings, encourage each other [scratched word]. And how beautiful it would be if one read some verses of the Koran, such as, "Let those fight in the cause of God who sell the life of this world for the Hereafter." (III-74) And: "Say not of those who are slain in the way of God, 'They are dead,' no, they are living." (II-154) And other similar verses that our forefathers used to mention in the battlefield, so that they bring peace to their brothers, and make tranquillity and happiness enter their hearts.

Do not forget to take some booty, even if it be a cup of water with which you drink and offer your brothers to drink, if possible. And then when the zero-hour comes, open your chest and welcome death in the cause of God, always remembering your prayers to ease your mission before the goal in seconds. And let your last words be, "There is no God but God and Muhammad is His Messenger." And then comes the meeting in the Highest Paradise with the mercy of God. When you see the masses of the infidels, remember those parties that numbered about 10,000 and how God granted victory to the believers. God said: "When the believers saw the confederate forces they said, 'This is what God and His Messenger promised, and God and His Messenger told us what was true.' And it only added to their faith and their submission." (XXXIII-22)

"Assassinations Using Poisons and Cold Steel"

The following excerpts are from a 172-page how-to manual used by the Al Qaeda group titled, "Military Studies in the Jihad Against the Tyrants." Seized in Manchester, England, the manual, written in Arabic, was translated and entered as evidence into the summer 2001 Federal trial against four Usamah Bin-Laden cohorts accused of involvement in the 1998 bombing of U.S. embassies in Kenya and Tanzania. Two sections of the manual, available to the public at the Federal Courthouse, were uploaded to the enterprising website, WWW.THESMOKINGGUN.COM.

In its November 26, 2001 issue, *Time* magazine reports that it has acquired the so-called *Encyclopedia of Jihad*, a 6,000-page text, also on CD-ROM. Says *Time*, "The manual instructs agents in the various arts of killing and self-defense." Six thousand pages? Could it be that this *Encyclopedia* contains the copies of US military manuals on CD-ROM that anyone can buy cheaply online, as suggested by the Azzam website article, "How Can I Train Myself for Jihad?" seen on page 264.

UK/BM-155 TRANSLATION

3- Grab the testicles by the hand and twist and squeeze.
4- Grab the rib cage with both hands and squeeze.

Assassinations with Poison: We will limit [the discussion] to poisons that the holy warrior can prepare and use without endangering his health.
First- Herbal Poisons: A- Castor Beans
The substance Ricin, an extract from Castor Beans, is considered one of the most deadly poisons. .035 milligrams is enough to kill someone by inhaling or by injecting in a vein. However, though considered less poisonous if taken through the digestive system, chewing some Castor Beans could be fatal. It is a simple operation to extract Ricin, and Castor Beans themselves can be obtained from nurseries throughout the country.
Symptoms: Need to vomit - diarrhea - unawareness of surroundings - the skin turns blue, leading to failure of blood circulation [sic] and finally ... death.
                        B- Precatory Beans
The herbal poison Abrin, extracted from Precatory Beans, is very similar to Ricin. The seeds of this plant are red and black and are used in prayer beads [TN: like a Rosary]. Prepare a very dark ink or refine some normal ink to
Dimothyl Sulfoxide
[Can be] found with horse breeders or veterinarians, and we can substitute Nitrobenzene or "cream" [PH]. The poison is mixed with this substance, and when the enemy touches the poison, he will die slowly within 15 minutes to an hour.

Nitrobenzene poison = external poison [by touching]

RICIN	One of these poisons is
ABIN	mixed with Nitrobenzene or
RCIN	DMSO or the "Cream".
Frog poison	

be as fine as possible while keeping it strong enough to
penetrate the shell of Precatory Beans. Put on a pair of leather
gloves and very carefully bore about twelve holes in each of the
prayer beads. After completing that, spray the prayer beads with
DMSO (Dimehtyl Sulfoxide). The Abrin will kill your victim
slowly, but relentlessly.

Extracting Abrin and Ricin

In order to facilitate removing the shells of these seeds, soak
3.2 ounces (an ounce = 31.1 milligrams) of castor-oil plant seeds
in about 10 ounces of water, adding two teaspoons of lyo [sic,
maybe meant lye] or an alkaline (a substance extracted from soap
powder). You need to submerge the seeds in the water, so cover
them with clean gravel or use marble. Let them soak for an hour,
then take out the seeds, clean them, and let the shells dry. They
can be easily removed after that.

Put the shelled seeds in a mixture four times their weight of
acetone, until they completely harden. Then put them in a covered
glass container, and leave them for 72 hours. After that,
transfer them to another container through a coffee filter. Put
on surgical gloves and a mask, and squeeze out as much of the
acetone as possible. Then add fresh acetone and repeat

the procedure of leaving them for 72 hours and straining them
through a coffee filter two more times. The final result will be
pure Eysein [PH] or Abrin.

C- The Water Hemlock Plant

A lethal dose is 3.2 grams. It has a palatable taste, and is very
similar to another plant, parsnip.

Symptoms: Nervous spasms within 15 to 60 minutes, including
severe locking and clenching of the jaw to the extent that the
tongue could be cut off.

D- The Tanj Oil Tree

Second- Semi-alkaline substances: They are highly solvent in
alcohol.

A- Tobacco

There is enough nicotine in three cigarettes to kill a person.
Sixty to 70 milligrams of pure nicotine will kill a person within
an hour if eaten.

B- Potato Sprout

The potato sprout (both rotten and green) contains Solanine.

How to Extract Poisonous Alkaline

Chop up the leaves finely. It is preferable to make a mixture,
and then put it in a drip coffee maker, through which the boiling
water can penetrate the coffee gradually.

Torture Methods: Secret agents use two methods of torture:

A. Physical torture.   B. Psychological torture

A.   Method of Physical Torture:
     1.   Blindfolding and stripping of clothes.
     2.   Hanging by the hands.
     3.   Hanging by the feet [upside down].
     4.   Beating with sticks and electrical wires.
     5.   Whipping and beating with sticks and twisted rubber belts.
     6.   Forcing the brother to stand naked for long periods of time.
     7.   Pouring cold water on the brother's head.
     8.   Putting out lighted cigarettes on the brother's skin.
     9.   Shocking with an electrical current.
     10. Kicking and punching.
     11. Attacking the brother with vicious dogs.
     12. Making the brother sit on a stake.
     13. Throwing in a septic tank.
     14. Pulling out the nails and hair.
     15. Dragging.
     16. Tying the hands and feet from behind.
     17. Utilizing sharp objects, such as a pocketknife or piece of glass.
     18. Burning with fire.
     19. Sleeping on a bare marble floor without a cover and flooding the cell with sewer water.
     20. Standing on toes and against a wall pressing with the fingers for long hours. The brother may be denied sleep, food, drink, and medicine.
     21. Beating on cuts and sore parts of the body.
     22. Giving the brother a lot of water or very watery fruits, such as watermelon, after denying him

          food and drink. After the brother drinks or eats the fruit, his hands and penis will be tied so the brother will not be able to urinate.
     23. Placing drugs and narcotics in the brother's food to weaken his will power.
     24. Placing the brother in solitary confinement where the cells are made of a special kind of cement that gets extremely hot in the summer and cold in winter.
     25. Hitting the brother's genitals with a stick or squeezing them by hand.
     26. Dragging the brother over barb wires and fragments of glass and metal.

B.   Methods of Psychological Torture:

     1.   Isolating the brother socially, cutting him off from public life, placing him in solitary confinement, and denying him news and information in order to make him feel lonely.
     2.   Forbidding calling him by name, giving the brother a number, and calling him by that number in order to defeat his morale.
     3.   Threatening to summon his sister, mother, wife, or daughter and rape her.
     4.   Threatening to rape the brother himself.
     5.   Threatening to confiscate his possessions and to have him fired from his employment.
     6.   Threatening to cause a permanent physical disability or life imprisonment.
     7.   Offer the brother certain enticements (apartment, car, passport, scholarship, etc.).
     8.   Using harsh treatment, insults, and curses to defeat his morale.

9. Controlling everything the brother does, even in
    private, whether he is awake or asleep, to convince him
    that they are in charge. They would force him to bow
    his head and look down while talking with the guards.

Further, let no one think that the aforementioned techniques are
fabrications of our imagination, or that we copied them from spy
stories. On the contrary, these are factual incidents in the
prisons of Egypt, Syria, Jordan, Saudi Arabia, and all other Arab
countries. Those who follow daily events and read the newspapers
and journals would be amazed to learn that:

    security personnel totally undressed veiled women in public.
    The security personnel arrested a brother's mother, a
    brother's sister, and a brother's wife and raped them.

    the wife of brother Saffout AbdulGhani - may Allah have him
    released - had a miscarriage when the government's dogs
    (i.e. cronies) beat and tortured her in front of her
    husband.

    the security personnel captured brother Hassan Al-Gharbawi's
    mother, who is older than 60 years, and hanged her by her
    feet [upside down]. The security personnel shaved the head
    of the wife of a brother who participated in the murder of
    Rif'at Al-Mahjoub [Egypt's former parliament speaker].

The stories are numerous and there is intense torture while
Muslims are in deep sleep.

O young men waging a holy war for the sake of Allah, there is
still hope in you. Your country awaits you, your brothers await
you, your wives wait you, the Muslim hostages await you.

UK/BM-173 TRANSLATION

Advice Taken from the book "Mothakkarat Fida'i Asir[a]" [Memoirs of a Captured Commando]: Concerning interrogation and questioning, paraphrased.

1. While being taken to the interrogation and torture areas, one should concentrate heavily on the route and try to memorize any signs in order to benefit operations and plan development.

2. In the beginning of the interrogation, a security officer (interrogator) would come to you with fatherly advice, deceitful phrases, and "crocodile tears" so you might confess and tell them everything.

3. It is necessary to secretly discard any document related to the work or anything else considered criminal evidence against you. Better, do not carry any documents concerning the work.

4. From the first moment in captivity, the brother should proudly take a firm and opposing position against the enemy and not obey the orders. The more firm and opposing the reaction, the more beneficial it is. These reactions will not lead to harsher treatment. Do not give the enemy an opportunity or an opening.

5. During the torture process, pretend that the pain is severe by bending over and crying loudly.

6. As the torture intensifies, its end nears.

7. Between torture sessions, the officers bargain with the brother and entice him with ending the torture if he supplies them with any information.

---

[a] This book is the memoirs of an Iranian Communist. All brothers should read it.

8. During the torture session, the counseling preacher may become a vicious beast.

9. The one who gives one piece of information to avoid the lashes of whips is deluding himself because the torture would intensify.

10. It is necessary that each brother plan for his interrogation and discuss it with his commander. He may be captured one day.

11. When I talk while under torture, I do not mention unknown dates and places to the security personnel, but well known ones.

12. When I mention dates or names, it is important to memorize them because they will ask about them again to know if I was truthful.

13. Pretending to be naive and ignorant during the questioning may lead to diverging from the plan, because all factors are against the brother: The place, the people, the situation. That leads to some or all the outcomes desired by the enemy. That is, it is important to remain psychologically and mentally calm and to maintain alertness and foresight.

14. Detailing events during the questioning, whether verbally or in writing, directly increases the crime. That person's situation is just like someone who falls in a swamp [quick sand]: the more he tries to save himself, the deeper he sinks.

15. The less information supplied during the torture, the lighter the judgement will be.

16. A devastating mistake that results in harsh judgement is that of a brother revealing information to others in his cell

not revealed during the torture. This is especially true when the interrogation is still going on, his fate has not been determined, and the case has not been closed.

17. Relating experiences should not take place prior to the judgement, but after it.

18. The interrogators may resort to planting suspicion and mistrust among the brothers. They may pretend that they have a friendly relationship with one of the brothers. It is necessary to think well of one another.

19. Do not accept humiliation and disgrace. Disobey orders and oppose them.

20. It is important to coordinate with your brothers before executing any operation (security plan).

21. The security personnel may leave you for long periods of time without asking you any questions in order to break your will and determination.

22. During the interrogation, say only the things that you agreed upon with your commander. Do not be concerned about other brothers.

BIN-LADEN THANKS ALLAH FOR 9/11/01
Al-Qaeda Press Release, 10/8/01

Here is America struck by God Almighty in one of its vital organs, so that its greatest buildings are destroyed. Grace and gratitude to God. America has been filled with horror from north to south and east to west, and thanks be to God that what America is tasting now is only a copy of we have tasted.

Our Islamic nation has been tasting the same for more than 80 years, of humiliation and disgrace, its sons killed and their blood spilled, its sanctities desecrated.

God has blessed a group of vanguard Muslims, the forefront of Islam, to destroy America. May God bless them and allot them a supreme place in heaven, for He is the only one capable and entitled to do so. When those have stood in defense of their weak children, their brothers and sisters in Palestine and other Muslim nations, the whole world went into an uproar, the infidels followed by the hypocrites.

A million innocent children are dying at this time as we speak, killed in Iraq without any guilt. We hear no denunciation, we hear no edict from the hereditary rulers. In these days, Israeli tanks rampage across Palestine, in Ramallah, Rafah and Beit Jala and many other parts of the land of Islam, and we do not hear anyone raising his voice or reacting. But when the sword fell upon America after 80 years, hypocrisy raised its head up high bemoaning those killers who toyed with the blood, honor and sanctities of Muslims.

The least that can be said about those hypocrites is that they are apostates who followed the wrong path. They backed the butcher against the victim, the oppressor against the innocent child. I seek refuge in God against them and ask Him to let us see them in what they deserve.

I say that the matter is very clear. Every Muslim after this event, after the senior officials in the United States of America, starting with the head of international infidels, Bush and his staff who went on a display of vanity with their men and horses, those who turned even the countries that believe in Islam against us — the group that resorted to God, the Almighty, the group that refuses to be subdued in its religion.

They have been telling the world falsehoods that they are fighting terrorism. In a nation at the far end of the world, Japan, hundreds of thousands, young and old, were killed and this is not a world crime. To them it is not a clear issue. A million children in Iraq, to them this is not a clear issue.

But when a few more than ten were killed in Nairobi and Dar es Salaam, Afghanistan and Iraq were bombed and hypocrisy stood behind the head of international infidels, the modern world's symbol of paganism, America, and its allies.

I tell them that these events have divided the world into two camps, the camp of the faithful and the camp of infidels. May God shield us and you from them.

Every Muslim must rise to defend his religion. The wind of faith is blowing and the wind of change is blowing to remove evil from the Peninsula of Mohammad, peace be upon him.

As to America, I say to it and its people a few words: I swear to God that America will not live in peace before peace reigns in Palestine, and before all the army of infidels depart the land of Mohammad, peace be upon him.

God is the Greatest and glory be to Islam.

Bin-Laden poster featuring Bert from *Sesame Street*

THE PROHIBITED VOICE OF AMERICA INTERVIEW WITH MULLAH OMAR MOHAMMAD

THIS INTERVIEW WITH MULLAH OMAR MOHAMMAD, THE TALIBAN LEADER, WAS CONDUCTED IN PASHTU FOR THE PUBLICLY-FUNDED RADIO CHANNEL VOICE OF AMERICA. THE BROADCAST WAS PULLED, FOLLOWING OBJECTIONS FROM THE US DEPUTY SECRETARY OF STATE AND SENIOR OFFICIALS OF THE NATIONAL SECURITY COUNCIL.

VOA: Why don't you expel Usamah Bin Laden?
Omar: This is not an issue of Usamah Bin Laden. It is an issue of Islam. Islam's prestige is at stake. So is Afghanistan's tradition.

VOA: Do you know that the US has announced a war on terrorism?
Omar: I am considering two promises. One is the promise of God, the other is that of Bush. The promise of God is that my land is vast. If you start a journey on God's path, you can reside anywhere on this earth and will be protected . . . The promise of Bush is that there is no place on earth where you can hide that I cannot find you. We will see which one of these two promises is fulfilled.

VOA: But aren't you afraid for the people, yourself, the Taliban, your country?
Omar: Almighty God . . . is helping the believers and the Muslims. God says he will never be satisfied with the infidels. In terms of worldly affairs, America is very strong. Even if it were twice as strong or twice that, it could not be strong enough to defeat us. We are confident that no one can harm us if God is with us.

VOA: You are telling me you are not concerned, but Afghans all over the world are concerned.
Omar: We are also concerned. Great issues lie ahead. But we depend on God's mercy. Consider our point of view: if we give Usamah away today, Muslims who are now pleading to give him up would then be reviling us for giving him up . . . Everyone is afraid of America and wants to please it. But Americans will not be able to prevent such acts like the one that has just occurred because America has taken Islam hostage. If you look at Islamic countries, the people are in despair. They are complaining that Islam is gone. But people remain firm in

their Islamic beliefs. In their pain and frustration, some of them commit suicide acts. They feel they have nothing to lose.

VOA: What do you mean by saying America has taken the Islamic world hostage?
Omar: America controls the governments of the Islamic countries. The people ask to follow Islam, but the governments do not listen because they are in the grip of the United States. If someone follows the path of Islam, the government arrests him, tortures him or kills him. This is the doing of America. If it stops supporting those governments and lets the people deal with them, then such things won't happen. America has created the evil that is attacking it. The evil will not disappear even if I die and Usamah dies and others die. The US should step back and review its policy. It should stop trying to impose its empire on the rest of the world, especially on Islamic countries.

VOA: So you won't give Usamah bin Laden up?
Omar: No. We cannot do that. If we did, it means we are not Muslims . . . that Islam is finished. If we were afraid of attack, we could have surrendered him the last time we were threatened and attacked. So America can hit us again, and this time we don't even have a friend.

VOA: If you fight America with all your might — can the Taliban do that? Won't America beat you and won't your people suffer even more?
Omar: I'm very confident that it won't turn out this way. Please note this: there is nothing more we can do except depend on almighty God. If a person does, then he is assured that the Almighty will help him, have mercy on him and he will succeed.

SUBJECT: BIN LADEN IS A "MOTHER FUCKER"

OHIO STATE UNIVERSITY'S MSA NEWS, ITS ISLAMIC NEWS SITE, RECEIVED A LOT OF HATE MAIL AFTER 9/11/01, ESPECIALLY ABOUT NEWS REPORTS REGARDING USAMAH BIN LADEN. HERE, AN MSA NEWS EDITOR, RESPONDS WITH A STRAIGHT FACE TO AN OUTRAGED READER.

Source: Direct Submission
Date: Fri, 28 Sep 2001 15:27:33 EDT
Text: Why do you have a page about this mother fucker! He deserves to die!!

Eds. Note: "Mother Fucker" reads in Dari, the second language of Afghanistan, "Mother-e-Qahba" (50% Indo-European, 50% Arabic). The Arabic "Qahba" means "prostitute." It is a very vulgar word today (and "vulgar" is a bigoted word), but this is not the case in classical Arabic. Thus it is found in the book called "Bayna al-Islam wal-Masihiyyah" ("Between Islam and Christianity") a 4th Century AH/10th century AD document recording eight epistles between the Muslim Spaniard al-Khazraji and a Christian authority in his native Andalusia comparing and contrasting their beliefs. It is used specifically in quotes from the book of Ezekiel (the stories about Ahola and Aholiba and the sperm of Foreign Invaders; modern translations use the word "zaniyah" [Hebrew Zonot, as in Bnei Zonot] in the copy we have). Ezekiel is buried in Afghanistan and his burial site is a Muslim "Mazar" or Shrine. In the 8-centuries old Encyclopedia Arabica called "Lisan al-Arab" by Imam al-Lughah Ibn Manzur al-Ifriqi al-Misri al-Gafsi (from the Punic city of Capsa), <http://lexicons.ajeeb.com>, we learn that "Qahbah" [prostitute] is well-known (you will not find it online because the editors of Ajeeb "cleaned it." See the 1880 AD Bulaq edition). FarsiDic.com, http://www.farsidic.com/FarsiDic.asp?farsi gives the meaning of "cuckold" (A man married to an unfaithful wife) for "qahbah" (and "zan qahbeh") and we know this is not the case, because we know the language. Ask your Iranian friends what "Mother-e-Qahba" means.

It is related to "Qahib" (masc.) and "Qahba" (fem.) with the meaning of "someone of old age." Lisan al-Arab says they are called so because they "cough too much." Thus "Quhb" is rooted in coughing in the most authentic Arabic derivation. Now, we will add to this that according to Kitab al-Aghani (The Book of Songs) of Abu al-Faraj al-Isphahani, a very ancient book that records all "Arab" antics (really not "Arab", but those of the lands between Alexandria and Bukhara), we read that "Quhb" was a form of marriage in pre-Islamic Arabia. A women who feels "horny" ("harna" in pure Arabic, we can expand here and give all the "juicy" meanings but we will not in respect to many on this list) would raise a black flag outside her tent. Men would stand outside in line. They would all copulate with her. To indicate that she is ready, she would cough, "taqhubu" in pure Arabic, (that the meaning of "qahbah" is elucidated). Then, when the baby is born, she would send it to any of the men who slept with her. He would accept it as a child of his own no questions asked ("yaleet" is the verb used). They see no shame in it (and Snoop DOGG says "it's your baby's mama" and advises you to treat her right). In order to understand Islam, you have to put it in contrast to pre-Islamic Arabic (yeah the "jahiliyah") says the late Maliki scholar al-Nayfar.

Also "Qahib" is an anagram for "Haqaba" which means era, thus the meaning of "age" is also confirmed. The days can mess with a human mind (or in the language of "Shaikh Zubair," the days can "*uck with you").

Moral of the story from all of this: Avoid vulgar language because it delivers nothing and you lose the argument. Better: analyze, express your feelings, share your honest thoughts, win a friend, extend a peaceful hand. Also, part of the exercise above is to elucidate that there is no "East" and there is no "West," but one "insanity" – "insaniyat" – the Arabic (and Hebrew) word for "humanity." Also, we add that the Arabs of North-Africa, to stress their point, in name calling would use the combination "Qahba-Butana" (and Butana, is Puta, Putain, Putana; any way you say it, it is the same). Please refrain from the use of this language because you see what happens. (eds.)

THE INFIDEL HELL
From *The Spectacle of Death* by K.M. Islam

In the Name of the Lord the Beneficent and the Merciful. We laud Him and shower blessings on His Messenger, the Gracious.

Hereafter have been described in plain language the circumstances of Hell which have been gleaned from the verses of the Holy Qur'an and the Hadith of the Holy Prophet (peace and blessings of Allah be upon him).

AN ESTIMATE OF THE TORMENTS IN HELL
The Holy Prophet (peace and blessings of Allah be upon him) has said: The lightest punishment would be inflicted on that sinner whose boots and straps would be filled with fire; and it will cause his mind to boil miserably. He will take this punishment for the severest, whereas it is the very first state of the hellish tortures.

The fire of Hell is 70 degrees hotter than the worldly fire. It has seven levels, and each level has a big entrance. The first level of Hell is reserved for those Muslim sinners and idolators who were polytheists, worshippers of fire, atheists, Jews, Christians and hypocrites respectively. These levels of Hell are known as (1) *Jaheem,* (2) *Jahannam* (3) *Sa'ir* (4) *Saqar* (5) *Nata* (6) *Haviya* and (7) *Hutama.* Every one of these extensive levels is replete with incalculable pains, tortures and torments, and multifarious houses. For instance, there is a house *Ghayy,* the severity of its torments is such that the denizens of other six levels pray 400 times daily for salvation from its tortures. There is another house, known as *Zamharir,* it is the region of extreme cold. There is still another house *Jubb-ul-Huzan,* i.e., well of griefs, wherein is a well called *Tinatul Khabal* — mire of pus and poison. There is a towering mountain, known as *Sau'ud,* its space equal to 70 years walking. Idolators would be thrown into the Fire of Hell from its peak. There is a pond, *Aab-I-hamim,* with water so hot that the moment a sinner drinks it, his upper lip swells to such an extent that it covers his nose and eyes; the lower, his chest. As this water passes down the throat, his tongue burns; mouth contracts and ultimately this boiling water tears apart the human lungs, stomach and intestines.. There is another tank Ghassaq wherein gathers the idolators' pus, sweat and blood. Another fountain, Ghisleen, serves the same purpose. Likewise, there are countless tormenting scenes in Hell. The size of the sinners' bodies would be stretched and broadened so as to magnify their sufferings and various types of tortures shall be inflicted on the exterior as well as the internal parts of each fiber and limb of their bodies. Burning, crushing, biting by poisonous snakes and scorpions, piercing with thorns, slashing of skin — these are the manifold modes of punishment in Hell. Due to the excess of heat in Hell, bodies of the sinners would melt, and they will be reborn and melt again. This process would be repeated for 700 times in the duration of a

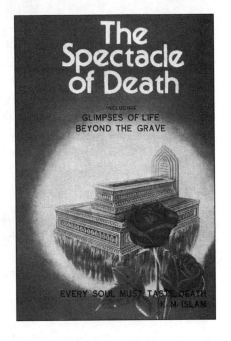

The
Spectacle
of Death

INCLUDING
GLIMPSES OF LIFE
BEYOND THE GRAVE

EVERY SOUL MUST TASTE DEATH
K. M. ISLAM

moment. But this point should not be ignored that the shape of the original limbs of their bodies would not undergo any change; flesh and skin would repeatedly be tortured. Skin of some infidels is said to be 42 yards thick; their teeth would resemble towering mountains, and their sitting would cover an unlimited space. After a long time, the pangs of hunger would be increased to such extremity that it will surpass all other torments. At last, the sinners would become terribly restless and demand food to satisfy their appetite. They would be given to eat *Zaqqum*, a thorny plant, which would get stuck in their throats. They would cry for water, as they used to do in the world when a morsel of food gets stuck in their throats. It shall be ordained that water be provided to them from *Jahim*, the very first level of Hell. It would cause their lips to swell, tongue to swindle, throat to break into pieces, and their intestines will be turn apart and excreted through their anuses. So, being in dire distress, they will supplicate to the Lord of Hell for death, so that their punishment may come to an end. After 1,000 years he will say: "You will always remain in Hell." After 1,000 years they will pray to God: "Deprive us of our lives, but have mercy and relieve us of this intolerable torment." After 1,000 years the Lord shall ordain: "Hold your tongue, and do not beg My pardon; you have been condemned forever." At last perforce they will say to one another: "Let us endure, for endurance may bear good fruit." They will continuously pray to the

Almighty for 1,000 years with extreme lamentation and entreaty, but all in vain. Ultimately when all hope is lost they will say to one another, restlessness or patience are one and the same for us. For us there is no means of salvation. They would be turned upside-down. The shape of their bodies would be distorted and they would assume the form of dogs, donkeys, monkeys, wolves, snakes and other beasts and animals. Those who are proud of their worldly pelf and power, would be trampled on the Day of Resurrection. Such is the description of the condition of the infidels on that Day.

TONGUE OF THE DENIZENS OF HELL

The Holy Prophet (peace and blessings of Allah be upon him) observed: "Verily, the sinner would stretch out his tongue to the length of three kos* and even six kos. The people will trample on his tongue and step on it." (*Tirmidhi*).

BODIES OF THE DENIZENS OF HELL

The Holy Prophet (peace and blessings of Allah be upon him) observed: "In hell, the part between the shoulders of an infidel would be equal to a distance of three days' journey, by a horse-rider. His jaw-tooth would be as big as the mountains of Uhud and the thickness of his skin would come up to a distance which can be covered in three days."

It is narrated on the authority of Hadrat Mujahid (may Allah be pleased with him) and Hadrat Ibn 'Abbas (may Allah be pleased with him) said: "Do you know the width of Hell?" I replied in the negative. He said: "Yes, by God! Verily there would be a distance of 70 years between the shoulder and the earlobe of a sinner, and therein would be running the streams of pus and blood." (*Targhib*)

---

* Kos is a measure of length about three English miles.

GLOSSARY

Alhamdulillah Praise be to Allah.

Allah the Name of the Creator of the universe.

asr late afternoon prayer.

Ayah verse of the Holy Quran.

'azl coitus interruptus.

baligh one who has attained the age of puberty.

barzakh period between death and resurrection; purgatory; isthmus.

bidah any innovated practices introduced in the religion of Islam. Considered heretical.

Bismallah in the name of Allah, this statement is usually made by Muslims who are about to indulge in a lawful task.

dajjal Anti-Christ. Thought to be Jewish.

dawah propagation of Islam through word and action, calling the people to follow the commandments of Allah.

deen usually translated as "religion". *Deen* is a comprehensive word, which means a total way of life, following the commandments of Allah.

dhikr mention of certain formulae like *"subhan Allah," "al-hamdu li-l-lah,"* etc.

diyah indemnity or compensation for injury or death.

dua supplication invoking Allah for whatever one desires.

eid religious festival.

Eid al Fitr three-day festival marking the end of Ramadan — the 9th month (the month of fasting).

Eid al Adha the feast of Sacrifice. This feast commemorates the Prophet Abraham's obedience to Allah by being prepared to sacrifice his only son Ishmael. A four-day festival that completes the rites of pilgrimage and takes place from the 10th–13th of *Duhl Hijjah* (the last Islamic month).

fajr early morning prayer.

faqih Islamic learned man, a lawyer or theologian qualified to give religious verdicts.

fasiq a reprobate individual, neglectful and careless in his dress and behavior whose evidence is not admissible if he becomes a witness.

Fatiha the opening Chapter of the Qur'an. *Fatiha* should be read in every prayer.

fiqh Islamic positive law.

ghusl full ritual washing of the body with water. *Ghusl* should be done after sexual intercourse, wet dreams, emission, menses, and childbirth.

hadath condition requiring *wudu'* or *ghusl.*

hadd punishment prescribed in textual sources (Qur'an and *Sunnah*) for certain violations.

hadd al-tarakhkhus point away from the boundary of a city whose inhabitants cannot be seen. Some jurists consider it to be a point from where the city's call to prayers (*adhan*) cannot be heard.

hadith sayings and traditions of the Holy Prophet Muhammad.

hajj pilgrimage to the Holy city of Mecca performed in the last month, *Dhu-l-Hijjah*, of the Islamic lunar calendar.

al-hakim al-shar'i religious authority, *mujtahid.*

haram forbidden, prohibited. It is necessary to abstain from the acts which are harmful. If someone performs a harmful act, he will be punished either by the Islamic court or in the hereafter or both. For example, stealing or eating pork.

hayd bleeding of a menstrual cycle.

hijab veil worn by Muslim women for reasons of modesty and protection.

hilal crescent.

hukm a judgement or legal decision by Allah. Order or command.

husna kindness.

ihram state of ritual consecration to perform major pilgrimage (*hajj*) or minor one (*'umrah*).

ihtiyat wajib precautionarily obligatory.

ijma unanimous consent of all learned men of Islam.

imam a person who leads the prayer and also for a famous Muslim scholar.

iman truth, faith, and acceptance.

isa Arabic word for Jesus Christ.

isha night prayer.

Islam literally means "submission to the will of Allah."

istihadah irregular bleeding other than the menstrual cycle.

istihalah transformation, chemical change.

istinqadh rescue, salvage.

janabah state after having sexual intercourse or ejaculation.

jahanam Hell.

Jahiliyyah Arabia in pre-Islamic times; adhering to *makkan* associationism.

ja'iz, halal, mubah permitted, allowed, lawful, legal. The acts or things which are permitted and lawful. There is no reward for performing it nor any punishment for neglecting it. *Mubah* is exclusively used for lawful things, not for permitted actions. An example, drinking tea.

jannah paradise.

jibreel Angel Gabriel.

jihad means struggling one's utmost to be a better person in the sight of Allah, and to establish Islamic way of life.

jinn a race of created beings that are made out of smokeless fire.

juma Friday, the Muslim's day of gathering on Friday noon prayers.

jumu'ah Friday.

kaba holiest, and first shrine constructed for the worship of One God, Allah. Muslims face towards the direction of the Kaba, Mecca. Also spelled Ka'bah, Qa'ba, Qa'aba.

kabirah grave or mortal sin (e.g., theft, homicide, adultery, false witness, etc.) which earns for its unrepentant perpetrator consignment to hellfire.

kaffarah expiation, compensation, penalty.

kafir unbeliever, who has rejected the truth of Islam.

khalifa a Muslim ruler of an Islamic State.

khums 20% tax levied on certain items.

khutba sermon.

kufr disbelief, infidelity, blasphemy.

maghrib sunset prayer.

mahram one who falls within the prohibited degree for marriage.

majhul al-malik unknown owner, derelict property.

majlis (pl. majalis) assembly to commemorate religious events.

makruh reprehensible, disliked, discouraged. It is used for the acts which are disliked but not harm. If someone does a *makruh* act, he will not be punished for it; however, if he refrains from it, then he will be rewarded. For example, eating before *ghusl janabat*.

malaikah angels.

marja the high ranking *mujtahid* is who is followed by the people. Literally, it means the point of reference. The high ranking *mujtahids* are called *marja'* because they are the point of reference for the people in the *shari'ah* matters.

maseeh a title which means "anointed" or Christ title given to Prophet Jesus.

masjid mosque, places of worship for the Muslims. In one sense the whole earth is a *Masjid* for the Muslims, the dome of the heavens is the roof.

Miraj the night journey of the Holy Prophet Muhammad (peace be upon him) from Mecca to Jerusalem and then through the realms of the seven heavens.

mufti the independent jurist assigned to the task of giving free juristic counsel.

Muhammad the name of the final Messenger and Prophet of God to Humanity.

Muharram the first month of the Islamic Calendar.

muhsanah (pl., *muhsanat*) literally, "protected"; name applied to the Muslim woman who is married, or to the Muslim virgin, or to the slave woman converted to Islam whose conversion makes marriage with her legitimate.

mujahideen warrior for the cause of Allah.

mukallaf one who is competent to undertake religious obligations; religiously accountable.

mu'min believer.

munafiq a person pretending falsely to be a Muslim.

Muslim literally means "submitting to the will", i.e., to the will of Allah, the Almighty.

mujtahid a religious scholar who is an expert of Islamic laws, the *shari'ah*. Usually, it is used for the high ranking *mujtahids* whose decrees are followed by the people.

nadhr solemn vow, pledge.

najasah ritual impurity.

najis ritually impure; not equivalent to unhygienic or unclean.

nifas bleeding of a woman after child-birth.

non-baligh one who has not attained the age of puberty.

non-mahram opposite of *mahram*. Obligatory precaution the follower (*muqallid*) has the discretion to revert to the ruling (fatwa) of the next high-ranking *mujtahid* on that particular issue only.

qada lapsed or due prayers, fasts, etc.

qadar divine providence, or God's disposition of any matter; divine decree.

qasr shortened prayers of a traveller.

qiblah direction in which all Muslims face when praying, which is the Kaba, in Mecca, Saudi Arabia The direction is north, east from New York.

qiyas to compare. Islamic jurisprudence's fourth foundation in which logical reasoning is used by learned men of Islam.

Quds Jerusalem.

Qur'an the last revelation of Allah given to Humanity, through his last Prophet and Messenger, Muhammad.

RAA abbreviation for *Radiya Allahu'anhu*.

Radiya *Allahu'anhu Allah* be pleased with him.

Ramadan the month of Fasting, the 9th month of the Islamic Calendar.

riba interest, usury.

riddah apostasy.

al-risalah al-'amaliyyah practical treatise prepared by the jurist for the laity.

ruku' genuflection practiced in *salat* or rite of worship.

SAAS abbreviation for *Salla Allahu alaihe wa Sallam*.

Safar second month of the lunar year; tampering by pre-Islamic Arabs with the calendar for the purpose of prolonging or shortening the previous

month (*muharram*) in which there is to be neither hunting nor war; also a disease thought to be contagious and consisting of a yellow worm in the digestive system.

Sahabi companion of Prophet Muhammad — peace be upon him.

sajda prostration, as in prayer.

salaam peace.

salaat prayer.

Salla Allahu alaihe wa Sallam means may the peace and blessings of Allah be upon him. This phrase is recited whenever the name of the Prophet Muhammad (peace and blessing of Allah be upon him) is mentioned.

saum fasting.

sa'y pacing back and forth seven times by a pilgrim between *Safa* and *Marwah*.

Shahada The creed of Islam: 'I bear witness that there is no deity worthy of worship except Allah, and I bear witness that Muhammad is the Messenger of Allah.'

Shaitan Satan.

shar'i lawful, legitimate

shar'ia or **shari'at** literally, the way. In Islamic terminology it means the laws of Islam, encompassing both the Quran and *Hadith*, the sayings of Prophet Muhammad (peace be upon him).

shaheed martyr; martyred.

Shawwal tenth month in the Islamic lunar calendar.

shirk associating partners with Allah. The grave sin of *shirk* is not forgiven if a person dies in that state.

siyam fasts.

Subhan Allah means "Glory be to Allah."

sunnat or **mustahab** recommended, desirable, better. It refers to the acts which are recommended but not *wajib*. If one neglects them, he will not be punished; however, if one performs them, he will be rewarded. For example, washing the hands before *wudu'*.

sura chapter of the Quran. Quran has 114 *suras* or chapters.

tahara purification of body, clothing and souls.

tahir ritually pure; not equivalent to hygienic or clean.

tamm complete prayers.

taqlid emulating the opinions of a religious authority.

taqsir cutting a piece of hair or nail by the pilgrim.

tathir ritual purification.

tawaf circumambulation around the *Kaba.*

tawhid the Divine Unity, in its utmost profound sense. Allah is One in His Essence and His attributes and His Acts.

tayammum dry purification when water is not available or is detrimental to health.

ta'zir discretionary punishment estimated by *al-hakim al-shar'i* or a judge that is not prescribed in the Quran or the *Sunnah*; chastisement.

ulema scholars, learned men, wise men.

ummah people bound together by ideology.

ummra a pilgrimage to Mecca, but not during the *hajj* period.

'urf convention, customary law.

wajib obligatory, necessary, incumbent. An act which must be performed. A person will be rewarded for performing it and punished for neglecting it, e.g., the daily prayers.

waqf property assigned for the service of Allah. An endowment.

witr a prayer which has an odd number of *rakat* (units). Usually referred to the last prayer of the night after the *isha* prayer.

wudu' purifying with water before performing prayers.

zakat wealth-sharing or institutionalized charity in Islam, consisting of an annual levy of 2½ percent on appropriated wealth, third pillar of Islam after confession of faith and *salaat.*

317

also available from feral house

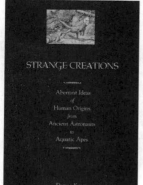